THE GEORGE GUND FOUNDATION
IMPRINT IN AFRICAN AMERICAN STUDIES

The George Gund Foundation has endowed
this imprint to advance understanding of
the history, culture, and current issues
of African Americans.

The publisher and the University of California Press Foundation gratefully acknowledge the generous support of the George Gund Foundation Imprint in African American Studies.

Social Movements and the Law

Social Movements and the Law

TALKING ABOUT BLACK LIVES MATTER
AND #METOO

EDITED BY
Lolita Buckner Inniss and Bridget J. Crawford

WITH CONTRIBUTIONS BY

Mehrsa Baradaran

Noa Ben-Asher

I. Bennett Capers

Linda S. Greene

Aya Gruber

Osamudia James

Keisha Lindsay

Ruthann Robson

Kathryn M. Stanchi

Lua Kamál Yuille

UNIVERSITY OF CALIFORNIA PRESS

University of California Press
Oakland, California

© 2025 by Lolita Buckner Inniss and Bridget J. Crawford

Library of Congress Cataloging-in-Publication Data

Names: Inniss, Lolita Buckner, editor. | Crawford, Bridget J., editor.
Title: Social movements and the law : talking about black lives matter
    and #metoo / edited by Lolita Buckner Inniss and Bridget J. Crawford.
Description: Oakland : University of California Press, 2024. |
    Includes bibliographical references and index.
Identifiers: LCCN 2024022956 (print) | LCCN 2024022957 (ebook) |
    ISBN 9780520385160 (cloth) | ISBN 9780520385177 (paperback) |
    ISBN 9780520385184 (ebook)
Subjects: LCSH: Race discrimination—Law and legislation—United
    States. | Discrimination in law enforcement—United States. |
    Discrimination in justice administration—United States. | African
    Americans—Violence against—United States. | African Americans—
    Civil rights. | Sexual harassment of women—Law and legislation—
    United States. | Social justice—United States. | Black lives matter
    movement—United States. | MeToo movement—United States. |
    BISAC: SOCIAL SCIENCE / Race & Ethnic Relations | SOCIAL
    SCIENCE / Ethnic Studies / American / African American & Black
    Studies
Classification: LCC KF4757 .S63 2024 (print) | LCC KF4757 (ebook) |
    DDC 342.7308/73—dc23/eng/20240528
LC record available at https://lccn.loc.gov/2024022956
LC ebook record available at https://lccn.loc.gov/2024022957

33   32   31   30   29   28   27   26   25   24
10   9   8   7   6   5   4   3   2   1

For myself, my children, my husband, and my mother
—LBI

For Mark and Devlin
—BJC

Contents

Preface

Black Lives Matter and #MeToo are two of the most prominent social movements of the twenty-first century. On the streets and on social media, more people have taken an active stand in support of either or both movements than almost any other in American history. The path this book takes is not via a single, continuous narrative, but rather by way of a series of exchanges that explore the following questions: How have the two movements unfolded—separately and together—and how do they enrich, inform, and complicate each other?

Apart from the introduction and conclusion, this book is written in the form of a conversation. While the participants are all professors, their dialogue and this book are intended for a general audience. The nontechnical conversation is clearly marked to indicate who is speaking; it is organized around metaphors of *internal* and *external* space.

Twelve scholars who care passionately about equality of all kinds begin by asking how one can understand the Black Lives Matter and

#MeToo movements internally, on their own terms. The conversation also turns to look at the movements from the outside. What happens when we apply the lens of intersectionality to the work that both movements are doing? Do the movements challenge what we thought we knew about an intersectional analysis that takes into account race *and* gender *and* other factors that go into each person's individual identity? How do Black Lives Matter and #MeToo actually influence the daily lives and concerns of students, community activists, lawyers, and scholars? Finally, looking outward and beyond Black Lives Matter and #MeToo, the participants consider how social movements impact law and culture, and how law and culture impact and change each other.

Over the course of the book, the contributors come together to offer a conscious, self-reflexive discussion that includes the voices of several participants on each topic, all while querying what voices are and are not heard in the shaping of the two movements under consideration. In many ways, the Black Lives Matter movement has come to be associated with an "underclass" Black male identity, while the #MeToo movement often is (mistakenly) attributed to white middle- and upper-class women. Yet Black women organized both movements and continue to serve in leadership roles.

What work needs to be done by those who want to make real the "more perfect union" envisioned by the Declaration of Independence? In these pages, interested readers will find dialogue participants who are not so different than themselves. The contributors acknowledge their own life experiences as they engage in difficult, and sometimes painful, discussions about race, gender identity, and other identity axes. Their conversation is motivated by a commitment to dialogue and community, and the belief that true freedom and equality requires all of us to participate.

This book shows—not tells—how people with different perspectives can disagree with open minds and a generosity of spirit. Targeted for a general audience, each chapter concludes with discussion questions and suggestions for further reading. The chapters also have informative text boxes and illustrations that provide the reader with additional context for the issues under discussion. This is a dialogue that is truly accessible by all and is sure to spark further conversation.

Acknowledgments

We have received support from multiple people in many corners of our professional and personal lives. Our project would not be possible without the thoughtful contributions and patience of our dialogue participants: Mehrsa Baradaran, Noa Ben-Asher, I. Bennett Capers, Linda S. Greene, Aya Gruber, Osamudia James, Keisha Lindsay, Ruthann Robson, Kathryn M. Stanchi, and Lua Kamál Yuille. Professor Linda S. Greene was one of the co-convenors of the symposium held at the University of Wisconsin Law School that gave rise to the essay, published in the *Wisconsin Journal of Law, Gender and Society*, which in turn led to the conception of this book. We thank the student editors who helped make that program and the related publication a reality.

We are grateful for the assistance of Jennifer Allison, Kate Babbitt, Colin Lingle, and Theresa Winchell in helping us think about the structure and contents of this book. For additional helpful comments and conversations, we thank Horace Anderson, Jim Theis, Dan Waterman, and faculty colleagues too numerous to thank at the

University of Colorado, Southern Methodist University, and Pace University. The production of this book was supported by funds from the University of Colorado School of Law and Pace University.

We thank Maura Roessner for her enthusiastic collaboration and patience at every stage of this project, as well as guidance and assistance throughout the publication process.

Lolita Buckner Inniss adds special personal thanks to Dr. Daryl Inniss for his scientific-technical, "get to the point" style of questioning that helped her to consider how this work might appeal to a person with a non-legal or non–social science background. She also thanks Marie Inniss for her insightful discussions about how to compare Black Lives Matter and #MeToo in meaningful ways. Bridget Crawford adds special personal thanks to Michèle Cone. For helpful conversations around race and gender that have unfolded over years—and even decades—Bridget Crawford also thanks Aurora, Maureen, Barry, Michelle, Martín, Sandra, Chris, Alexis, Johya, Judy, Treva, Reaver, and the Ursuline Sisters of Cleveland.

Contributors

VOLUME EDITORS

LOLITA BUCKNER INNISS is the Dean and Provost's Professor of Law at the University of Colorado Boulder. Her scholarship focuses on legal history, and the intersection of race, gender, and law. She has taught across the law school curriculum, including property law, comparative racism and the law, real estate transactions, and immigration clinical practice. Dean Inniss attended Princeton University and UCLA Law School, and earned LLM and PhD degrees from Osgoode Hall, York University, in Canada. Growing up in Los Angeles, Dean Inniss aspired to be a citizen of the world, all while being grounded by ancestors who were present in the United States since the late 1600s, and who experienced some of the country's most traumatic events, including the Confederate battle and surrender at Appomattox, and the Tulsa race massacre. Her guidestar is the notion that there can be no fixity even in the past—our constantly changing recollections and understandings cause us to reinterrogate the present and re-envision the future on a regular basis.

BRIDGET J. CRAWFORD is a University Distinguished Professor at the Elisabeth Haub School of Law at Pace University. She writes about taxes, inheritance, property, and gender. Professor Crawford grew up in Cleveland Heights, Ohio, a community of 8.2 square miles. For most of her childhood, there were eight Jewish temples, five Catholic churches, and twenty-seven other places of worship serving a population of approximately sixty thousand people. Professor Crawford attended Saint Ann's School from 1974 to 1983. Beginning in 1972, the Parish Social Action Committee of Saint Ann's dedicated itself to racial integration in housing. That group became the Heights Community Congress, which is still going strong more than fifty years later.

ADDITIONAL CONTRIBUTORS

MEHRSA BARADARAN is a Professor of Law at UCI Law. Baradaran writes about banking law, financial inclusion, inequality, and the racial wealth gap. Born in Iran, Professor Baradaran immigrated to the United States with her parents when she was nine years old. She is a member of the Church of Jesus Christ of Latter-day Saints and the author of three books: *How the Other Half Banks: Exclusion, Exploitation, and the Threat to Democracy* (2015); *The Color of Money: Black Banking and the Racial Wealth Gap* (2017); and *The Quiet Coup: Neoliberalism and the Looting of America* (2024).

NOA BEN-ASHER is a Professor of Law at St. John's University. Professor Ben-Asher teaches Torts; Family Law; and Sexuality, Gender, and the Law. They were raised in a Zionist Orthodox Jewish family and community in Israel. Professor Ben-Asher writes broadly about jurisprudence and queer theory.

I. BENNETT CAPERS is a Professor of Law and the Director of the Center of Race, Law and Justice at Fordham University School of

Law, where he teaches Evidence; Criminal Law and Criminal Procedure; and a seminar on Race, Gender, and Crime. His academic interests include the relationship between and among race, gender, technology, and criminal justice, and he is a prolific writer on these topics. Professor Capers formerly served as an Assistant United States Attorney in the Southern District of New York. Professor Capers integrates his experiences as a Black gay man and as a federal prosecutor into his writing about the law.

LINDA S. GREENE is the 1855 Professor and MSU Foundation Professor of Law at Michigan State University, where she served as the Dean from 2021 to 2024. Her teaching and academic scholarship focus on Constitutional Law, Civil Procedure, Legislation, Civil Rights, and Sports Law. Professor Greene is a former elite middle-distance runner. She served on the United States Olympic Committee and was Counsel to the United States Senate Judiciary Committee. Before her teaching career, Professor Greene was an attorney at the NAACP Legal Defense and Education Fund. She became the first African American woman to teach at Temple University School of Law in 1978 and at Harvard Law School in 1984.

AYA GRUBER is a Professor of Law at the USC Gould School of Law. She teaches courses in Criminal Law and Criminal Procedure. She is an expert on criminal law and procedure, violence against women, and critical theory. Her scholarship focuses primarily on feminist efforts to strengthen criminal law responses to crimes against women. Professor Gruber is a former public defender. Her mother is a second-generation Japanese American, and her father is a second-generation Russian American. She was born and raised in Miami, Florida.

OSAMUDIA JAMES is a Professor of Law at the University of North Carolina School of Law. Professor James writes and teaches in the areas of Education Law, Race and the Law, Administrative Law, and Torts. Her scholarship explores the interaction of law and identity in the context of public education.

KEISHA LINDSAY is a Professor in the departments of Gender and Women's Studies and Political Science at the University of Wisconsin–Madison. Professor Lindsay's research and teaching interests include feminist political theory, Black feminism, Black masculinity, and gender-based politics in the African diaspora.

RUTHANN ROBSON is a Professor of Law and University Distinguished Professor at City University of New York (CUNY) School of Law, where she has taught since 1990 in the fields of Constitutional Law and Sexuality and Law. Her books include *Dressing Constitutionally: Hierarchy, Sexuality and Democracy* (2013). Professor Robson has centered the experiences of lesbians, gay men, and other sexual minorities in her academic work as well as her award-winning creative writing.

KATHRYN M. STANCHI is the E. L. Cord Professor of Law at William S. Boyd School of Law, University of Nevada, Las Vegas. She writes widely on persuasion, rhetoric, and feminist theory. She is the co-convener of the U.S. Feminist Judgments Project and an executive editor of the Feminist Judgments Series, which includes volumes on tax law, family law, employment discrimination, and reproductive justice. Professor Stanchi has written that her parents grew up "in a time and culture that believed it was a waste of time and money to educate girls" and she is deeply grateful to her parents for nevertheless sacrificing for her education.

LUA KAMÁL YUILLE is a Professor of Law and Business at Northeastern University. Her work connects property theory, economics, business law, critical pedagogy, and group identity. Before becoming a law professor, Professor Yuille was a federal law clerk, Latin Americanist socioeconomic development lawyer, Wall Street corporate transactional attorney, public school teacher, pro bono immigration litigation practitioner—all of which provide a strong foundation for her engaged scholarship on a wide range of questions.

Locating Black Lives Matter and #MeToo in Social and Legal Reform Movements

Lolita Buckner Inniss
Bridget J. Crawford

> A social movement that only moves people is
> merely a revolt. A movement that changes both
> people and institutions is a revolution.

> Martin Luther King Jr., *Why We Can't Wait*

A social movement is any collective action by an engaged and organized group aimed at changing institutional or societal behaviors.[1] Social movements are rooted in critiques of institutionalized models; they have as their ultimate aim the transformation of prevailing norms into new ones.[2] Social movements may be formal or informal, and often bring together individuals from seemingly disparate social groups that either share common objectives or are working in parallel to challenge the legitimacy of the status quo. Social movements grow out of the naming of political, economic, social, and, especially, legal injustices—harms that often are intertwined. Following the naming of injustices and any efforts to increase awareness of the pernicious effects of those injustices, social movements often seek remediation via the revision and reclamation of negative ideologies; they do so by naturalizing discourses and scripts promoted by dominant forces.³ This type of pushback was seen, for example, in the creation of self-affirming, self-ratifying representative slogans, such as the 1960s Black civil rights chant of "Black Is Beautiful," seeking to overturn centuries of dominant voices that made opposite claims.⁴ It is also evident in the popular 1970s assertion, "A woman's place is in the house . . . and in the Senate," which seized on longstanding masculinist notions about women's proper roles and their alleged incapacities for political leadership.⁵

In the hands of astute organizers, slogans, often memorable and succinct, can become protest themes that effectively capture and communicate the essence of a particular issue or cause. Such slogans galvanize people around a common goal, raise awareness about a particular problem, and create a sense of urgency for change. In like fashion come the contemporary protest cries of "Black Lives Matter" and "#MeToo," together with the social movements they herald for legal and social reckoning.

SOCIAL MOVEMENTS, PROTEST, AND LEGAL CHANGE

Not surprisingly, *protest* is a deeply fraught word, as it is frequently deployed to describe acts of physical violence and social upheaval wrought via public disorder, vandalism, and other tangible harms. To be sure, some protest involves physical rather than figurative intervention. However, focusing on violence ignores the extent to which protest far more frequently encompasses orderly, measured, peaceful, and nonviolent efforts to effect change by voicing opposition to oppressive norms, policies, and practices. Protest is often a means of initiating dialogue among same-side stakeholders, as well as with those on opposing sides of an issue. Protest has the potential to foster greater understanding and empathy between opposing sides, as well as the opportunity to find common ground and potential solutions. Furthermore, even in instances where those on

opposite sides of an issue are unmoved by the concerns at its foundation, protest can still bring attention to an issue that it previously
lacked, and spur discussion and debate.

This more benign form of protest in the context of social movements is essential to democratic societies, as it allows individuals to
express their dissatisfaction with the status quo, advocate for social
justice and, notably, to embrace and incorporate law as a tool for
change. Within the framework of social movements, protest often is
grounded in the view that changing law or society is a long, slow,
devolutionary process, but that some transformations can be more
revolutionary in nature, and encompass more rapid, even chaotic
change.[6] The relationship between law and social movements is not,
however, unidirectional. Law helps to shape social movements, and
social movements are, in reciprocal fashion, often crucial in helping
to accelerate matters within the legal domain, especially those that
would be difficult or even impossible to achieve via litigation or
other traditional legal tools.[7]

Perhaps no better example of this mutual relationship between
law and social movements is the civil rights movement in the United
States. One can trace a clear (and often brutal) line between, for
example, Black people's sitting in at a lunch counter to protest segregation and changes to public accommodation laws.[8] There is a direct
connection between widespread media images of police officers turning dogs or firehoses on peaceful Black protestors and the ensuing
(although rarely immediate) changes in school segregation laws.
These images sparked outrage among many viewers, and thereby
served as a means of creating support for the civil rights movement.

A similar journey may be seen in the contemporary women's
movement, which was spurred in part by events such as the discard-
ing of objects into the "Freedom Trash Can" at the 1968 Miss America
contest and the sit-in a few years later at the offices of the *Ladies'
Home Journal* magazine. Each event was designed to challenge the
values and ideals that defined women's "proper" roles, and each
played a central role in the law reform that, for example, ultimately

enabled married women to open credit accounts in their own names.[9]

Indeed, several scholars have addressed how the Black civil rights movement, the feminist movement of the 1960s and 1970s, and other rights-oriented social movements have mobilized law as an instrument of reform.[10] In the relationship between and among adherents of social movements, protest, and law—many of whom were interdisciplinary figures and not lawyers—reciprocity has played a critical role: the identities of movement members are key drivers of change, and change in turn reshapes the identities of those activists. When legal scholars and social reformers begin engaging in theoretical and pragmatic work together, they can forge a more comprehensive understanding of the legal system and its practical implications. Legal scholars bring their expertise in jurisprudence and analysis to the table, while social reformers provide valuable insight into the practical implications of legal issues in society. By working together, they can identify areas where legal theory can be applied to improve the functioning of the legal system and ensure that the law is serving the needs of society. This collaboration leads not only to the development of new legal theories, but also to the refinement of existing ones, culminating in the implementation of practical solutions to legal problems. Ultimately, the relationship between social movements and legal theory serves as an important mechanism for shaping some doctrinal and methodological departures or "turns" in law.[11]

TURNS IN THE LAW

The law has experienced numerous "turns" in recent decades—that is, departures from standard jurisprudential considerations. We identify multiple turns: critical, ethical, global, empirical, pragmatic, cultural, law and society, legal-historical, and legal-geographical. Consider first the critical turn, which involves fostering a "disposition of wary skepticism and critical vigilance" toward the law, and focuses instead on the ways in which law is used to maintain social hierarchies and power imbalances, as well as the need to develop strategies for challenging and transforming these structures.[12] Another is the ethical turn, which involves a renewed emphasis on two important factors: (1) the ethical dimensions of legal decision-making, and (2) the recognition that legal rules and institutions are deeply intertwined with broader social and moral values. The global turn encompasses the increasing interconnectedness of legal systems and the recognition that legal problems often require global solutions that transcend national borders.[13] In addition, there are empirical turns involving the study of law by way of direct, more social scientific methods rather than via secondary texts,[14] and pragmatic turns that advocate for more action-oriented approaches to law.[15] Cultural turns, which assume the substantial interaction between law and culture, are also often seen in legal discussions.[16] There are also broad law and society turns, in which interactions between law and society are centered; legal-historical turns, where time and its passage are made paramount considerations; and legal-geographic turns, where spatial considerations are principal concerns.[17]

Overall, these turns reflect a growing recognition that law is not a neutral or static set of rules, but rather an evolving and dynamic system that is shaped by broader social and political forces. Indeed, there are so many "turns" that a cynic might wonder whether the practice of law and its theoretical underpinnings is, at bottom, a decidedly dizzying enterprise full of pirouettes. With too many serially taken turns, can the focus on *law* lead to meaningful reform, as opposed to a return to the status quo? Ultimately, in bringing any mode of analysis—regardless of whether the academic banner is "law and social science," "law and culture," or "law and society"—it is useful to study how legal change can and does happen. Legal change and turns that stem from the power of social movements, and in turn, social movements that invoke law, help to enshrine law as a tool of progress, not regression.

It is important to note, however, that reliance on the legal system can be both a strength and a weakness of social movements. On the one hand, it can provide a platform for activists to make their case and to push for change. On the other hand, it can also reinforce existing power structures and limit the scope of the movement's demands. Additionally, legal victories can sometimes be limited in their impact and fail to address the underlying issues that gave rise to the movement in the first place.

Nonetheless, the study of Black Lives Matter and #MeToo implicates many, if not most, of the turns we have identified. Each is an example of how social movements challenge law, while simultaneously relying on it as a transformational force. The historic foundations of the turns on which both these movements are based give them heft and depth, and the contemporary framing of each social movement further enhances their power to bring about change.

BLACK LIVES MATTER AND #METOO AS RELATED NEW SOCIAL MOVEMENTS

Although social movement turns in law and society are not novel, Black Lives Matter and #MeToo are often described and analyzed as "new" social movements, and thus many discussions are centered in terms of their novelty.[18] As we detail in the introduction to chapter 2, both movements became popularized through twenty-first-century social media hashtags. And while these two distinct (yet, as we will show, sometimes interlocking) social movements grew out of long-standing historical oppressions and harms, they are, in many ways, new in force and effect. We understand both Black Lives Matter and #MeToo as decidedly modern movements united by three aspects: (1) their search for meaning, (2) the challenge they mount to the dominant culture, and (3) their roles in the formation of new individual and collective identities.[19] Both movements are undergirded by the belief that individual freedom is coextensive with the pursuit of liberation for all people. The movements seek to empower survivors and potential victims; raise awareness about issues; and challenge the structures and attitudes that enable, if not demand, harmful individual and structural behavior.

Both Black Lives Matter and #MeToo represent challenges to prevailing social and legal norms that have historically marginalized and oppressed people based on their race, gender, or other characteristics. By bringing attention to the experiences and perspectives of marginalized communities, these movements have the potential to transform the dominant culture and create a more just and equitable society. Moreover, the movements intersect in important ways; for example, Black women are uniquely marginalized because they often experience both racism and sexism.

The two campaigns have had some success in achieving legal reforms, while exercising an even greater influence on public opinion. Although there has been, and continues to be, significant backlash against both movements, and there are some who consider them to be polarizing and divisive, there have also been successes, especially in garnering public support for what are broad-based rights claims.

Black Lives Matter is a social, political, economic, and, ultimately, legal movement whose chief goal is eradicating systemic racism in all its manifestations. The Black Lives Matter movement originated in the United States in 2013 following the acquittal of George Zimmerman, a neighborhood watch volunteer who stalked, shot, and killed an unarmed Black teenager in Florida.[20] The teen, Trayvon Martin, was on his way back from a local store after purchasing snacks.[21] Despite the heinousness of the killing, Zimmerman was not charged with any crime until almost two months later, and the charge of second-degree murder came only after a social media campaign by activists. At his criminal trial, Zimmerman was acquitted of both second-degree murder and manslaughter for Trayvon Martin's death. Incensed by this outcome, a group of three friends and activists—Alicia Garza, Patrisse Cullors, and Opal Tometi—came together to craft the hashtag #BlackLivesMatter on social media in response to the verdict. Their intention with this social justice campaign was to draw attention to the systemic racism and violence that Black people face in the United States.

The Black Lives Matter movement quickly gained momentum, with protests and demonstrations taking place across the country, especially after a white police officer shot and killed a Black teenager, Michael Brown, in Ferguson, Missouri, in 2014. Black Lives Matter became a call to figurative arms for activists and advocates seeking to address police brutality and anti-Black racial injustice in the criminal justice system and beyond. A key concern of Black Lives Matter is the elimination of violence that Black people have frequently suffered at the hands of both the state and non-state actors. The movement's seemingly self-evident rallying call is a necessary reminder of the humanity of Black people in a society where that humanity is all too often denied.[22]

#MeToo, like Black Lives Matter, is a multifaceted movement with significant legal, social, political, and economic implications. It was first introduced by Tarana Burke in 2006.[23] Burke developed the phrase to instill a sense of solidarity among survivors of sexual violence, especially the young girls with whom she worked in low-income communities in Alabama. She created the #MeToo movement as a way to empower these survivors and raise awareness about the prevalence of sexual violence. #MeToo developed a second life when it came to the fore as a social media hashtag that swept across the world in the wake of multiple allegations that film producer Harvey Weinstein had sexually harassed (and, in some cases, sexually abused) women. Actress Alyssa Milano invited women to denounce sexual harassment of which they were victims on Twitter (now known as X) using the hashtag #MeToo. Many women received more attention when they took to social media to announce their experiences of harassment or abuse than when they had reported the same events to friends, family members, co-workers, bosses, or law enforcement. Weinstein ultimately was convicted of sex crimes in 2020 in both

New York and California. In April 2024, New York's highest court overturned Weinstein's conviction, although the California conviction still stands as of this writing.[24]

In sum, the #MeToo movement, like Black Lives Matter, is an organic movement that grew from popular support. Both movements were born out of grassroots activism and social media and gained momentum through the participation and support of millions of people around the world. Both Black Lives Matter and #MeToo have a significant similarity well beyond their origin stories: they are social movements that help to emphasize the harm that individuals experience while at the same time framing and naming collective identities and injuries. The cumulative effect of repeated retellings of individual killings, brutality, abuse, or suffering heightens the recognition that such atrocities are not merely "private" harms, but rather part of a larger structure of inequality, indifference, and inhumanity that allows them to happen in the first place. And yet, in as many ways as Black Lives Matter and #MeToo are similar, there are also profound distinctions between the movements.

DIFFERENCES BETWEEN THE MOVEMENTS

This book takes as its central focus many of the differences in the ways that the Black Lives Matter and #MeToo movements have unfolded and are perceived. To frame it in very simple terms, as we are writing in the third decade of the new millennium, Black Lives Matter often raises an image of Black people, violence, and tenuous claims. #MeToo, in contrast, frequently envisages white women, sexualized injustice, and redress. Further, Black Lives Matter is often castigated as a "bad" social movement, one that is purely reactionary, lacks moral and ethical grounding, is without clear purpose, is guided by unprincipled leaders, is premised on deviance from "legitimate" social and legal norms, and/or has no significant hope of emancipatory change. Even some self-proclaimed Black Lives Matter allies,

while acknowledging the fact that values within the movement reciprocally legitimize societal norms, have decried the extent to which
the movement's goals deviate from the conformity with mainstream
institutionalized values. Black Lives Matter has even been called, at
the extreme edges, "a terrorist movement."[25] The claim that Black
Lives Matter activists were terrorists was sometimes tied to the now
mostly discredited, apocryphal descriptor "Black Identity Extremist,"
or BIE, a label that has been used by some law enforcement groups
to describe a supposed threat posed by individuals or groups who
hold extreme views about Black empowerment.[26]

#MeToo, in contrast, is more frequently seen as seen as a "good"
social movement that emerged from the ground up (as opposed to
being instigated by "outside agitators"). With #MeToo, there is often
a utopian vision at play that lends itself to more generic and abstract
desires for gender equality and social justice. These goals are deemed
not only less disruptive to, but sometimes fully in line with, established social, legal, and cultural frames. Because #MeToo has been
able to deploy symbols such as freedom, justice, social inclusion, and
redress—as opposed to radical social transformation—it has been
more typically framed as in accord with the existing order. Hence,
#MeToo is frequently seen as an expression of the legitimate hopes
of participants and of society more broadly for tangible, meaningful,
long-lasting systemic change for women.[27]

Many Black Lives Matter protesters are often assailed for being
loud and overly insistent, while #MeToo adherents are often hailed
for having the courage to speak at all. Women from all walks of life,
from the famous to the obscure, are honored for speaking up and out
in response to the #MeToo call. #MeToo often foregrounds people—
typically women—as victims, offering a statement that they, too,
have been subjected to sexual harassment, abuse, or neglect.[28] While
a key goal of the #MeToo campaign is to show just how pervasive
sexual assault and harassment are, another is to lend support for and
credibility to the individual women who share their stories of sexual
harassment and abuse.

In contrast, Black Lives Matter is, at least linguistically, a collective claim, an assertion of humanity and dignity on behalf of an entire group of people. In response, Black people are often excoriated for giving voice in this way to their concerns.[29] Furthermore, the emerging public perception of Black Lives Matter is associated with an "underclass" Black male identity, whereas #MeToo is coming to have an externally facing association with people who identify as white, cisgendered female, and middle and upper class.

The divergent perceptions of Black Lives Matter and #MeToo confound, given that Black women organized both movements. Black women, however, have long understood that advocating in the areas of sex, sexual identity, or related issues has meant compromises about Blackness, or gender, or both.[30] While it is not uncommon to encounter challenges to the predominant Black-white binary in American racial discourse, there is a startling failure to acknowledge what is effectively a sex-race binary in civil rights work. Historically, many Black women working within Black rights movements have been told to suppress their concerns about gender equality in order to present a "united front" on issues of racial injustice, as if race has no place in gender equality projects.[31]

While there is no doubt that, for example, gendered violence harms Black women as much as white women (and vice versa), concerns about the inadequacies of state-based responses to such violence are frequently captured by the forces of "millennial feminism" that use #MeToo as a tool to advocate for a "get tough on crime" approach. This perspective is counter to the Black Lives Matter calls for reshaping what is viewed as excessive and anti-Black policing.[32] Consider also that equal protection jurisprudence in this country is designed to recognize race or sex as an invidious classification; it is not equipped to recognize discrimination at the intersection of race and sex (or other protected characteristics).

For these reasons, one wonders how well law is equipped to effect justice in our time. Understandably, law is sometimes discarded in favor of social actions that seemingly lie within public reach. Central among our goals in initiating the work leading to this book is to query both similarities and divergences between Black Lives Matter and #MeToo, and to assess the role of law in both movements, all while understanding that we, and other scholars, come at this topic from varying subject-based positioning.

POSITIONALITY OF THE INTERLOCUTORS AND THE ORIGINS OF THIS BOOK

The positionality of interlocutors refers to the social, cultural, and individual positions and identities that people, including conversation starters and interviewers, occupy in society. These positions can include aspects such as race, gender, age, socioeconomic status, education level, and many other factors. The social location of interlocutors can have a significant impact on conversations in a number of ways, starting first and foremost with how varying perspectives and experiences shape conversations. Next, the positionality of interlocutors can affect the level of comfort and trust between and among discussants. Finally, and perhaps most importantly, this positionality can also influence the power dynamics within a conversation, and determine whether, in fact, there is even anything to talk about.

In our case, we as editors come from overlapping, yet decidedly different, subject positions. We are two cis women entrenched in academic feminist movements. One of us is Black. The other of us is white. Within these identities, both shared and separate, we found that there was most assuredly something to talk about in the context of Black Lives Matter and #MeToo.

We have chosen to use our shared and divergent social identities, professional experiences, and divergent racial backgrounds to critically reflect on these matters. Despite what seem to be consistent setbacks in racial and gender advancement, we are *skeptical optimists:* we are convinced that visiting and revisiting the intersectional nature of movements like Black Lives Matter and #MeToo may still provide a foundation for sociolegal solutions. We are also deeply committed to the work of achieving the more perfect union of which we believe our great country is capable.

The issues embraced by the Black Lives Matter and #MeToo movements are ripe for a robust intersectional analysis, given the interlocking nature of racial and gender oppression. We are joined in this endeavor by a group of scholars who first came together for conversations in a symposium sponsored by the *Wisconsin Journal of Gender, Law and Society* in 2019 that was co-convened by the two of us and Linda Greene. That journal published those conversations in dialogue form. The contributors to this book include the initial contributors to the Wisconsin symposium and several other legal scholars with wide-ranging teaching and scholarly interests— including critical race theory, feminist theory, violence against women, the criminal justice system, policing, human and legal geography, structural marginalization, and constitutional and civil rights law. The conversations in the original 2019 essay are broadened and deepened in this book. Further, additional invited colleagues have enriched the discussion with their own perspectives not only on both movements, but also with attention to the nation-wide protests in 2020 in the aftermath of the deaths of unarmed Black Americans at the hands of the police. Our contributors also make trenchant observations about the way the media covered Black Lives Matter protests compared to its coverage of the insurrection riots at the United States Capitol on January 6, 2021. All movements are contextualized by the COVID-19 pandemic that lingers, as well as by the fits and starts in the U.S. economy that have characterized the years since 2020. These plural scholarly voices and perspectives further enhance, enrich, deepen, and complicate the project.

Continuing with the form seen in the initial journal article, most of this book is presented in the style of a dialogue. It was, however, written asynchronously and at different times. Authors answered questions on their own and sent them to us. Our task, as editors, was to attempt to bring some "flow" and coherence to a long

conversation that evolved over time, distance, and multiple varia-
tions. In the case of participants who were part of the original 2019
Wisconsin Journal of Gender, Law and Society essay, some chose to
revisit their work, and expanded or reshaped it as they saw fit. New
participants were free to write with or without explicit knowledge of
others' contributions. In any case, all participants had multiple
opportunities to refine and change their work, after seeing each other's answers and our editorial interventions.

HOW THIS BOOK IS DIFFERENT

There are a number of works that query contemporary racial and
gender issues. This book is located in the context of other works that
theorize the Black Lives Matter movement, while also giving particular emphasis to the movement's breadth, depth, and origins,
along with considerations of its internal and external perceptions.[33]
We have also learned from prior work on the #MeToo movement, as
well as from scholarship that not only interrogates contemporary
debates in anti-sexual violence activism and justice seeking, but also
engages with late-twentieth-century efforts to identify sexual harassment as a long-standing societal problem.[34]

One of the most unique aspects of this book is its use of dialogue
between and among scholars. We two act as editors, narrators, and
co-authors when we gather the voices of others and participate in
conversations. We are thus moving frequently between the mono-
logic, the dialogic, and the polyphonic, following the example of several excellent books that convent dialogues between and among
scholars and intellectuals on issues of gender and/or race and ethnicity.[35] One thing we note is that, while there are invariably differences in approach to some of the questions, we have the privilege of
writing within a context that largely lacks the dialogic constraints
found among people who share sharply contrasting views on race

and gender.[36] In instances where there are large differences in perspective, there are differing burdens on participants when they speak at all, and especially when they serve as interlocutors or conversation leaders.

While most of this book follows in the dialogic vein seen elsewhere, it intentionally explores the interrelationships and differences between the Black Lives Matter movement and the #MeToo movement. Specifically, this book is one of the first to provide academic—yet broadly accessible—context for the two movements generally, as well as the widespread protests in the summer of 2020 during the height of the COVID-19 pandemic. We seek to explore the similar origins and methods of the Black Lives Matter and #MeToo movements and consider their relative success (or lack thereof) in achieving their stated aims.

This book also shines new light on what is at stake when those who have experienced sexual harassment or abuse raise their voices against members of groups who have their own experience with oppression. For example, which stories are told, and whose stories are heard, are important considerations when it comes to discussing sexual abuse cases involving Black men like Bill Cosby and R. Kelly.[37]

By showing how the Black Lives Matter and #MeToo social justice movements intersect, this book seeks to illuminate important questions and foster necessary conversations about how social and legal change can be achieved in an era in which media, especially social media, play a large role in shaping public opinion. The pages that follow are intended to offer discussion and inquiry for consideration by a large and diverse readership. Accordingly, each chapter concludes with further discussion questions designed to provoke thoughtful contemplation of the law's potential and limitations, as well as the law's relationship to social change. The discussion questions make this book appropriate for the solo reader, students, and book clubs alike, as they embrace discussions of the present, and how it is informed by the past.

THE LONG ARC OF HISTORY

Recent years have witnessed an overwhelming outcry from activists who have protested seemingly never-ending instances of unjustified police and vigilante detentions, assaults, and murders of Black people. These tragedies cross class and gender lines, as Black people from all walks of life seem at all times prone to being summarily judged, and even executed, by agents of the state or by self-deputized private citizens.

That said, the Black Lives Matter movement is the most recent iteration of organized protests against police violence, which have a long history and have been at the heart of Black American activism for a more than a century. In the years after the Civil War, Black people and their allies decried the absence of Black rights, an absence that extended even, at least in context, to where those rights had been framed by post–Civil War amendments.[38] Indeed, mere decades after the ratification of those amendments, and despite the initial optimism they engendered, the reality was that Black people faced oppression in almost every facet of life. It eventually came to the point that the National Association for the Advancement of Colored People, an organization that has historically advocated for the rights of Black people, was forced to denounce the collusion between certain police and justice services and white supremacist organizations such as the Ku Klux Klan (KKK), which were then all-powerful in the Deep South.[39]

During the same period that Black Lives Matter came to prominence, we experienced a cultural watershed moment, as women have begun (or begun again) to fight loudly and publicly against sexual harassment, violence, and abuse by powerful men, and have done so under the umbrella of the #MeToo movement. As is true with Black Lives Matter, prior generations of women also launched protests against pervasive masculinist norms that limited women's possibilities. However, in the protests of decades past, women frequently felt pressured to suffer sexual harassment and assault, as well as other gender-based violations and indignities, in silence. Popular culture even incorporated these harms as part of what was to be expected when women left their homes.[40] Women employed in workplaces alongside men, especially male bosses, sometimes became "office wives" to such men.[41] "Office wife" is a phrase that conveys mixed notions of work, domesticity, and sexual promise.[42] This silence grew out of fear that formal or informal complaints might endanger their jobs or relationships with co-workers, or even attract more harassment or abuse.

While both these movements are critical reflections on compelling legal and social issues, there are some who suggest that the Black Lives Matter movement is fading into obscurity, along the lines of the Occupy movement,[43] as the minor rumblings of a few disaffected activists who have maximized their media exposure. In contrast, the #MeToo movement has spread and flourished across industries in the United States and even around the globe, seeming to reshape the culture and causing many to question the impact of unequal gender relations, and to challenge notions of power and sexual autonomy. Not coincidentally, perhaps, the "Karen" label entered the popular lexicon around the same time, signifying an entitled (typically middle-aged) white woman who asserts her racial and gender privileges in order to police the public behavior and actions of others, especially Black people.[44]

What accounts for the difference in how the Black Lives Matter and #MeToo movements have unfolded and been received by the public? A possible answer may lie in the persistent failure to understand the interlocking nature of racial and gender oppression, combined with a dearth of a robust intersectional analysis. *Intersectionality* is a term popularized by legal scholar Kimberlé Crenshaw in an article published in 1989 in the *University of Chicago Legal Forum*, in which she wrote, "Because the intersectional experience [of Black women] is greater than the sum of racism and sexism, any analysis that does not take intersectionality into account cannot sufficiently address the particular manner in which Black women are subordinated. . . . Discrimination, like traffic through an intersection, may flow in one direction, and it may flow in another."[45]

To a certain extent, the national collective consciousness seems capable of understanding the horrors of violence against Black men or discrimination against white women, but not the multiple vectors of discrimination experienced by women, trans, and gender diverse people of all races and ethnicities. What this means is that the legal issues growing out of or related to Black Lives Matter and #MeToo are sometimes similarly insufficiently inclusive in their framing. This calls for deeper interrogation of the relevance of law to address harms described by both movements.

RELEVANCE OF LEGAL ISSUES IN SOCIAL MOVEMENTS

The failure to understand the interconnectedness of gender and racial oppression in the context of legal or social justice issues is not new. In 1992, Nobel prize-winning author Toni Morrison edited a groundbreaking collection that brought together scholars across multiple disciplines to discuss another watershed moment in the United States: Professor Anita Hill's 1991 allegations of sexual harassment against U.S. Supreme Court nominee Clarence Thomas. In that volume, titled *Race-ing Justice, En-Gendering Power: Essays on Anita Hill, Clarence Thomas, and the Construction of Social Reality* (Pantheon, 1992), scholars examined the racial and sexual aspects of the Hill-Thomas debacle, as well as the legal, historical, and cultural contexts for Hill's claims and the response to them. While some of the authors took a decidedly intersectional approach to their analysis, others seemed to call into question the wisdom of framing Hill's claims as a matter of gender instead of race (or vice versa), while others even doubted whether her claims raised sufficient issues of law and justice at all. So, too, in the twenty-first century, scholars engaged in understanding the legal, social, political, and cultural significance of the Black Lives Matter and #MeToo movements vary in their understandings not only of the movements themselves, but also how they engage law or justice, and differ on whether to engage with the movements alone or in tandem.

In assessing Black Lives Matter, #MeToo, and other complex social justice movements, some lawyers and legal scholars prefer to assess racial and gender harms on separate axes, whereas others believe that only an intersectional approach—one not embraced by the current law—can achieve meaningful justice. Furthermore, questions about the roles of class privilege, money, and power run like an operating system in the background of any analysis. Assessing social justice movements like Black Lives Matter and #MeToo requires a nuanced understanding of how systemic inequalities impact different communities.

Those who assess racial and gender harms as occurring on separate axes often focus on addressing one issue at a time, such as racial discrimination or gender discrimination. They believe that this approach allows for a more targeted response to specific forms of injustice, and that addressing each axis separately can lead to more effective solutions. On the other hand, those who advocate for an intersectional approach believe that racial and gender harms are inextricably linked and cannot be fully understood or addressed without taking into account the ways in which different forms of oppression intersect. This latter approach recognizes that individuals can experience multiple forms of discrimination, and that the intersections of race, gender, class, sexuality, and other identities create unique experiences of marginalization and exclusion.

Regardless of whether Black Lives Matter and #MeToo are viewed individually or intersectionally, one thing is very clear: there has been, and will likely continue to be, legal and social backlash to both movements.

BACKLASH TO BLACK LIVES MATTER AND #METOO AND THE ROLE OF LAW

The Black Lives Matter and #MeToo movements have both brought significant attention to issues of social justice, particularly around the experiences of Black people and survivors of sexual harassment and assault. However, both movements have also faced extensive legal and social backlash.

Black Lives Matter has been met with strong public pushback from those who disagree with its message or tactics. Some critics have argued that the movement is anti-police, despite the fact that it focuses specifically on addressing systemic racism and the problem of police brutality. Others have criticized the looting and property damage that has occurred during some protests, broadly characterizing these events as "riots," even though the majority of protests have been peaceful. Additionally, some have accused the movement of being divisive or promoting violence, despite its efforts to promote equality and justice for all. In terms of legal backlash, there have been efforts to restrict or criminalize Black Lives Matter protests, including laws that increase penalties for obstructing traffic and even targeting protesters with violence. There have also been cases of police using excessive force against protesters or using surveillance to monitor Black Lives Matter activists.

Similarly, the #MeToo movement has also faced some strong counterresponses from those who disagree with its message or methods. Some have argued that the movement has led to a "witch hunt" mentality, in which those accused of sexual misconduct are immediately assumed to be guilty. Others have suggested that some accusations may be false or exaggerated, and that the movement could unfairly damage the reputations of innocent individuals.

Regarding the law-related backlash to #MeToo, there have been defamation lawsuits brought by those accused of sexual misconduct, as well as efforts to weaken Title IX protections (i.e., federal requirement that institutions protect against sex-based discrimination) for survivors of sexual assault on college campuses. Few movements for liberation can proceed without opposition, and that is certainly true of the Black Lives Matter and #MeToo movements. Those who proclaim "All Lives Matter," for example, seek to untether Black Lives Matter from its historical roots. Instead of understanding "Black Lives Matter" as a simple claim of humanity in a society that has historically denied it, detractors falsely interpret the phrase as one of comparative worth. And with counter slogans like "Blue Lives Matter," conservatives seek to exalt the importance of present-day sacrifices of police officers and mute the emphasis on decades, and indeed, centuries of private and state violence against Black people in the United States.

Correspondingly, the "not all men" reaction to #MeToo seeks to take an empirically grounded argument—that most sexual harassment and violence is inflicted by men on women—and reduce it to an individual problem without gendered dimensions. Indeed, these detractors of the #MeToo movement might even be understood as asserting an empirical counterclaim—that most men are not harassers or perpetrators of violence. Others are quick to raise doubts about #MeToo accusers' veracity, framing men as unwitting dupes of sexual sirens, or as hapless victims of "scorned women" extracting revenge.[46]

Perhaps one of the most pernicious backlashes to both Black Lives Matter and #MeToo are the so-called anti-woke laws that have been written in jurisdictions across the country. For example, the Florida legislature passed a bill that limits the way schools can teach about race, gender, or other aspects of identity.[47] The word *woke* is part of African-American parlance, and refers to the trait of being socially, culturally, and politically aware, especially as it concerns injustices like structural racism.[48] In recent years it has been adopted into white mainstream culture, and soon thereafter corrupted to refer to narrow, partisan, countercultural concerns, particularly by those who claim to not be racists because they never consider race. Indeed, for some critics, Black Lives Matter and #MeToo are key examples of all of the ills of "wokeism."

To be sure, the movements have not been helped by accusations of financial wrongdoing or revelations that several prominent women associated with the #MeToo movement had been involved in efforts by (now former) New York Governor Andrew Cuomo to discredit a woman who had accused him of sexual harassment.[49] Even the most well-intentioned progressive social leaders may be revealed to have very real human weaknesses. This may be especially true in instances where some movement leaders have had little access to traditional forms of power, such as political or economic influence, and so they are more susceptible to error. To dwell on such matters, however, ignores many of the social, legal, political, and economic improvements that have grown from Black Lives Mater and #MeToo in a relatively short time. It is thus essential to focus on the greater meaning and positive impact of these movements.

STRUCTURE OF THIS BOOK

This book is built around a written dialogue among twelve professors, most of whom are trained as lawyers, who teach at universities in the United States. The contributors to this book have different perspectives, backgrounds, and races. We note at the outset, though, that no one should be interpreted as speaking "for" members of a particular group. Nor do the participants represent of full range of viewpoints, political affiliations, ethnic backgrounds, or racial identities found in the diverse U.S. (and global) population. Six of the twelve contributors to the dialogue are Black; ten of twelve contributors identify as women. This book unapologetically elevates Black American women's voices—without excluding others—in the discussion and analysis of about two movements founded and sustained by Black American women.

Each chapter begins with a brief contextual note written by the editors. It then presents the questions posed to the contributors and the edited dialogue that ensued, with each contributor's contribu-

tion marked with their name. This allows the reader to readily identify the topic under discussion and the "speaker." The reader can
trace the evolution of ideas and various points where authors agree
or take different views. Interspersed in each chapter are textual
notes and illustrations to provide the reader with necessary context.
Where we have excerpted law review articles, we have eliminated
footnotes and made certain deletions, without indicating what those
are, to keep the excerpts readable. All material otherwise remains as
the author wrote it. Each chapter concludes with a series of questions for reflection or discussion as well as a list of suggested further
readings for those who want to learn more.

Chapter 1 explores the origins of Black Lives Matter and #MeToo,
asking whether the two movements represent twenty-first-century
ideological combustion, or can be better understood as a flare in a
continuous burning of earlier movements. Contributor Keisha
Lindsay takes the view that both Black Lives Matter and #MeToo are
powerful, autonomous movements created by Black feminists who
set out to intentionally challenge white patriarchy.

Chapter 2 proceeds to a more explicit comparison of the goals,
assumptions, and methods of the two movements. One of the most
salient differences, says contributor Noa Ben-Asher, is their framing: #MeToo is a message of shared suffering, which Black Lives
Matter is an ethical demand. While there is some overlap between
the two movements, their differing framings and goals have led to
different priorities and strategies for creating change.

Chapter 3 seeks to co-locate Black Lives Matter and #MeToo in
the larger field of feminist thought and explores how feminist theory
and aspirations about law itself shape both movements. In this
regard, intersectionality is a central concept; it undergirds much of
what mediates and sustains progress for women, in addition to trans
and nonbinary people, in legal and law-like settings. As contributor
Lua Yuille observes, intersectionality demands that justice be multivalent. In this respect, we estimate that both movements have some
distance to go. We trace a self-reflexive dimension within both Black

Lives Matter and #MeToo that tends to exclude those deemed to be outside the goals of each movement.

Chapter 4 considers which voices are missing from the two movements and what we can learn from their absence. Contributor Ruthann Robson notes that processes of theory building and movement building often leave someone or something out of the final product. Where there is exclusion, this may be due to a range of factors, including the selection and prioritization of ideas and perspectives, power dynamics, and structural inequalities. Such omissions, while at times problematical and hurtful, may also be vitally necessary to achieve ultimate success.

Chapter 5 turns to a metaphoric spatial query with an external, forward-looking question about what the next steps are for both movements, and what lies at the end of each movement's journey. This taxonomy considers that the Black Lives Matter and #MeToo movements have individual locations in cultural discourse, but that they also are mutually and jointly co-located.

Chapter 6 offers vital predictions about where both movements may go in the future. This concern comes in the guise of two questions. What defines success? How will we know if there is victory? Is success, as contributor Bennett Caper opines, when the movements no longer are necessary? And if so, does the absence of a necessity for such movements raise the specter of a colorblind, genderblind society where there are no downsides to difference, but upsides, as contributor Osamudia James writes?

SPATIAL TURNS IN LAW

As alluded to above, this book embraces, among other turns, spatial turns in law. That is, the book makes ample use of internal and external spatial metaphors. This "spatial turn" is not unusual in humanistic, legal, or social scientific endeavors more broadly.[50] Race and gender identities especially have been and are markers of the spaces that people inhabit. These spaces tend to reify difference, and, in a seemingly endless iterative process, the spaces are, in turn, formed and reformed by the people who occupy them.[51] In deploying spatial metaphors, the book proceeds along five multiple dimensions.

The first move is internal, in the sense of comparing Black Lives Matter and #MeToo to each other, in terms of their definitions, goals, and ideas of success. The second move is external: the lens of intersectionality—one that has a theoretical history and present vitality outside the movements—leads to new perspectives. Intersectionality reveals lesser-understood dimensions of Black Lives Matter and #MeToo, while the movements, in turn, suggest that intersectional analysis may obscure the popular legibility of the movements' messages. Third, a meta-internal spatial framework invites inquiry into how the movements shape the daily work of scholars, teachers, lawyers, and community activists. Fourth, a dialectical external-internal frame drives questions about the movements' effects on law and popular culture, and the reciprocal effects between those external influences and the movements themselves.

The final spatial arrangements, which we classify as "material," are understood as giving rise to some of the concerns at the heart of the #MeToo and Black Lives Matter movements and are best explained by offering concrete examples. For #MeToo, harassment, assault, and other forms of gender discrimination occur outside what some people deem to be women's primary place: the home. Today, women work in private *and* public workplaces. Women are frequently found at many levels of company hierarchy, but workplaces are (one of many) sites of sexualized harassment and violence.

Likewise, there are material spatial aspects to the harms caused to Black people that are the subject of the Black Lives Matter movement. Black people have long been restricted in where they have been legally permitted to live, work, attend school, or simply be present in public spaces. A further intricacy in these narratives of Black spatial constraint and displacement are the ways in which white women have sometimes been complicit in policing such norms, ranging from white women's leadership in schools and neighborhood racial segregation schemes in the post–World War II period to their involvement in noted recent efforts to enlist police to oust Black people from spaces to which they have rights (so-called Karen incidents, which are described briefly earlier in this introduction).

FINAL NOTES

In closing, Black Lives Matter and #MeToo are both social movements heralded by protest slogans that were developed in response to trauma and tragedy. In order for protest slogans to be effective in developing social and legal movements, they must be used strategically and consistently over time. These social movements, however, are not premised only on breaches of legal or sublegal norms or failures of social integration. Instead, these social movements are vital territories of struggle for sociolegal power and narrative. They are not merely examples of the idea of a social movement turn in law—they are central to it.

Furthermore, this turn is ever more important as we look out upon contemporary assaults upon women's rights and autonomy that have particular potential to harm Black women. As we write today, we are faced with the unfolding legacy of *Dobbs v. Jackson Women's Health Organization*, the 2022 Supreme Court case that invalidated *Roe v. Wade*.[52] *Dobbs* is a harbinger not only of the loss of abortion rights, but also signals that other crucial rights protected by the Fourteenth Amendment, a key source of Black rights, may be under assault, as it may be considered to legally validate future claims that such protection is absent from the text of the amendment. Claims about women's reproductive autonomy, like many other women's rights issues, are frequently premised on religious, normative, narrow, or race-centric moral concerns about social change, all while being disguised as positive, broad-based, secular, purely descriptive, race-blind civic concerns. The conversations in this book help to make these points. We need to embrace the potential of Black Lives Matter and #MeToo, separately and together, to combat such changes.

We add a final note on language. Throughout the book, we follow the convention adopted by several major news outlets and scholars to use an initial capital letter in the word *Black* to describe individuals, groups of people, and cultures of the African diaspora, even though centuries of racism and white supremacy have denied many people accurate information about their origins and culture. If using a lowercase letter in "black" refers to a color, then we understand using an initial capital letter in "Black" as appropriate when describing people by reference to an identity axis.[53] This embrace of the initial capital letter as a sign of respect is not new. Writing in 1929, W. E. B. Du Bois had argued that "the use of a small letter for the name of twelve million Americans and two hundred million human beings is a personal insult."[54] Recognizing that language is constantly in flux, we are persuaded by Du Bois' reasoning.

Note also that we generally refer to the movements "Black Lives Matter" (without using a hashtag) and "#MeToo" (with a hashtag), although both movements use hashtags on social media. This is not to create a rank between the two movements, but the choice is informed by two factors. First, many people have an embodied experience with the Black Lives Matter movement on account of the 2020 protests following George Floyd's death, whereas many people's participation in the movement against sexual assault and harassment is limited to social media. Second, Black Lives Matter, with its initial capital letters, is understood by most readers as a signifier for a movement, whereas the hashtag in #MeToo (alternately, "Me Too," "MeToo," "Metoo," or "metoo") improves its legibility.

NOTES

Epigraph: Martin Luther King Jr., *Why We Can't Wait* (New York: New American Library, 1963), 116.

1. See generally Laura Beth Nielsen, "Social Movements, Social Process: A Response to Gerald Rosenberg," *John Marshall Law Review* 42, no. 3 (2009).

2. See generally Amna A. Akbar, Sameer M. Ashar, and Jocelyn Simonson, "Movement Law," *Stanford Law Review* 73, no. 4 (2021).

3. See Lolita Buckner Inniss, "While the Water Is Stirring: Sojourner Truth as Proto-Agonist in the Fight for (Black) Women's Rights," *Boston University Law Review* 100, no. 5 (2020): 1647 ("Naturalizing discourses are intentional representations of particular social identities as if they were a result of biology or nature, rather than history or culture which made them appear permanent and unalterable").

4. The slogan "Black Is Beautiful" emerged in the United States during the civil rights movement of the 1960s. The phrase was used in shorthand to revalorize Black bodies and as a rallying cry for Black people to embrace their natural features, including their dark skin and natural hair, as symbols of pride and tools to advance the Black cultural nationalist project that grew out of political and legal events. Paul C. Taylor, *Black Is Beautiful: A Philosophy of Black Aesthetics* (Malden, MA: Wiley, 2016), 16.

5. These slogans, for all of their self-laudatory content, were sometimes co-opted by media forces. Consider the 1970s slogan "You've Come a Long Way, Baby," which served as a cigarette maker's slogan to entice women to smoke, all while also acting as an unofficial rallying cry of second wave feminism. See, for example, Lolita Buckner Inniss, "Roxanne Shanté's 'Independent Woman': Making Space for Women in Hip-Hop," in *Fight the Power: Law and Policy through Hip Hop Songs*, ed. Gregory S. Parks and Frank Rudy Cooper (Cambridge: Cambridge University Press, 2021), 175–86.

6. The sociolegal revolution is, of course, not new. For instance, the substantial doctrinal changes in the contemporary world of property law have frequently led to this area of law being described as revolutionary. See, for example, Lolita Buckner Inniss, "Property Law Revolution, Devolution and Feminist Legal Theory," in *Feminist Judgments: Rewritten Property Opinions*, ed. Eloisa C. Rodriguez Dod and Elena Maria Marty-Nelson (Cambridge: Cambridge University Press, 2021), 10–18.

7. See, for example, Michael McCann, "Law and Social Movements," in *The Blackwell Companion to Law and Society*, ed. Austin Sarat (Malden, MA: Blackwell, 2004), 506.

8. Christopher W. Schmidt, "Divided by Law: The Sit-ins and the Role of the Courts in the Civil Rights Movement," *Law and History Review* 33, no. 1 (2015): 93, 94 (describing how 1960s Black civil rights campaigns in the

courts were supported by already mobilized social protest movements of the era). And there are yet other examples of how other types of social movements were direct antecedents of or impetuses for social change. See, for example, Ahmed White, "Its Own Dubious Battle: The Impossible Defense of an Effective Right to Strike," *Wisconsin Law Review* 6 (2018): 1083 (discussing how the labor federation social movement of the 1930s established its "campaign to organize the industrial workforce in large part on a mutual embrace of the New Deal state and its legal system").

9. In 1974 the Equal Credit Opportunity Act granted women the right to obtain credit cards separate from their husbands. Banks and other financial institutions denied married women in the U.S. credit cards or loans in their own names; single women also sometimes had difficulty opening credit accounts. See, for example, Winnie F. Taylor, "The ECOA and Disparate Impact Theory: A Historical Perspective," *Journal of Law and Policy* 26, no. 2 (2018).

10. See, for example, Scott L. Cummings, "The Social Movement Turn in Law," *Law and Social Inquiry* 43, no. 2 (2018): 361. See also Catherine L. Fisk and Diana S. Reddy, "Protection by Law, Repression by Law: Bringing Labor Back into the Study of Law and Social Movements," *Emory Law Journal* 70, no. 1 (2020): 63.

11. See, for example, Cummings, "Social Movement Turn," 361.

12. See Michelle Madden Dempsey, "On Finnis's Way In," *Villanova Law Review* 57, (2012): 827, 828.

13. See Marjorie Garber, Beatrice Hanssen, and Rebecca L. Walkowitz, eds., *The Turn to Ethics* (New York: Routledge, 2000).

14. See Bryant Garth and Elizabeth Mertz, "Introduction: New Legal Realism at Ten Years and Beyond," *UC Irvine Law Review* 6, no. 2 (2016): 122.

15. See, for example, Bridget J. Crawford, "The Profits and Penalties of Kinship: Conflicting Meanings of Family in Estate Tax Law," *Pittsburgh Tax Review* 3, no. 1 (2005).

16. See, for example, Jessica Silbey, "The Politics of Law and Film Study: An Introduction to the Symposium on Legal Outsiders in American Film," *Suffolk University Law Review* 42, no. 4 (2009): 756.

17. See, for example, Irus Braverman, Nicholas Blomley, David Delaney, and Alexandre Kedar, "Expanding the Spaces of Law," in *The Expanding Spaces of Law: A Timely Legal Geography*, ed. Irus Braverman, Nicholas Blomley, David Delaney, and Alexandre Kedar (Stanford, CA: Stanford Law Books, 2014), 1–2.

18. See generally Nelson A. Pichardo, "New Social Movements: A Critical Review," *Annual Review of Sociology* 23 (1997): 411–30.

19. See Alberto Melucci, *Nomads of the Present: Social Movements and Individual Needs in Contemporary Society* (Philadelphia: Temple University Press, 1989).

20. Angela Onwuachi-Willig, "Childress Lecture: The CRT of Black Lives Matter," *St. Louis University Law Journal* 66, (2018) 663, (2018).

21. See Charles Tilly, Ernesto Castañeda, and Lesley J. Wood, *Social Movements, 1768—2018* (New York: Routledge, 2020), 241.

22. Based on anecdotal observation, we note that there are even Black Lives Matter signs that permeate mostly white, upper-class neighborhoods, like in Boulder County, Colorado. These same neighborhoods are often deeply uneasy with the presence of actual Black people. As one writer observes, there are times when "Black Lives Matter signs have replaced actual Black lives."

23. See, for example, Holly Corbett, "#MeToo Five Years Later: How the Movement Started and What Needs to Change," *Forbes*, October 27, 2022, https://www.forbes.com/sites/hollycorbett/2022/10/27/metoo-five-years-later-how-the-movement-started-and-what-needs-to-change/?sh=4b34e9595afe [https://perma.cc/VJC5-T6GD] (describing Burke's coining the phrase "me too" in 2006 connection with her advocacy on behalf of sexual assault survivors).

24. See Jan Ransom, "Mr. Weinstein's Criminal Convictions in California Still Stand," *New York Times*, April 25, 2024, https://www.nytimes.com/live/2024/04/25/nyregion/harvey-weinstein-appeal [https://perma.cc/D3R2-K95V].

25. See, for example, Daniel Byman, "Who Is a Terrorist, Actually?" *Vox*, September 22, 2020, https://www.vox.com/identities/21449415/antifa-terrorists-violence-patriot-prayer-black-lives-matter-protests-portland-kenosha [https://perma.cc/FW2R-SG7L] ("When I write about the threat of white supremacist terrorism, I often receive complaints from readers that I am focusing on the wrong problem and that my articles are ill-informed and misleading (I'm putting the complaints politely). Instead of focusing on white supremacists, they argue, I should instead write about the 'real' terrorists like antifa and Black Lives Matter.").

26. The term "Black Identity Extremist" was reportedly first used internally by the FBI in August 2017, but it gained public attention in an FBI intelligence assessment leaked to the media later that year. See Wadie Said, "Law Enforcement in the American Security State," *Wisconsin Law Review*

2019, no. 4 (2019): 819–33, citing Hannah Allam, "5 Takeaways about the Trump Administration's Response to Far-Right Extremis*m*," *NPR*, June 7, 2019, https://www.npr.org/2019/06/07/730346019/5-takeaways-about-the-trump-administrations-response-to-far-right-extremism [https://perma.cc/DF5S-XMM5]. The concept of the Black Identity Extremist has been criticized by civil rights groups and activists who argue that it is a vague and racially charged label that is used to target Black activists and suppress dissent. Many have also pointed out that the FBI has historically targeted Black activists and civil rights leaders, such as via the 1950s and 1960s FBI COINTELPRO (an acronym for counterintelligence program) campaign that monitored allegedly subversive groups, including several Black organizations, under the guise of national security concerns. See, for example, Richard E. Morgan, *Domestic Intelligence: Monitoring Dissent in America* (Austin: University of Texas Press, 1980).

27. See, for example, William A. Gamson, "Social Movements and Cultural Change," in *From Contention to Democracy*, ed. Marco G. Giugini, Doug McAdam, and Charles Tilly (Lanham, MD: Rowman & Littlefield, 1998), 57–79.

28. Lolita Buckner Inniss, "Me, One: Sexual Harassment and the Single Voice," *Ain't I a Feminist Legal Scholar Too?* (blog), October 16, 2017, http://innissfls.blogspot.com/2017/10/me-one-sexual-harassment-and-single.html [https://perma.cc/Z2BH-2557].

29. For a discussion of the value of coming to voice, see Dallel Sarnou, "The Polyphonic, Dialogic Feminine, Narrative Voice in Anglophone Arab Women's Writings," *Rupkatha Journal on Interdisciplinary Studies in Humanities* 7, no. 3 (2016).

30. See, for example, Gloria Hull, Patricia Bell Scott, and Barbara Smith, eds., *All the Women Are White, All the Blacks Are Men, but Some of Us Are Brave* (New York: Feminist Press, 1982), 13–22.

31. See, for example, Lolita Buckner Inniss, "Toward a Sui Generis View of Black Rights in Canada? Overcoming the Difference-Denial Model of Countering Anti-Black Racism," *Berkeley Journal of African-American Law and Policy* 9 (January 2007): 32–73 (discussing the pressure on some North American Black women to ignore gendered racism in order to support "racial uplift" projects for Black men and women).

32. Aya Gruber describes the concerns about the inadequacies of state-based responses to gendered violence as part of a "millennial feminism" that occupies the space of "an uncomfortable equilibrium of distaste for gender crimes and punishments. On one side of the scale is a Black Lives Matter–

informed belief that policing, prosecution, and incarceration are racist, unjust, and too widespread. . . . On the other side is a #MeToo-informed preoccupation with men's out-of-control sexuality and abuse of power. This side wants to get tough." Aya Gruber, *The Feminist War on Crime: The Unexpected Role of Women's Liberation in Mass Incarceration* (Oakland: University of California Press, 2020), 5.

33. See, for example, Barbara Ransby, *Making All Black Lives Matter* (Oakland: University of California Press, 2018); Keeanga-Yamahtta Taylor, *From #BlackLives Matter to Black Liberation* (Chicago: Haymarket Books, 2016); and Christopher J. Lebron, *The Making of Black Lives Matter: A Brief History of an Idea* (New York: Oxford University Press, 2017).

34. See, for example, Biana Fielborn and Rachel Loney-Howes, *#MeToo and the Politics of Social Change* (Cham, Switzerland: Palgrave Macmillan, 2019); Laurie Collier Hillstrom, *The #MeToo Movement* (Santa Barbara, CA: ABC-CLIO, 2019); and Judith Rudakoff, *Performing #MeToo: How Not to Look Away* (Bristol, UK: Intellect Books, 2021).

35. See, for example, S. J. Kleinberg, Eileen Boris, and Vicki Ruíz, *The Practice of U.S. Women's History: Narratives, Intersections, and Dialogues* (New Brunswick, NJ: Rutgers University Press, 2007); Marcelo Suarez-Orozco, Vivian Louie and Roberto Suro, *Writing Immigration: Scholars and Journalists in Dialogue* (Berkeley, CA: University of California Press, 2011) (asking central questions surrounding immigration, and exploring topics including illegal immigration, enduring myths, and fallacies regarding immigration).

36. Leland Harper and Jennifer King, *Racist, Not Racist, Antiracist: Language and the Dynamic Disaster of American Racism* (Lanham, MD: Rowman & Littlefield, 2022), 73–80.

37. See, for example, Lisa Respers France, "Black Women Would Not Rest until R. Kelly Was Investigated," *CNN*, September 27, 2021, https://www.cnn.com/2019/02/22/entertainment/black-women-r-kelly/index.html [https://perma.cc/Y82P-CSRL] (referencing both the R. Kelly and the Bill Cosby cases).

38. Shortly after the Civil War, the Thirteenth, Fourteenth, and Fifteenth Amendments to the Constitution and the Civil Rights Act of 1866 offered African Americans freedom from the most onerous indicia of servitude, the chance to be treated as members of the polity, and the right to vote and participate in the political process, among other rights. See generally Eric Foner, *A Short History of Reconstruction, 1863–1877*, updated ed. (New York: Harper Perennial Modern Classics, 2015).

39. See, for example, Michael German, "Hidden in Plain Sight: Racism, White Supremacy and Far-Right Militancy in Law Enforcement," *Brennan Center for Justice*, August 27, 2020, https://www.brennancenter.org/our-work/research-reports/hidden-plain-sight-racism-white-supremacy-and-far-right-militancy-law [https://perma.cc/L3FK-YW75]. ("By the 1920s, the KKK alone claimed 1 million members nationwide from New England to California, and had fully infiltrated federal, state, and local governments to advance its exclusionist agenda.")

40. See generally Bonnie J. Dow, *Prime-Time Feminism: Television, Media Culture, and the Women's Movement since 1970* (Philadelphia: University of Pennsylvania Press, 1996).

41. The phrase "office wife" has been common in the United States and Canada since at least the 1930s, popularized by Faith Baldwin's 1930 novel *The Office Wife* (New York: Dodd, 1930) and its 1930 movie adaptation *The Office Wife*, directed by Lloyd Bacon. The notion of the "office wife" has been rendered more gender neutral via "office spouse" (or the addition of "cubicle hubby"). See also Wendy Leung, "The Office Wife and Cubicle Hubby: Till Downsizing Do Us Part," *The Globe and Mail*, March 8, 2010, https://www.theglobeandmail.com/life/the-office-wife-and-cubicle-hubby-till-downsizing-do-us-part/article4309413/ [https://perma.cc/DB5X-6GD9]. Some modern renditions view such relationships as reciprocally beneficial for men and women. However, many commentators have observed that notwithstanding a move toward gender neutrality, women are still often expected to be subservient to men in office settings. Even in modern times women secretaries and assistants are often constructed as office wives who are "deferential and ladylike" and who act as "loyal, trustworthy and devoted" extensions of their usually male bosses. Rosemary Pringle, "What Is a Secretary?," in Linda McDowell and Rosemary Pringle, eds., *Defining Women: Social Institutions and Gender Divisions* (Cambridge: Polity Press, 1992), 170, 173–75. See also Ann Eyerman, *Women in the Office: Transitions in a Global Economy* (Toronto, Canada: Sumach Press, 2000), 87.

42. Philip Hanson, *This Side of Despair: How the Movies and American Life Intersected during the Great Depression* (Madison, NJ: Fairleigh Dickinson University Press, 2008), 123.

43. See, for example, James A. Anderson, "Some Say Occupy Wall Street Did Nothing. It Changes Us More Than We Think," *Time*, November 15, 2021, https://time.com/6117696/occupy-wall-street-10-years-later/ [https://perma.cc/3TJM-GNHS].

44. See, for example, Willa Paskin, "The Karen: Rise of the Karen," *Decoder Ring*, podcast, July 13, 2020, MP3 audio, 39:18, https://slate.com /podcasts/decoder-ring/2020/07/decoder-ring-the-karen.

45. Kimberlé Crenshaw, "Demarginalizing the Intersection of Race and Sex: A Black Feminist Critique of Antidiscrimination Doctrine, Feminist Theory, and Antiracist Politics," *University of Chicago Legal Forum* 140 (1989): 149.

46. In 1991, Senator Howell Heflin (R-AL) said to Anita Hill, "Now, in trying to determine whether you are telling falsehoods or not, I have got to determine what your motivation might be. Are you a scorned woman?" See Grace Segers, "Here Are Some of the Questions Anita Hill Answered in 1991," *CBS News*, September 18, 2018, https://www.cbsnews.com/news/here-are-some-of-the-questions-anita-hill-fielded-in-1991/ [https://perma.cc/M94V-ZX78].

47. See Tim Craig, "Florida Legislature Passes Bill That Limits How Schools and Workplaces Teach about Race and Identity," *Washington Post*, March 10, 2022, https://www.washingtonpost.com/nation/2022/03/10/florida-legislature-passes-anti-woke-bill/.

48. See, for example, Tehama Lopez Bunyasia and Candis Watts Smith, *Stay Woke: A People's Guide to Making All Black Lives Matter* (New York: New York University Press, 2019), 156 (noting that "staying woke means recognizing that the dominant mode of racial ideology is colorblind, and racism, generally speaking, is best understood as deeply embedded in our society").

49. On accusations of financial wrongdoing, see, for example, Sean Campbell, "Black Lives Matter Secretly Bought a $6 Million House," *New York Magazine*, April 4, 2022, https://nymag.com/intelligencer/2022/04 /black-lives-matter-6-million-dollar-house.html [https://perma.cc/M2JZ-TMRY]; Tat Bellamy-Walker, "Black Lives Matter Activists Accuse Executive of Stealing $10 Million in Donor Funds," *NBC News*, September 7, 2022, https://www.nbcnews.com/news/nbcblk/black-lives-matter-activists-accuse-executive-stealing-10-million-dono-rcna46481 [https://perma .cc/3HYS-A69Q]. On events surrounding #MeToo and Cuomo, see Jodi Kantor and Michael Gold, "Roberta Kaplan, Who Aided Cuomo, Resigns from Time's Up," *New York Times*, August 9, 2011, https://www.nytimes. com/2021/08/09/nyregion/roberta-kaplan-times-up-cuomo.html [https:// perma.cc/KNP3-EN4K].

50. See, for example, Edward Soja, "Afterword," *Stanford Law Review* 48, no. 5 (1996): 1423. ("The spatial turn—or what might be called the spatialization of critical studies—reflects the growing interest in the power of space and spatial thinking as a way of interpreting not just the contemporary world, but

of dealing with critical questions of all kinds—including those addressed by critical legal scholars. Increasing attention is being given to the problems of the city, urban and regional issues, to locality, to the body, to place, to the relationships between the local and the global, to boundaries, to borders, to what can most broadly be described as the spatiality of human life.")

51. See, for example, Lolita Buckner Inniss, "'From Space-Off to Represented Space.' Review of *Reimagining Equality: Stories of Gender, Race, and Finding Home*, by Anita Hill," *Berkeley Journal of Gender Law and Justice* 28, no. 1 (2013): 147.

52. Dobbs v. Jackson Women's Health Organization, 142 S. Ct. 2228 (2022); Roe v. Wade, 410 U.S. 113 (1973).

53. See, for example, Nancy Coleman, "Why We're Capitalizing Black," *New York Times*, July 5, 2020, https://www.nytimes.com/2020/07/05/insider/capitalized-black.html [https://perma.cc/X43W-WXPG].

54. See, for example, Lori L. Tharps, "The Case for Black with a Capital B," *New York Times*, November 18, 2014, https://www.nytimes.com/2014/11/19/opinion/the-case-for-black-with-a-capital-b.html [https://perma.cc/6WZP-DLD9] (quoting W. E. B. Du Bois).

BIBLIOGRAPHY

Akbar, Amna A., Sameer M. Ashar, and Jocelyn Simonson. "Movement Law." *Stanford Law Review* 73, no. 4 (2021): 821–84.

Allam, Hannah. "5 Takeaways about the Trump Administration's Response to Far-Right Extremism," *NPR*, June 7, 2019. https://www.npr.org/2019/06/07/730346019/5-takeaways-about-the-trump-administrations-response-to-far-right-extremism [https://perma.cc/DF5S-XMM5].

Anderson, James A. "Some Say Occupy Wall Street Did Nothing. It Changes Us More Than We Think." *Time*, November 15, 2021. https://time.com/6117696/occupy-wall-street-10-years-later/ [https://perma.cc/3TJM-GNHS].

Bacon, Lloyd, dir. *The Office Wife*. Burbank, CA: Warner Bros. Pictures, 1930.

Baldwin, Faith. *The Office Wife*. New York: Dodd, 1930.

Bellamy-Walker, Tat. "Black Lives Matter Activists Accuse Executive of Stealing $10 Million in Donor Funds." *NBC News*, September 7, 2022.

https://www.nbcnews.com/news/nbcblk/black-lives-matter-activists-accuse-executive-stealing-10-million-dono-rcna46481 [https://perma.cc/3HYS-A69Q].

Braverman, Irus, Nicholas Blomley, David Delaney, and Alexandre Kedar. "Expanding the Spaces of Law." In *The Expanding Spaces of Law: A Timely Legal Geography*, edited by Irus Braverman, Nicholas Blomley, David Delaney, and Alexandre Kedar, 1–29. Stanford, CA: Stanford University Press, 2014.

Bunyasia, Tehama Lopez, and Candis Watts Smith. *Stay Woke: A People's Guide to Making All Black Lives Matter.* New York: New York University Press, 2019.

Byman, Daniel. "Who Is a Terrorist, Actually?" *Vox*, September 22, 2020. https://www.vox.com/identities/21449415/antifa-terrorists-violence-patriot-prayer-black-lives-matter-protests-portland-kenosha [https://perma.cc/FW2R-SG7L].

Campbell, Sean. "Black Lives Matter Secretly Bought a $6 Million House." *New York Magazine*, April 4, 2022. https://nymag.com/intelligencer/2022/04/black-lives-matter-6-million-dollar-house.html [https://perma.cc/M2JZ-TMRY].

Coleman, Nancy. "Why We're Capitalizing Black." *New York Times*, July 5, 2020. https://www.nytimes.com/2020/07/05/insider/capitalized-black.html [https://perma.cc/X43W-WXPG].

Corbett, Holly. "#MeToo Five Years Later: How the Movement Started and What Needs to Change." *Forbes*, October 27, 2022. https://www.forbes.com/sites/hollycorbett/2022/10/27/metoo-five-years-later-how-the-movement-started-and-what-needs-to-change/?sh=4b34e9595afe [https://perma.cc/VJC5-T6GD].

Craig, Tim. "Florida Legislature Passes Bill That Limits How Schools and Workplaces Teach about Race and Identity." *Washington Post*, March 10, 2022. https://www.washingtonpost.com/nation/2022/03/10/florida-legislature-passes-anti-woke-bill/.

Crawford, Bridget J. "The Profits and Penalties of Kinship: Conflicting Meanings of Family in Estate Tax Law." *Pittsburgh Tax Review* 3, no. 1 (2005): 1–70.

Crenshaw, Kimberlé. "Demarginalizing the Intersection of Race and Sex: A Black Feminist Critique of Antidiscrimination Doctrine, Feminist Theory, and Antiracist Politics." *University of Chicago Legal Forum* 1989, no. 1 (1989): 139–68.

Cummings, Scott L. "The Social Movement Turn in Law." *Law and Social Inquiry* 43, no. 2 (2018): 360–416.

Dempsey, Michelle Madden. "On Finnis's Way In." *Villanova Law Review* 57 (2012): 827–43.

Dobbs v. Jackson Women's Health Organization, 142 S. Ct. 2228 (2022).

Dow, Bonnie J. *Prime-Time Feminism: Television, Media Culture, and the Women's Movement since 1970.* Philadelphia: University of Pennsylvania Press, 1996.

Eyerman, Ann. *Women in the Office: Transitions in a Global Economy.* Toronto: Sumach Press, 2000.

Fielborn, Biana, and Rachel Loney-Howes. *#MeToo and the Politics of Social Change.* Cham, Switzerland: Palgrave Macmillan, 2019.

Fisk, Catherine L., and Diana S. Reddy. "Protection by Law, Repression by Law: Bringing Labor Back into the Study of Law and Social Movements." *Emory Law Journal* 70, no. 1 (2020): 63–152.

Foner, Eric. *A Short History of Reconstruction, 1863–1877.* Updated edition. New York: Harper Perennial Modern Classics, 2015.

France, Lisa Respers. "Black Women Would Not Rest until R. Kelly Was Investigated." *CNN*, September 27, 2021. https://www.cnn.com/2019/02/22/entertainment/black-women-r-kelly/index.html [https://perma.cc/Y82P-CSRL].

Gamson, William A. "Social Movements and Cultural Change." In *From Contention to Democracy*, edited by Marco G. Giugini, Doug McAdam, and Charles Tilly, 57–78. Lanham, MD: Rowman & Littlefield, 1998.

Garber, Marjorie, Beatrice Hanssen, and Rebecca L. Walkowitz, eds. *The Turn to Ethics.* New York: Routledge, 2000.

Garth, Bryant, and Elizabeth Mertz. "Introduction: New Legal Realism at Ten Years and Beyond." *UC Irvine Law Review* 6, no. 2 (2016): 121–36.

Gay, Roxane. "Fifty Years Ago, Protestors Took on the Miss America Pageant and Electrified the Feminist Movement." *Smithsonian Magazine*, January 2018. https://www.smithsonianmag.com/history/fifty-years-ago-protestors-took-on-miss-america-pageant-electrified-feminist-movement-180967504/ [https://perma.cc/Z2H8-B5UL].

German, Michael. *Hidden in Plain Sight: Racism, White Supremacy and Far-Right Militancy in Law Enforcement.* Brennan Center for Justice, August 27, 2020. https://www.brennancenter.org/our-work/research-reports/hidden-plain-sight-racism-white-supremacy-and-far-right-militancy-law [https://perma.cc/L3FK-YW75].

Gruber, Aya. *The Feminist War on Crime: The Unexpected Role of Women's Liberation in Mass Incarceration.* Oakland: University of California Press, 2020.

Hanson, Philip. *This Side of Despair: How the Movies and American Life Intersected during the Great Depression.* Madison, NJ: Fairleigh Dickinson University Press, 2008.

Harper, Leland, and Jennifer King. *Racist, Not Racist, Antiracist: Language and the Dynamic Disaster of American Racism.* Lanham, MD: Rowman & Littlefield, 2022.

Hillstrom, Laurie Collier. *The #MeToo Movement.* Santa Barbara, CA: ABC-CLIO, 2019.

Hull, Gloria, Patricia Bell Scott, and Barbara Smith, eds. *All the Women Are White, All the Blacks Are Men, but Some of Us Are Brave.* New York: Feminist Press, 1982.

Inniss, Lolita Buckner. "'From Space-Off to Represented Space.' Review of *Reimagining Equality: Stories of Gender, Race, and Finding Home* by Anita Hill." *Berkeley Journal of Gender Law and Justice* 28, no. 1 (2013): 138–51.

———. "Me, One: Sexual Harassment and the Single Voice." *Ain't I a Feminist Legal Scholar Too?* (blog). October 16, 2017. http://innissfls .blogspot.com/2017/10/me-one-sexual-harassment-and-single.html [https://perma.cc/Z2BH-2557].

———. "Property Law Revolution, Devolution and Feminist Legal Theory." In *Feminist Judgments: Rewritten Property Opinions*, edited by Eloisa C. Rodriguez Dod and Elena Maria Marty-Nelson, 10–18. Cambridge: Cambridge University Press, 2021.

——— "Roxanne Shanté's 'Independent Woman': Making Space for Women in Hip-Hop." In *Fight the Power: Law and Policy through Hip Hop Songs*, edited by Gregory S. Parks and Frank Rudy Cooper, 175–186. Cambridge: Cambridge University Press, 2021.

———. "Toward a Sui Generis View of Black Rights in Canada? Overcoming the Difference-Denial Model of Countering Anti-Black Racism." *Berkeley Journal of African-American Law and Policy* 9 (January 2007): 32–73.

———. "While the Water Is Stirring: Sojourner Truth as Proto-Agonist in the Fight for (Black) Women's Rights." *Boston University Law Review* 100, no. 5 (2020): 1637–664.

Kantor, Jodi, and Michael Gold. "Roberta Kaplan, Who Aided Cuomo, Resigns from Time's Up." *New York Times*, August 9, 2011. https://

www.nytimes.com/2021/08/09/nyregion/roberta-kaplan-times-up-cuomo.html [https://perma.cc/KNP3-EN4K].

Kleinberg, S. J., Eileen Boris, and Vicki Ruíz. *The Practice of U.S. Women's History: Narratives, Intersections, and Dialogues.* New Brunswick, NJ: Rutgers University Press, 2007.

Lebron, Christopher J. *The Making of Black Lives Matter: A Brief History of an Idea.* New York: Oxford University Press, 2017.

Leung, Wendy. "The Office Wife and Cubicle Hubby: Till Downsizing Do Us Part." *Globe and Mail*, March 8, 2010. https://www.theglobeandmail.com/life/the-office-wife-and-cubicle-hubby-till-downsizing-do-us-part/article4309413/ [https://perma.cc/DB5X-6GD9].

Lichtenstein, Grace. "Feminists Demand 'Liberation in *Ladies' Home Journal* Sit-In." *New York Times*, March 19, 1970.

McCann, Michael. "Law and Social Movements." In *The Blackwell Companion to Law and Society*, edited by Austin Sarat, 506–22. Malden, MA: Blackwell, 2004.

Melucci, Alberto. *Nomads of the Present: Social Movements and Individual Needs in Contemporary Society.* Philadelphia: Temple University Press, 1989.

Morgan, Richard E. *Domestic Intelligence: Monitoring Dissent in America.* Austin: University of Texas Press, 1980.

Nielsen, Laura Beth. "Social Movements, Social Process: A Response to Gerald Rosenberg." *John Marshall Law Review* 42, no. 3 (2009): 671–84.

Onwuachi-Willig, Angela. "Childress Lecture: The CRT of Black Lives Matter." *St. Louis University Law Journal* 66, no. 4 (2022): 663–76.

Paskin, Willa. "The Karen: Rise of the Karen." *Decoder Ring*, podcast, July 13, 2020. MP3 audio, 39:18. https://slate.com/podcasts/decoder-ring/2020/07/decoder-ring-the-karen.

Pichardo, Nelson A. "New Social Movements: A Critical Review." *Annual Review of Sociology* 23 (1997): 411–30.

Pringle, Rosemary. "What Is a Secretary?" In *Defining Women: Social Institutions and Gender Divisions*, edited by Linda McDowell and Rosemary Pringle, 170–76. Cambridge: Polity Press, 1992.

Ransby, Barbara. *Making All Black Lives Matter.* Oakland: University of California Press, 2018.

Ransom, Jan. "Mr. Weinstein's Criminal Convictions in California Still Stand." *New York Times*, April 25, 2024. https://www.nytimes.com/live/2024/04/25/nyregion/harvey-weinstein-appeal [https://perma.cc/D3R2-K95V].

Rudakoff, Judith. *Performing #MeToo: How Not to Look Away.* Bristol, UK: Intellect Books, 2021.

Said, Wadie. "Law Enforcement in the American Security State." *Wisconsin Law Review* 2019, no. 4 (2019): 819–33.

Sarnou, Dallel. "The Polyphonic, Dialogic Feminine, Narrative Voice in Anglophone Arab Women's Writings." *Rupkatha Journal on Interdisciplinary Studies in Humanities* 7, no. 3 (2016): 202–12.

Schmidt, Christopher W. "Divided by Law: The Sit-ins and the Role of the Courts in the Civil Rights Movement." *Law and History Review* 33, no. 1 (2015): 93–149.

Segers, Grace. "Here Are Some of the Questions Anita Hill Answered in 1991." *CBS News*, September 18, 2018. https://www.cbsnews.com/news/here-are-some-of-the-questions-anita-hill-fielded-in-1991/ [https://perma.cc/M94V-ZX78].

Silbey, Jessica. "The Politics of Law and Film Study: An Introduction to the Symposium on Legal Outsiders in American Film." *Suffolk University Law Review* 42, no. 4 (2009): 755–68.

Soja, Edward. "Afterword." *Stanford Law Review* 48, no. 5 (1996): 1421–430.

Suarez-Orozco, Marcelo, Vivan Louie, and Roberto Suro. *Writing Immigration: Scholars and Journalists in Dialogue.* Berkeley: University of California Press, 2011.

Taylor, Keeanga-Yamahtta. *From #BlackLives Matter to Black Liberation.* Chicago: Haymarket Books, 2016.

Taylor, Paul C. *Black Is Beautiful: A Philosophy of Black Aesthetics.* Malden, MA: Wiley, 2016.

Taylor, Winnie F. "The ECOA and Disparate Impact Theory: A Historical Perspective." *Journal of Law and Policy* 26, no. 2 (2018): 573–636.

Tharps, Lori L. "The Case for Black with a Capital B." *New York Times*, November 18, 2014. https://www.nytimes.com/2014/11/19/opinion/the-case-for-black-with-a-capital-b.html [https://perma.cc/6WZP-DLD9].

Tilly, Charles, Ernesto Castañeda, and Lesley J. Wood. *Social Movements, 1768–2018.* New York: Routledge, 2020.

White, Ahmed. "Its Own Dubious Battle: The Impossible Defense of an Effective Right to Strike." *Wisconsin Law Review* 6 (2018): 1065–131.

Historical and Contemporary Contexts of the Black Lives Matter and #MeToo Movements

WITH CONTRIBUTIONS BY

Mehrsa Baradaran   *Aya Gruber*
Noa Ben-Asher   *Lolita Buckner Inniss*
I. Bennett Capers   *Osamudia James*
Bridget J. Crawford   *Keisha Lindsay*
Linda S. Greene

BACKGROUND

What does it mean to offer historic or contemporary context to any movement, much less to the Black Lives Matter and #MeToo movements? At the center of the endeavor is the effort to offer a temporal framework to the movements—that is, to fix them in both time and space. This may be an effort to channel the power of chronological assessments, and hence, to take control over historical judgments.[1] Black people have far too often been invisible in history, and so, too, have women of all backgrounds. To have one's actions fixed in time is to have one's presence acknowledged.

In this chapter, the dialogue participants explore the historical and contemporary contexts of the Black Lives Matter and #MeToo movements. Both are examples of radical practices and philosophies that seek substantial social, legal, and economic transformations in the lives of Black people and women of all racial and ethnic identities. These transformations have most assuredly been shaped by past techniques, strategies, and discourses, as well as by current events.

It is worth observing that in June 2020, as the COVID-19 pandemic continued to spread in the United States and around the world, millions of people across the globe protested the police killing of George Floyd, an unarmed forty-six-year-old Black man in Minneapolis, Minnesota.[2] In Australia, Belgium, Brazil, Bulgaria, England, France, Germany, Hong Kong, Ireland, Italy, Japan, Kosovo, the Netherlands, Portugal, Scotland, South Africa, South Korea, Spain, Switzerland, Tunisia, and Wales, people took to the streets to express their outrage, often in defiance of legal and social norms.[3]

The protests after George Floyd's murder were a visible manifestation of the pent-up frustrations and rage that many Black Americans had felt for generations. Black people were not alone in feeling this way; for some white Americans, and people of other racial backgrounds, the repeated footage of Mr. Floyd's killing finally led them to acknowledge the truth of what their Black counterparts had been saying for years: police violence unfairly targets and brutalizes Black people in this country. In many respects, the killing of George Floyd crystallized what it means to be an ally to Black people—not just engaging in educative or philosophical projects for equality, but also working to support and advocate for the rights and equality of Black individuals, both in personal interactions and in larger systems of power and oppression. This newly realized allyship also meant to actively work to dismantle systems of oppression that disproportionately affected Black people.

So, in the summer of 2020, people of all racial and ethnic identities joined together in unprecedented numbers to proclaim that "Black Lives Matter," with banners, posters, and chants in the streets. This slogan had first entered the popular imagination in the months after the 2012 the killing of seventeen-year-old Trayvon Martin, an unarmed Black boy, by a neighborhood vigilante. This individual thought that Martin, who was wearing a hoodie and walking home from the store where he had bought Skittles and a fruit drink, looked suspicious.[4]

Reacting on Facebook to the acquittal of Martin's killer, self-described "radical Black organizer" Alicia Garza wrote what she called "a love letter to [B]lack people," using the hashtag "#blacklivesmatter."[5] The hashtag caught on and inspired the creation of multiple, decentralized racial justice organizations, loosely guided by a standard set of guiding principles.[6]

Like the Black Lives Matter movement, the #MeToo movement gained momentum because of a social media hashtag. In 2017, the *New York Times* published an article revealing that film producer Harvey Weinstein had entered into confidential agreements to settle claims that he sexual harassed several employees or members of the film industry, including actress Ashley Judd.[7] In response, actress Alyssa Milano's exhortation on Twitter (now known as X), which read, "If you've been sexually harassed or assaulted write 'me too' as a reply to this tweet," went viral.[8] Milano, however, had not coined the term "#MeToo." Activist Tarana Burke, a Black woman, had been using the phrase on social media since 2006 in her work with sexual assault victims as a form of "empowerment through empathy."[9] Milano, who had been unaware that the term actually originated with Burke, soon linked to Burke's organization and the "heartbreaking and inspiring" origin of the Burke's use of the phrase.[10] The hashtag remains popular; it is thought to have had widespread impact on public awareness of the problem of sexual harassment and sexual assault, with over half of all U.S. Facebook users estimated to be friends with someone who posted about this issue.[11]

While the Black Lives Matter and #MeToo movements have distinct origins and focuses, they share some similarities in their approaches. Both movements have been driven by grassroots organizing, as well as the use of social media to amplify voices and tell the stories of those who have long been marginalized. Additionally, both movements have faced criticism and pushback from those who argue that they are overly divisive or that their demands are unrealistic. Although the history behind each movement is different, both Black Lives Matter and #MeToo have similar contemporary claims and deploy modern tools, such as social media, to obtain deep change.

We asked our participants this question:

> Do you view the Black Lives Matter and #MeToo movements as autonomous phenomena or as outgrowths, evolutions, extensions, or departures from prior social or legal movements?

DIALOGUE

Bennett Capers: Organizers are aware of what worked, and what didn't, for other movements. Can we really think of Black Lives Matter and #MeToo without thinking of how they build on, and learn lessons from, movements that came before them? Remember Occupy Wall Street? Remember SlutWalks? I think of #NeverAgain following the mass shooting at Stoneman Douglas High School. I take it as a given that no social movement is truly an autonomous phenomenon. I'm not suggesting this is done consciously, but everything seeps in.

I'll go a step further and suggest that the #MeToo movement likely learned a thing or two from the Black Lives Matter movement. The latter was immediately attacked for not being inclusive enough; hence, the emergence of the counterclaims of "All Lives Matter" and "Blue Lives Matter," as well as adjacent claims like "Trans Lives Matter." #MeToo, as a matter of branding, first by Tarana Burke and then Alyssa Milano, is as inclusive—and thus made to go viral—as it can get. There's certainly no demographic that cannot claim #MeToo. This is just one example of a "lesson" its organizers likely learned from thinking about Black Lives Matter.

ABOUT SLUTWALKS

In order not to be raped, women should "avoid dressing like sluts." When a Toronto police officer made this observation in January 2011, he galvanized a worldwide protest known as SlutWalk. In less than a year, the grassroots initiative spread to over one hundred cities, including New York, Berlin, Cape Town, New Delhi, London, Chicago, Mexico City, Vienna, Helsinki, Buenos Aires, and Singapore, as well as smaller towns and college campuses across the United States. To date, tens of thousands of people, mostly women—many of whom disavow any attempt to reclaim the word slut—have participated in the effort, and the mobilization continues.

SlutWalk is premised on the ubiquity of rape, most of it inflicted by acquaintances, dates, and intimates. In the words of one participant, "Let's acknowledge that sexual violence exists everywhere." Another explains that she is walking "because this kind of thing has happened to about half of the women I know." Participants find the status quo unacceptable. Often angry and defiant, they decry rape and the culture of victim-blaming that surrounds it. Some wear the clothes they had on when raped.

SlutWalk seeks to contest cultural formulations of "bad victims," women unworthy of protection from sexual violence.

Excerpt from Deborah Tuerkheimer, "Slutwalking in the Shadow of the Law," *Minnesota Law Review* 98, no. 4 (2014): 1458–59, 1469–71, 1473.

Osamudia James: In its radicality, Black Lives Matter does draw heavily on the provocative aims and goals of movements like Occupy Wall Street or even SlutWalk, so I understand why you mention those, Bennett. As an aside, I'll say it is sobering to think that wanting all Black people, including queer folks, to be free, could be properly characterized as "radical," but here we are.

Lolita Buckner Inniss: It's definitely true that when people describe Black Lives Matter, or even #MeToo, as "radical," they are speaking pejoratively. Black Lives Matter has even, at times, been described as a "terrorist" organization.[12]

I see the value in reclaiming the word *radical*. In general, radical means being thorough in the pursuit of a particular goal or ideology. In politics, a "radical" is someone who advocates for significant or fundamental changes to society or the political system. It literally means "pertaining to roots," from the Latin *radix*. To me, the "radical" movement often offers a vision for change that is explicitly ameliorative, redemptive, and inclusive. To me, that is revelatory of these movements' genealogies and fundamental understandings. In both the Black Lives Matter and #Me Too movements, we see this yearning for democratic change and broadly inclusive participatory governance in civil society.

Osamudia James: In the Black Lives Matter movement in particular, I see a movement for Black liberation. Certainly, the contemporary movement is anchored in the same themes as earlier civil rights movements. If the insistence on recognizing the value of Black lives might be characterized as plaintive, it is more akin to the peaceful protests of the early to mid-twentieth century, led by Martin Luther King Jr. and the Southern Christian Leadership Conference, and less to the more assertive Black Power movement, led by the Student Non-Violent Coordinating Committee, the Black Panthers, and others.[13] But Black Lives Matter makes key departures from the rhetoric and platforms of those earlier movements, starting with leadership:

ABOUT THE BLACK POWER MOVEMENT

The black nationalist position received its first modern wave of sustained mass exposure in 1966 when Willie Ricks and Stokely Carmichael began using the term "Black Power" during the March Against Fear in Mississippi. Tension between integrationist and nationalist approaches had already erupted within and between various civil rights organizations. But the high-profile and polarized controversy over the term "Black Power" transformed what had been largely an underground conflict into a full-scale, highly-charged public debate over the fundamental direction and conception of the civil rights movement.

The mainstream reactions to the idea of comprehending the civil rights movement as a struggle for Black Power reflect the discourse associated with the marginalization of nationalist race consciousness in the dominant cultural rhetoric. Both black and white integrationists equated Black Power with white supremacy.

The integrationists saw two problems with Black Power. First, the concept assumed that power should be distributed on a racial basis, thereby assuming that American society should be thought of in terms of separate white and black communities. Black Power thus violated both the integrationist principle to transcend race consciousness at the ideological level and the integrationist program to end the segregation of whites and blacks at the institutional and community level.

Excerpt from Gary Peller, "Race Consciousness," *Duke Law Journal* 1990, no. 4 (1990): 787–88, 790.

ABOUT MICHAEL BROWN AND FERGUSON, MISSOURI

From the events in Ferguson, a new language of protest and resistance was born. The events gave voice to a new generation of protesters under the banner of slogans and hashtags such as "Hands Up! Don't Shoot!" and "#Black Lives Matter." On Saturday, August 9, 2014, Michael Brown, an unarmed black teenager, was shot and killed by Darren Wilson, a white police officer, in Ferguson, Missouri, a suburb of St. Louis. The circumstances of Michael Brown's death were disputed. Earlier reports indicated that Wilson initially approached Brown for jaywalking, and the interaction escalated into an altercation. Ferguson police state that Brown was shot while leaning into Wilson's car and struggling for the officer's gun. Some witnesses maintained that Brown's hands were raised, indicating surrender, when Wilson fired the fatal shots.

The killing resulted in a series of protests throughout the community, both peaceful and violent. In addition to outrage over Brown's death, local and county police were widely criticized for a forceful and militarized response to the protests, including the use of armored vehicles, smoke canisters, and tear gas to dispel the crowds.

Following Michael Brown's death [and the absence of any state prosecution], U.S. Attorney General Eric Holder announced that he would launch a separate investigation into the conduct of the Ferguson, Missouri, and St. Louis County police departments. The City of Ferguson, a majority African-American suburb, has only three African-American officers out of fifty-three members of the department. At the conclusion of the investigation, the DOJ issued a scathing report criticizing the Ferguson Police Department and the municipal court system in Ferguson, as well as provided recommendations for reform. The question, however, is whether the report and the responses to the unrest will result in profound changes and lessen the mistrust between citizens and police or will merely be ignored.

Excerpt from S. David Mitchell, "Ferguson: Footnote or Transformative Event?," *Missouri Law Review* 80, no. 4 (2015): 946, 950–52.

Black Lives Matter leadership is not only Black, but very intentionally female and queer.[14]

Keisha Lindsay: Definitely true, Osamudia. Unlike previous movements, Black Lives Matter and #MeToo were founded by self-identified Black feminists who explicitly articulated their intention to challenge white supremacist, patriarchal power.

Osamudia James: Also, Black Lives Matter is the first (or maybe the second) major movement for Black liberation in which religion in general, and the Black church, in particular, doesn't feature prominently, either intellectually or physically. Possibly the only movement that can claim that mantle, having the distinction of "first," might be the Black Power movement that operated alongside the traditional civil rights movement of the twentieth century.

Why does the Black church not feature as prominently? Americans overall may be less religious now than in the 1960s, although it is not necessarily true that Black Americans are less religious.[15] I think it is because the patriarchal, hierarchical, and socially conservative traditions of the Black church don't work with the more radical goals of Black Lives Matter.

Noa Ben-Asher: I want to pick up on Osamudia's insight about the non-religiosity of the Black Lives Matter movement. I think we

AN EARLY STATEMENT ON WOMEN'S RIGHTS

When, in the course of human events, it becomes necessary for one portion of the family of man to assume among the people of the earth a position different from that which they have hitherto occupied, but one to which the laws of nature and of nature's God entitle them, a decent respect to the opinions of mankind requires that they should declare the causes that impel them to such a course.

We hold these truths to be self-evident; that all men and women are created equal; that they are endowed by their Creator with certain inalienable rights; that among these are life, liberty, and the pursuit of happiness; that to secure these rights governments are instituted, deriving their just powers from the consent of the governed. Whenever any form of Government becomes destructive of these ends, it is the right of those who suffer from it to refuse allegiance to it, and to insist upon the institution of a new government, laying its foundation on such principles, and organizing its powers in such form as to them shall seem most likely to effect their safety and happiness. Prudence, indeed, will dictate that governments long established should not be changed for light and transient causes; and accordingly, all experience hath shown that mankind are more disposed to suffer, while evils are sufferable, than to right themselves, by abolishing the forms to which they are accustomed. But when a long train of abuses and usurpations, pursuing invariably the same object, evinces a design to reduce them under absolute despotism, it is their duty to throw off such government, and to provide new guards for their future security. Such has been the patient sufferance of the women under this government, and such is now the necessity which constrains them to demand the equal station to which they are entitled.

> The history of mankind is a history of repeated injuries and usurpations on the part of man toward woman, having in direct object the establishment of an absolute tyranny over her.
>
> Excerpt from *Declaration of Sentiments* (1848).

should distinguish religious *authority* from religious *values*. In both Black Lives Matter and #MeToo, there are certainly religious values that are endorsed (even celebrated).

Bridget Crawford: Religious values most certainly infused the language and thought of both nineteenth-century woman suffrage activists and abolitionists.[16] The Declaration of Sentiments, which was adopted at the first major women's rights gathering at Seneca Falls, New York, in 1848, modeled itself on the Declaration of Independence. It asserted that "all men and women are created equal; that they are endowed by their Creator with certain inalienable rights."[17]

Lolita Buckner Inniss: That's definitely true of many nineteenth-century activists. It is worth recalling that women activists like Sojourner Truth had a "womanist" vision of rights. This meant an approach to civil rights that was premised not only an intense desire to improve the plight of women, especially Black women, but also an explicit, activist religiosity. This religious approach to women's rights had, however, a practical foundation that looked at the context of women's lives and the barriers they faced.[18] Sojourner Truth and others did not ask women to seek heavenly rewards only—the earth could also be a place of enjoyment.

While more contemporary women's movements also brought clear ideological goals to bear, and understood women's situations in context, I think the religious language had mostly dropped out of women's rights advocacy by the 1970s and 1980s, though.

Bridget Crawford: Fair point. What feminists in the late twentieth century had in common with their counterparts from the nineteenth century was a certain optimism about the law. For first-wave feminists, that optimism was borne out. Women received the right to vote in federal elections with the ratification of the Nineteenth Amendment in 1920. For Black women, that right was not made more meaningful until additional voter protection laws were passed in the 1960s.[19] And although there is still no federal Equal Rights Amendment, second-wave feminists did succeed in making sexual harassment a harm that was cognizable under the law.[20] Without second-wave feminists' embrace of the law, there would be no #MeToo movement.

Mehrsa Baradaran: I want to amplify these lineage points. The Black Lives Matter movement built upon and learned from the preceding movements, but there is not a direct lineage to trace either movement to those that directly preceded it. I think there was a spark that lit both movements: In the case of #MeToo, I think it was Trump's election and Harvey Weinstein. As for Black Lives Matter, it was Trayvon Martin's killing and Zimmerman's acquittal—then the movement went nationwide after Michael Brown and the protests in Ferguson.

Noa Ben-Asher: Mehrsa, I am compelled by your suggestion that the two movements reveal a current cultural and political "breakdown." It seems that we are indeed in the midst of a loss of faith in the democratic process yielding fair results, and in so-called democratic institutions providing fairness and equality for all.

Linda Greene: I agree with Mehrsa and Noa that both movements arise from contemporary circumstances. But both were also foreshadowed by significant prior movements. Remember that, at the March on Washington in 1963, Martin Luther King said, "We can never be satisfied as long as the Negro is the victim of the unspeakable horrors of police brutality."[21] The 1966 Black Panther Ten Point Program demanded "an immediate end to police brutality and murder of black people."[22] Several of the sixties' Black urban rebellions—in New York, the Harlem riots (1964); in Los Angeles, the Watts riots (1965); the Detroit riots (1967); the Newark riots (1967)[23]—arose proximately from police abuse of Blacks. The same is true of Black Lives Matter.

Lolita Buckner Inniss: I'm happy that you brought up those moments in the civil rights movement, Linda, because in my mind, Black Lives Matter and #MeToo are both related to the long-standing relationship between Black civil rights and the quest for women's (often understood as white women's) equality.[24] Interestingly, the Black civil rights movement has functioned historically as an explicitly acknowledged paradigm for women's rights, but some contemporary work around women's rights has at times disdained what has been described as "reasoning from race."[25]

At first, the reluctance of white people—and remember that the majority of white women voted for Trump for president in both 2016 and 2020[26]—meant that Black Lives Matter might be less sustainable as a social movement. But it is both noteworthy and sad that the Black Lives Matter movement has gained a place of greater social prominence in the wake of the COVID-19 crisis that began in 2020, during which Black people died at rates far higher than whites, and in the protests that were triggered by not only the May 2020 police killing of George Floyd, but also the fact that so many other Black people have been killed without justification by police and vigilantes. Black people have long been the too-frequent victims of formal and extralegal violence and killing. White people now are marching about it and talking about it.

Figure 1. A memorial placed after the shooting of Michael Brown in Ferguson, Missouri, 2014. Photo by Jamelle Bouie.

Aya Gruber: I think that's important, Lolita. Black Lives Matter originated as a reaction to George Zimmerman's outrageous slaying of Trayvon Martin for doing nothing more than walking home from a store with Skittles and a drink. In the years following Martin's death, several police killings of innocent Black men and women made the rounds on social media, and federal investigations of police departments in towns like Ferguson confirmed that policing is a deliberate, efficient, and effective method of maintaining Black residents' marginalized status and economic insecurity.[27] I sensed a shift in the discourse of Black Lives Matter: from a focus on particular cops and white vigilantes who committed unjustified murders, toward a larger, more radical indictment of American carceral system.

Also, the founders of Black Lives Matter—Alicia Garza, Patrisse Cullors, and Opal Tometi—are always identified as "radical Black" activists.[28] People within the Black Lives Matter movement made it clear that they regarded the criminal system's tendency to wound, control, and thus maintain the subordinate status of people of color not as a *malfunction*, but as the system's *function*. And over time, the mantra "Black lives matter" has come to encompass more than just a critique of the criminal system. To give just one example, the movement was at the fore of condemning the Trump administration for genocidally enabling the coronavirus to decimate Black communities.[29]

Lolita Buckner Inniss: Let me also add that insurrection has been at the heart of many U.S. liberation movements, beginning with the Boston Tea Party and coming down through United States history. Social upheavals often fuel fundamental changes in the way a society is organized and governed, and in many cases lead to the recognition, if not the empowerment, of marginalized groups.

This is no less true of the Black Lives Matter and #MeToo movements. Linda Greene mentioned earlier that the Black Lives Matter movement is, in some ways, a legacy of the urban unrest of the 1960s. Those were termed "riots" by authority figures, as they were demonstrations that, in some cases, went beyond plaintive protest and erupted into violence.[30] In the twenty-first century, we have seen that too. Sometimes, contemporary protestors have used force to tear down Confederate monuments and other public reminders of Black subordination.[31]

But let's be clear: sometimes the protesters who took part in the 1960s civil rights demonstrations were not responsible for violent or destructive eruptions—it was not unusual for authorities to provoke violent responses, sometimes by means of covert agents acting as members of the protesting groups. We saw the same thing in the summer of 2020 with protests around the death of George Floyd.[32] Let's also acknowledge that ostensibly allied groups have sometimes sought to "hijack" Black Lives Matter protests, using them to center an alternate set of concerns or simply as cover for their own wrongdoing.[33]

Bridget Crawford: In-person demonstrations are not an ongoing salient feature of the #MeToo movement. To be sure, the 2017

Figure 2. Women's March in Washington, DC, 2017. Photo by S. Pakhrin.

Women's March on Washington, conceived as a demonstration against the rhetoric and misogynistic views of President Donald Trump, attracted approximately 470,000 people to the nation's capital.[34] Combined with the numbers of participants in marches that took place elsewhere in the United States and around the globe at that time, an estimated seven million people took part in protests.[35] Historically speaking, these were numbers that, at least up until the time of the Black Lives Matter protests in 2020, hadn't been seen in the United States since the Vietnam War era.[36] The more powerful work of the #MeToo movement is happening online, rather than in workplaces and courts of law.

It's worth noting that those who are credited with founding and popularizing the movement respectively—Tarana Burke (born in 1973) and Alyssa Milano (born in 1972)—fall squarely within the demographic associated with the initial development of a "third wave" of feminism.[37] Third-wave feminism differs from the movements that preceded it in many ways, including its embrace of a broader social justice agenda and its reliance, in large part, on non-legal tools (like social media) for addressing gender inequality.[38]

In response to the U.S. Supreme Court's 2022 decision in *Dobbs v. Jackson Women's Health Organization*,[39] which overturned *Roe v. Wade*, there were no massive street demonstrations. Where people did make their views known, however, was at the ballot box. In Kansas, Montana, and Kentucky, voters have since rejected anti-abortion measures that were placed on the ballot. Furthermore, in Vermont, California, and Michigan, citizens voted to amend their state constitutions to protect the right to abortion.[40] Those actions are all a direct legacy of preceding generations of women and their allies who worked for gender justice. Each movement builds on the other.

Lolita Buckner Inniss: As we consider historical antecedents to Black Lives Matter and #MeToo, it is so very relevant, Bridget, to think about how *Dobbs* fits into this equation. In the Court's opinion, there is reliance not on *the* history of abortion, but rather on *a* history of abortion jurisprudence. Justice Alito seems to entirely omit a discussion of abortion's history as a decidedly sublegal undertaking by and for women.[41] And as a sublegal undertaking, very often abortion providers were Black women and other "outsiders."[42]

DISCUSSION QUESTIONS

1. Bennett Capers makes the point that "Black Lives Matter" has been criticized, as a slogan, for not being inclusive enough, whereas #MeToo is an inclusive "brand," insofar as anyone can use the hashtag to describe their own individual experience. Do you think that, in creating the hashtag #blacklivesmatter, the movement's founders were focused on inclusivity? How much is inclusiveness a key to a social movement's success?

2. What does Osamudia James mean when she says that "the insistence on recognizing the value of Black lives might be characterized as plaintive"? From your perspective, is this a fair characterization?

3. Noa Ben-Asher says that both Black Lives Matter and #MeToo endorse and celebrate religious values. What values are they talking about? Do you agree or disagree?

4. Lolita Buckner Inniss comments that "it is both noteworthy and sad that the Black Lives Matter movement has gained a place of greater social prominence in the wake of the COVID-19 crisis that began in 2020." What relationship, if any, was there between the COVID-19 crisis and the June 2020 worldwide street demonstrations against police brutality?

5. Bridget Crawford observes that in-person demonstrations are not the ongoing hallmark of the #MeToo movement. Why do you think that is?

6. In your view, what is at stake in analyzing Black Lives Matter and #MeToo in relationship to prior social or legal movements? In other words, why do we care whether they are outgrowths, evolutions, extensions, or departures from what came before?

NOTES

1. See generally Lolita Buckner Inniss, "It's about Bloody Time and Space," *Columbia Law Journal* 41, no. 1 (2021): 147.

2. Evan Hill, Ainara Tiefenthäler, Christiaan Triebert, Drew Jordan, Haley Willis, and Robin Stein, "How George Floyd Was Killed in Police Custody," *New York Times*, updated January 2, 2022, https://www.nytimes.com/2020/05/31/us/george-floyd-investigation.html?smid=url-share [https://perma.cc/XLU5-MJNH].

3. See, for example, Larry Buchanan, Quoctrung Bui, and Jugal K. Patel, "Black Lives Matter May Be the Largest Movement in U.S. History," *New York Times*, July 3, 2020, https://www.nytimes.com/interactive/2020/07/03/us/george-floyd-protests-crowd-size.html [https://perma.cc/9PVN-ZWFW]; "Protests Across the Globe after George Floyd's Death," *CNN*, June 13. 2020, https://www.cnn.com/2020/06/06/world/gallery/intl-george-floyd-protests

/index.html [https://perma.cc/4DVV-LUB6]. In the United States, estimates are that between 15 million and 26 million participated in public demonstrations, making it "the largest movement in the country's history." On June 6, 2020, alone, more than 500,000 people participated in over 500 different locations all over the United States (Buchanan et al. "Black Lives Matter"). By way of comparison, an estimated 3 million participated in the Women's March of 2017 (Buchanan et al. "Black Lives Matter"); see also History.com Editors, "Civil Rights Movement," History.com, updated January 22, 2024, https://www.history.com/topics/black-history/civil-rights-movement [https://perma.cc/9PWF-3364]. Between 200,000 and 300,000 participated in the August 28, 1963, March on Washington led by A. Philip Randolph, Bayard Rustin, Martin Luther King Jr., and others.

4. President Obama called for both peace and "soul searching" when Martin's killer, who claimed self-defense, was acquitted of second-degree murder and manslaughter. See Adrian Campo-Flores and Lynn Waddell, "Jury Acquits Zimmerman of All Charges," *Wall Street Journal*, July 14, 2013, https://www.wsj.com/articles/SB10001424127887324879504578603562762064502?mod=WSJ_hpp_LEFTTopStories [https://perma.cc/RZ4A-EYBZ].

5. See generally Jelani Cobb, "The Matter of Black Lives," *New Yorker*, March 14, 2016, http://www.newyorker.com/magazine/2016/03/14/where-is-black-lives-matter-headed [https://perma.cc/HU9D-GHEH].

6. "Black Lives Matter . . . What We Believe," University of Central Arkansas, accessed February 6, 2023, https://perma.cc/4SD8-Z8A6.

7. See, for example, Jodi Kantor and Megan Twohey, "Harvey Weinstein Paid Off Sexual Harassment Accusers for Decades," *New York Times*, October 5, 2017, https://www.nytimes.com/2017/10/05/us/harvey-weinstein-harassment-allegations.html [https://perma.cc/5F88–4Y8D].

8. Alyssa Milano (@Alyssa_Milano), "If you've been sexually harassed or assaulted write 'me too' as a reply to this tweet," Twitter tweet, October 15, 2017, https://twitter.com/Alyssa_Milano/status/919659438700670976 [https://perma.cc/MPU4-QMJV].

9. See Cristela Guerra, "Where'd the #MeToo Initiative Really Come From? Activist Tarana Burke, Long Before Hashtags," *Boston Globe*, October 17, 2017, https://www.bostonglobe.com/lifestyle/2017/10/17/alyssa-milano-credits-activist-tarana-burke-with-founding-metoo-movement-years-ago/o2Jv29v6ljObkKPTPB9KGP/story.html?event=event12 [https://perma.cc/R59J-AVBU].

10. Guerra, "Where'd the #MeToo Initiative Really Come From."

11. See Ashwinin Tambe, "Reckoning with the Silences of #MeToo," *Feminist Studies* 44, no. 1 (2018): 197–202.

12. See, for example, Reena Flores, "White House Responds to Petition to Label Black Lives Matter a 'Terror' Group," *CBS News*, July 17, 2016, https://www.cbsnews.com/news/white-house-responds-to-petition-to-label-black-lives-matter-a-terror-group/ [https://perma.cc/NZ6Q-3C92] (reporting that the White House declined to act on a petition "asking for the federal government to formally label the Black Lives Matter movement as a 'terror group'" because the White House is not responsible for designations of groups as domestic terrorist organizations).

13. William N. Eskridge Jr., "Noah's Curse: How Religion Often Conflates Status, Belief, and Conduct to Resist Antidiscrimination Norms," *Georgia Law Review* 45, no. 3 (2011): 678–79.

14. Leader Alicia Garza has explained, "This movement has insisted on making sure that queer black people are playing a central leadership role in the social and political change that we are trying to achieve." At the same time, she acknowledges aspects of her background that make her privileged: "Being queer, being black, being a woman all comes with particular experiences that either benefit me at the expense of others, or where others benefit at my expense. For example, I have a college degree and class privilege, even though my access to these things is not common for most black folks, queer folks, trans folks, and cisgender women." Les Fabian Brathwaite, "The New Black Vanguard: Alicia Garza on What Really Matters," *Out*, May 18, 2016, https://www.out.com/news-opinion/2016/5/18/new-black-vanguard-alicia-garza-matters [https://perma.cc/YSV2-QPNX] (quoting Alicia Garza).

15. Pew Research Center, *Modeling the Future of Religion in America*, September 13, 2022, https://www.pewresearch.org/religion/2022/09/13/modeling-the-future-of-religion-in-america/ [https://perma.cc/6A7N-EYHX].

16. See, for example, Elizabeth B. Clark, "'The Sacred Rights of the Weak': Pain, Sympathy, and the Culture of Individual Rights in Antebellum America," *Journal of American History* 82, no. 2 (1995): 463–93.

17. Carrie Cokely, *Declaration of Sentiments*, Britannica Encyclopedia, updated April 19, 2024, https://www.britannica.com/event/Declaration-of-Sentiments.

18. See, for example, Lolita Buckner Inniss, "While the Water Is Stirring: Sojourner Truth as Proto-Agonist in the Fight for (Black) Women's Rights," *Boston University Law Review* 100, no. 5 (2020): 1653–54.

19. See, for example, Paul K. Stafford, "'Men, Their Rights and Nothing More; Women, Their Rights and Nothing Less': The Fifteenth Amendment at 150 and the 19th Amendment at 100," *Texas Bar Journal* 83, no. 6 (2020): 372–75.

20. On the Equal Rights Amendment, see, for example, Martha F. Davis, "The Equal Rights Amendment: Then and Now." *Columbia Journal of Gender and Law* 17, no. 3 (2008): 419–60. On sexual harrassment, see Catharine A. MacKinnon and Thomas I. Emerson, *The Sexual Harassment of Working Women: A Case of Sex Discrimination* (New Haven, CT: Yale University Press, 1979).

21. See Michelle Garcia, "3 Often Forgotten Parts of Martin Luther King's I Have a Dream Speech," *Vox*, January 17, 2019, https://www.vox.com/2016 /1/18/10785618/martin-luther-king-dream-speech [https://perma.cc /44RH-USU6] (quoting Dr. King).

22. Huey P. Newton and Bobby Seale, *The Black Panther Party for Self-Defense Ten-Point Platform and Program*, October 15, 1966.

23. On the Harlem riots, see, for example, August Meier and Elliott M. Rudwick, *CORE: A Study in the Civil Rights Movement, 1942–1968* (Urbana: University of Illinois Press, 1975). On the Watts riots, see, for example, Eric Bennett, "Watts Riot of 1965," *Oxford African American Studies Center*, updated December 1, 2006, https://doi.org/10.1093 /acref/9780195301731.013.43843. On the Detroit riots, see Hubert Locke, *The Detroit Riot of 1967* (Detroit, MI: Wayne State University Press, 2017). On the Newark riots, see Rick Rojas and Khorri Atkinson, "Five Days of Unrest That Shaped, and Haunted, Newark," *New York Times*, July 11, 2017, https://nytimes.com/2017/07/11/nyregion/newark-riots-50-years.html [https://perma.cc/982U-XL9Q].

24. See Lolita Buckner Inniss, "A Review of *Reasoning from Race: Feminism, Law, and the Civil Rights Revolution*, by Serena Mayeri." *Texas Law Review* 91 (2011), https://scholar.smu.edu/law_faculty/451/.

25. Inniss, 2–3.

26. See, for example, Angelina Chapin, "Of Course White Women Voted for Trump Again," *The Cut*, November 17, 2020, https://www.thecut .com/2020/11/many-white-women-still-voted-for-trump-in-2020.html [https://perma.cc/A5A3–4YAK].

27. See, for example, United States Department of Justice Civil Rights Division, *Investigation of the Ferguson Police Department*, March 4, 2015, https://www.justice.gov/sites/default/files/opa/press-releases

/attachments/2015/03/04/ferguson_police_department_report.pdf [https://perma.cc/T4K5-7PC3].

28. See Black Lives Matter, "Herstory," accessed February 6, 2023, https://blacklivesmatter.com/herstory/.

29. See, for example, David Nakamura, "Trump Struggles to Convince Black Leaders His Administration Will Respond to Racial Inequities on Coronavirus," *Washington Post*, April 17, 2020, https://www.washingtonpost.com/politics/trump-struggles-to-convince-black-leaders-his-administration-will-respond-to-racial-inequities-on-coronavirus/2020/04/17/5939873e-7ffa-11ea-8013-1b6da0e4a2b7_story.html [https://perma.cc/Q2TJ-J9A5]; Adam Serwer, "The Coronavirus Was an Emergency until Trump Found Out Who Was Dying," *The Atlantic*, May 8, 2020, https://www.theatlantic.com/ideas/archive/2020/05/americas-racial-contract-showing/611389/ [https://perma.cc/7DK6-9SER].

30. See, for example, Nick Robinson, "Rethinking the Crime of Rioting," *Minnesota Law Review* 107, no. 1 (2022): 85–87 (discussing history of race riots in the United States).

31. See, for example, Jennifer Henderson, "Protestors Tear Down Statues from Confederate Monuments in DC and North Carolina," *CNN*, June 20, 2020, https://www.cnn.com/2020/06/20/us/north-carolina-confederate-monument/index.html [https://perma.cc/9MG6-YUH6].

32. See, for example, Buchanan et al. "Black Lives Matter."

33. See Olga Khazan, "Why People Loot," *The Atlantic*, June 2, 2020, https://www.theatlantic.com/health/archive/2020/06/why-people-loot/612577/ [https://perma.cc/T3TH-Z3LY].

34. See Tim Wallace and Alicia Parlapiano, "Crowd Scientists Say Women's March in Washington Had 3 Times as Many People as Trump's Inauguration," *New York Times*, January 22, 2017, https://www.nytimes.com/interactive/2017/01/22/us/politics/womens-march-trump-crowd-estimates.html [https://perma.cc/Y44K-Q84T].

35. See Anemona Hartocollis and Yamiche Alcindor, "Women's March Highlights as Huge Crowds Protest Trump: 'We're Not Going Away,'" *New York Times*, January 21, 2017, https://www.nytimes.com/2017/01/21/us/womens-march.html [https://perma.cc/4YW4-C27U].

36. "Protests across the Globe after George Floyd's Death," *CNN*, June 13, 2020, https://www.cnn.com/2020/06/06/world/gallery/intl-george-floyd-protests/index.html [https://perma.cc/4DVV-LUB6].

37. See Leslie Heywood and Jennifer Drake, "Introduction," in *Third Wave Agenda: Being Feminist, Doing Feminism*, ed. Leslie Heywood and

Jennifer Drake, 1–20 (Minneapolis: University of Minnesota Press, 1997), 4 (defining third-wave feminists as those "whose birthdates fall between 1963 and 1973").

38. Bridget J. Crawford, "Toward a Third-Wave Feminist Legal Theory: Young Women, Pornography, and the Praxis of Pleasure," *Michigan Journal of Gender and Law* 14, no. 1 (2007): 102–104.

39. Dobbs v. Jackson Women's Health Organization, 142 S. Ct. 2228 (2022).

40. See Amy Littlefield, "Democrats Need to Realize How Much *Dobbs* Mattered," *New York Times*, November 19, 2022, https://www.nytimes .com/2022/11/19/opinion/midterm-election-abortion-roe-dobbs-democrats .html [https://perma.cc/J2GP-TWYJ].

41. See, for example, Lolita Buckner Inniss, "Abortion Law as Protection Narrative," *Oregon Law Review* 101, no. 2 (2023): 213–55.

42. See, for example, Lolita Buckner Inniss, "Bridging the Great Divide—A Response to Linda Greenhouse and Reva B. Siegel's 'Before (and after) *Roe v. Wade:* New Questions about Backlash,'" *Washington University Law Review* 89, no. 4 (2012): 968 (noting that Black grannies and midwives played a prominent role in abortion care in the nineteenth century).

BIBLIOGRAPHY

Brathwaite, Les Fabian. "The New Black Vanguard: Alicia Garza on What Really Matters." *Out*, May 18, 2016. https://www.out.com/news-opinion /2016/5/18/new-black-vanguard-alicia-garza-matters [https://perma.cc /YSV2-QPNX].

Bennett, Eric. "Watts Riot of 1965." *Oxford African American Studies Center*. Updated December 1, 2006. https://doi.org/10.1093/acref /9780195301731.013.43843.

Black Lives Matter. "Herstory." Accessed February 6, 2023. https:// blacklivesmatter.com/herstory/ [https://perma.cc/3N5H-VH57].

"Black Lives Matter . . . What We Believe." University of Central Arkansas. Accessed February 6, 2023. https://perma.cc/4SD8-Z8A6.

Buchanan, Larry, Quoctrung Bui, and Jugal K. Patel. "Black Lives Matter May Be the Largest Movement in U.S. History." *New York Times*, July 3, 2020. https://www.nytimes.com/interactive/2020/07/03/us/george -floyd-protests-crowd-size.html [https://perma.cc/9PVN-ZWFW].

Campo-Flores, Adrian, and Lynn Waddell. "Jury Acquits Zimmerman of All Charges." *Wall Street Journal*, July 14, 2013. https://www.wsj.com /articles/SB10001424127887324879504578603562762064502?mod= WSJ_hpp_LEFTTopStories [https://perma.cc/RZ4A-EYBZ].

Chapin, Angelina. "Of Course White Women Voted for Trump Again." *The Cut*, November 17, 2020. https://www.thecut.com/2020/11/many-white-women-still-voted-for-trump-in-2020.html [https://perma.cc /A5A3-4YAK].

Clark, Elizabeth B. "'The Sacred Rights of the Weak': Pain, Sympathy, and the Culture of Individual Rights in Antebellum America." *Journal of American History* 82, no. 2 (1995): 463–93.

Cobb, Jelani. "The Matter of Black Lives." *New Yorker*, March 14, 2016. http://www.newyorker.com/magazine/2016/03/14/where-is-black-lives-matter-headed [https://perma.cc/HU9D-GHEH].

Cokely, Carrie. *Declaration of Sentiments*, Britannica Encyclopedia. Updated April 19, 2024. https://www.britannica.com/event/Declaration -of-Sentiments.

Conner, Jewell. "Black Lives Matter Protest Comes to IUS." *Horizon: The Student Voice of Indiana University Southeast*, November 9, 2016. https://iushorizon.com/19590/news/black-lives-matter-protest -comes-to-ius/ [https://perma.cc/56Y5-T5AR].

Crawford, Bridget J. "Toward a Third-Wave Feminist Legal Theory: Young Women, Pornography, and the Praxis of Pleasure." *Michigan Journal of Gender and Law* 14, no. 1 (2007): 99–168.

Davis, Martha F. "The Equal Rights Amendment: Then and Now." *Columbia Journal of Gender and Law* 17, no. 3 (2008): 419–60.

Dobbs v. Jackson Women's Health Organization, 142 S. Ct. 2228 (2022).

Eskridge, William N., Jr. "Noah's Curse: How Religion Often Conflates Status, Belief, and Conduct to Resist Antidiscrimination Norms." *Georgia Law Review* 45, no. 3 (2011): 657–720.

Flores, Reena. "White House Responds to Petition to Label Black Lives Matter a 'Terror' Group." *CBS News*, July 17, 2016. https://www .cbsnews.com/news/white-house-responds-to-petition-to-label-black -lives-matter-a-terror-group/ [https://perma.cc/NZ6Q-3C92].

Francis, Megan Ming. "The Price of Civil Rights: Black Lives, White Funding, and Movement Capture." *Law and Society Review* 53, no. 1 (2019): 275–309.

Garcia, Michelle. "3 Often Forgotten Parts of Martin Luther King's I Have a Dream Speech." *Vox*, January 17, 2019. https://www.vox

.com/2016/1/18/10785618/martin-luther-king-dream-speech [https:// perma.cc/44RH-USU6].

Guerra, Cristela. "Where'd the #MeToo Initiative Really Come From? Activist Tarana Burke, Long before Hashtags." *Boston Globe*, October 17, 2017. https://www.bostonglobe.com/lifestyle/2017/10/17/alyssa -milano-credits-activist-tarana-burke-with-founding-metoo -movement-years-ago/o2Jv29v6ljObkKPTPB9KGP/story. html?event=event12 [https://perma.cc/R59J-AVBU].

Hartocollis, Anemona, and Yamiche Alcindor. "Women's March High- lights as Huge Crowds Protest Trump: 'We're Not Going Away.'" *New York Times*, January 21, 2017. https://www.nytimes.com/2017/01/21/us /womens-march.html [https://perma.cc/4YW4-C27U].

Henderson, Jennifer. "Protestors Tear Down Statues from Confederate Monuments in DC and North Carolina." *CNN*, June 20, 2020. https:// www.cnn.com/2020/06/20/us/north-carolina-confederate-monument /index.html [https://perma.cc/9MG6-YUH6].

Heywood, Leslie, and Jennifer Drake. "Introduction." In *Third Wave Agenda: Being Feminist, Doing Feminism*, edited by Leslie Heywood and Jennifer Drake, 1–20. Minneapolis: University of Minnesota Press, 1997.

Hill, Evan, Ainara Tiefenthäler, Christiaan Triebert, Drew Jordan, Haley Willis, and Robin Stein. "How George Floyd Was Killed in Police Custody." *New York Times*, updated January 2, 2022. https://www .nytimes.com/2020/05/31/us/george-floyd-investigation.html?smid= url-share [https://perma.cc/XLU5-MJNH].

Hillstrom, Laurie Collier. *Black Lives Matter: From a Moment to a Movement*. Santa Barbara, CA: ABC-CLIO, 2019.

History.com Editors. "Civil Rights Movement." History.com. Updated January 22, 2024. https://www.history.com/topics/black-history/civil- rights-movement [https://perma.cc/9PWF-3364].

———. "Women's Suffrage." History.com. Updated February 30, 2024. https://www.history.com/topics/womens-history/the-fight-for-womens -suffrage [https://perma.cc/GC7X-VUVZ].

Hobson, Janell, ed. *Are All the Women Still White? Rethinking Race, Expanding Feminisms*. Albany: State University of New York Press, 2016.

Inniss, Lolita Buckner. "Abortion Law as Protection Narrative." *Oregon Law Review* 101, no. 2 (2023): 213–55.

———. "Bridging the Great Divide—A Response to Linda Greenhouse and Reva B. Siegel's 'Before (and after) *Roe v. Wade*: New Questions about

Backlash.'" *Washington University Law Review* 89, no. 4 (2012):
963–72.

———. "It's about Bloody Time and Space." *Columbia Law Journal* 41, no.
1 (2021): 146–57.

———. "A Review of *Reasoning from Race: Feminism, Law, and the Civil
Rights Revolution,* by Serena Mayeri." *Texas Law Review* 91 (2011).
https://scholar.smu.edu/law_faculty/451/.

———. "While the Water Is Stirring: Sojourner Truth as Proto-Agonist in
the Fight for (Black) Women's Rights." *Boston University Law Review*
100, no. 5 (2020): 1637–64.

Kantor, Jodi, and Megan Twohey. "Harvey Weinstein Paid Off Sexual
Harassment Accusers for Decades." *New York Times,* October 5, 2017.
https://www.nytimes.com/2017/10/05/us/harvey-weinstein-harass-
ment-allegations.html [https://perma.cc/5F88–4Y8D].

Khazan, Olga. "Why People Loot." *The Atlantic,* June 2, 2020. https://
www.theatlantic.com/health/archive/2020/06/why-people-loot
/612577/ [https://perma.cc/T3TH-Z3LY].

Littlefield, Amy. "Democrats Need to Realize How Much *Dobbs* Mattered." *New York Times,* November 19, 2022. https://www.nytimes
.com/2022/11/19/opinion/midterm-election-abortion-roe-dobbs
-democrats.html [https://perma.cc/J2GP-TWYJ].

Locke, Hubert G. *The Detroit Riot of 1967.* Detroit, MI: Wayne State
University Press, 2017.

MacKinnon, Catharine A., and Thomas I. Emerson. *Sexual Harassment
of Working Women: A Case of Sex Discrimination.* New Haven, CT:
Yale University Press, 1979.

Meier, August, and Elliott M. Rudwick. *CORE: A Study in the Civil Rights
Movement,* 1942–1968. Urbana: University of Illinois Press, 1975.

Milano, Alyssa (@Alyssa_Milano). "If you've been sexually harassed or
assaulted write 'me too' as a reply to this tweet." Twitter, October 15,
2017. https://twitter.com/Alyssa_Milano/status/919659438700670976
[https://perma.cc/MPU4-QMJV].

Mitchell, S. David. "Ferguson: Footnote or Transformative Event?"
Missouri Law Review 80, no. 4 (2015): 943–60.

Nakamura, David. "Trump Struggles to Convince Black Leaders His
Administration Will Respond to Racial Inequities on Coronavirus."
Washington Post, April 17, 2020. https://www.washingtonpost.com
/politics/trump-struggles-to-convince-black-leaders-his-administration
-will-respond-to-racial-inequities-on-coronavirus/2020/04/17/5939873e

-7ffa-11ea-8013-1b6da0e4a2b7_story.html [https://perma.cc/Q2TJ -J9A5].

Newton, Huey P., and Bobby Seale. *The Black Panther Party for Self-Defense Ten-Point Platform and Program*. October 15, 1966.

New-York Historical Society. "Women and the American Story (WAMS)." Accessed February 6, 2023. https://wams.nyhistory.org/ [https://perma.cc/56RW-SZP8].

Peller, Gary. "Race Consciousness." *Duke Law Journal*, no. 4 (1990): 758–847.

Pew Research Center. *Modeling the Future of Religion in America*. September 13, 2022. https://www.pewresearch.org/religion/2022/09/13/modeling-the-future-of-religion-in-america/ [https://perma.cc/6A7N-EYHX].

"Protests across the Globe after George Floyd's Death." *CNN*, June 13, 2020. https://www.cnn.com/2020/06/06/world/gallery/intl-george-floyd-protests/index.html [https://perma.cc/4DVV-LUB6].

Robinson, Nick. "Rethinking the Crime of Rioting." *Minnesota Law Review* 107, no. 1 (2022): 77–138.

Rojas, Rick, and Khorri Atkinson. "Five Days of Unrest That Shaped, and Haunted, Newark." *New York Times*, July 11, 2017. https://nytimes.com/2017/07/11/nyregion/newark-riots-50-years.html [https://perma.cc/982U-XL9Q].

Serwer, Adam. "The Coronavirus Was an Emergency until Trump Found Out Who Was Dying." *The Atlantic*, May 8, 2020. https://www.theatlantic.com/ideas/archive/2020/05/americas-racial-contract-showing/611389/ [https://perma.cc/7DK6-9SER].

Stafford, Paul K. "'Men, Their Rights and Nothing More; Women, Their Rights and Nothing Less': The Fifteenth Amendment at 150 and the 19th Amendment at 100." *Texas Bar Journal* 83, no. 6 (2020): 372–75.

Sullivan, Patricia. *Lift Every Voice: The NAACP and the Making of the Civil Rights Movement*. New York: New Press, 2009.

Tambe, Ashwinin. "Reckoning with the Silences of #MeToo." *Feminist Studies* 44, no. 1 (2018): 197–202.

Taylor, Keeanga-Yamahtta. *From #BlackLives Matter to Black Liberation*. Chicago: Haymarket Books, 2016.

Tuerkheimer, Deborah. "Slutwalking in the Shadow of the Law." *Minnesota Law Review* 98, no. 4 (2014): 1453–511.

United States Department of Justice Civil Rights Division. *Investigation of the Ferguson Police Department*. March 4, 2015. https://www.justice

.gov/sites/default/files/opa/press-releases/attachments/2015/03/04/ferguson_police_department_report.pdf [https://perma.cc/T4K5-7PC3].

Wallace, Tim, and Alicia Parlapiano. "Crowd Scientists Say Women's March in Washington Had 3 Times as Many People as Trump's Inauguration." *New York Times*, January 22, 2017. https://www.nytimes.com/interactive/2017/01/22/us/politics/womens-march-trump-crowd-estimates.html [https://perma.cc/Y44K-Q84T].

Watters, Jessica. "Pink Hats and Black Fists: The Role of Women in the Black Lives Matter Movement." *William and Mary Journal of Women and the Law* 24, no. 1 (2017): 199–208.

Comparing the Movements

GOALS, ASSUMPTIONS, AND METHODS OF
BLACK LIVES MATTER AND #METOO

WITH CONTRIBUTIONS BY

Mehrsa Baradaran	*Aya Gruber*
Noa Ben-Asher	*Lolita Buckner Inniss*
I. Bennett Capers	*Osamudia James*
Bridget J. Crawford	*Keisha Lindsay*
Linda S. Greene	*Kathryn M. Stanchi*

BACKGROUND

Both the past and present contribute to the shape of any social or legal movement. As seen in the previous chapter, the Black Lives Matter and #MeToo movements both draw on elements of the past and the present to bring attention to their concerns. For Black Lives Matter, pivotal issues of racial discrimination and police brutality have served as catalysts for policy changes and societal reforms. In like fashion, the #MeToo movement has been spurred on by calls for changes in societal attitudes toward sexual harassment and assault. The previous chapter identified the 2012 killing of teenager Trayvon Martin as the spark for the contemporary Black Lives Matter movement, and a 2017 post on Twitter (now called X) as the impetus for a popular #MeToo movement, which had deeper origins in and drew from earlier work against sexual violence.

Broadly understood, both movements are justice seeking: they seek remedy for past harms and change going forward. They aim to change laws, workplace policies, and societal attitudes to ensure not only that survivors are supported, but also that perpetrators are held accountable for their actions. The movements employ various means for accomplishing these goals.

This chapter features a conversation about these goals, and the specific methods used by both Black Lives Matter and #MeToo, including social media campaigns, public demonstrations, and legislative advocacy.

We asked our dialogue participants these questions:

> What are the goals of these movements? What are the
> assumptions of the Black Lives Matter and #MeToo
> movements? What are methods employed by these
> movements to attain their goals? What are the
> similarities between the two movements? How do they
> differ?

DIALOGUE

Goals

Bennett Capers: We tend to associate the Black Lives Matter movement with eradicating "blue on Black" violence—police brutality against Black people—and making law enforcement officers accountable. But the movement has developed a much broader and more ambitious agenda. For a long time, the Black Lives Matter website contained a section highlighting "What We Believe." Here are some of the movement's core beliefs that were listed on that page:

> Every day, we recommit to healing ourselves and each other, and to
> co-creating alongside comrades, allies, and family a culture where
> each person feels seen, heard, and supported.

We acknowledge, respect, and celebrate differences and commonalities.

We work vigorously for freedom and justice for Black people and, by extension, all people.

We intentionally build and nurture a beloved community that is bonded together through a beautiful struggle that is restorative, not depleting.

We are unapologetically Black in our positioning. In affirming that Black Lives Matter, we need not qualify our position. To love and desire freedom and justice for ourselves is a prerequisite for wanting the same for others.

We build a space that affirms Black women and is free from sexism, misogyny, and environments in which men are centered.

We practice empathy. We engage comrades with the intent to learn about and connect with their contexts.[1]

These goals are not only ambitious, but revolutionary in a good way, and on their face would seem to have commonalities with the #MeToo movement, which takes as its focus ending sexual violence.

Bridget Crawford: Interestingly, the Black Lives Matter website no longer includes the "What We Believe" section. I don't know why that is. Maybe it is that some of Black Lives Matter's "revolutionary" goals have been the source of public criticism. For example, at one point, this "What We Believe" page included the statement:

We disrupt the Western-prescribed nuclear family structure requirement by supporting each other as extended families and "villages" that collectively care for one another, especially our children, to the degree that mothers, parents, and children are comfortable.[2]

I suspect that Black Lives Matter took down the page—and scrubbed that language from its website entirely—in response to criticism from conservatives. For example, former NFL player Marcellus Wiley, who is Black, went on national television and criticized the group for having "anti-family values," while he extolled the virtues of traditional two-parent homes.[3] Of course, this is playing on old stereotypes and pathologizing of Black American families, especially those led by single mothers, as deviant, without acknowledging the deeply racist and sexist systems and policies that contribute to family structures.[4]

Linda Greene: The goals are now in shorter form on the website under "About." They explain that Black Lives Matter's mission is "to eradicate white supremacy and build local power to intervene in violence inflicted on Black communities by the state and vigilantes."[5] But regardless of what is written where, I think that Black Lives Matter, in the popular imagination at least, is most associated with efforts to stop the explicit or implicit racial bias that results in the discriminatory deployment of deadly force.[6]

In a similar way, #MeToo focuses on the gendered power structures in the workplace that sustain a gender subordination conducive to sexual harassment, an abuse of that power.[7] So both movements really challenge the current allocation of power to the white patriarchy in society.

Lolita Buckner Inniss: Bennett and Linda, I am struck by your comments about the importance of eliminating police and other state violence in the Black Lives Matter movement. While, as you seem to imply, Bennett, "blue on Black" violence represents violence by white law enforcers against Black people, it is vital to recognize that white supremacist violence, whether practiced by the state or by private actors, is not just the province of white people. Consider the killing of Tyre Nichols by Memphis, Tennessee, police in January 2023.[8] All of the five officers charged in his death were Black. White supremacy culture and anti-Blackness are perils that affect people of all races—even, most sadly of all, Black people.

I will also add, in comparing the two movements' goals, that both movements engage in efforts to realign notions of property as it concerns women and Black people. Much of United States law and society rests upon early notions of both Black people and all women as property—as things to be controlled and enjoyed by men, as beings without the capacity for fully rational thought, as implements to used and discarded as needed. Property could not, of course, own property, and hence white women and Black people in the early history of our country occupied a shared status of being bereft of anything truly their own. Throughout U.S. history, women of all races and ethnicities, and Black people of all gender identities, have been systematically denied access to property ownership. Laws and customs have also restricted women's ability to inherit, own, or control property. Through practices such as redlining and discriminatory lending, Black people have been especially harmed. Such harms have had lasting impacts on the economic well-being of both groups and have contributed to the persistence of gender and racial disparities in wealth and poverty.

In the past several decades, white women, and women in general, have been accorded the formal right to earn and own their own wages and their own property. But structural inequalities have meant that white women still own and earn less than white men, and Black women and other women of color earn and own even less. The #MeToo movement, while its primary goals are eliminating sexual harassment and sexual violence, also understands implicitly that part of what makes women vulnerable to men is their economic subordination.

For Black people, who, as a group, are among the poorest in the United States, it is no wonder that an important, although lesser publicized, goal of the Black Lives Matter movement is to address some of the distortions in Black access to property, whether in the form of wages or capital.

Kathy Stanchi: As a student of rhetoric, I think the rhetorical differences between the movements are interesting. When we talk about the goals of the Black Lives Matter and #MeToo movements, one of first things that stands out to me is their names. Laid side by side, the names of the two movements suggest an obvious and stark difference.

#MeToo is a *quantitative* movement, one that is based in solidarity in numbers. I see the strong influence of the feminist method of consciousness raising in the #MeToo methodology: women coming together to share experiences as a way of constructing and validating their lived realities.

Black Lives Matter, on the other hand, as a label, is a *qualitative* statement—it asserts the meaningfulness and importance of Black lives. On that "About" page on its website, the Black Lives Matter organizers say, "We affirm our humanity, our contributions to this society, and our resilience in the face of deadly oppression."[9]

The fact that a statement about the humanity of Black people is controversial—specifically, the fact that such an understated and modest argument that "Black Lives Matter" could be controversial— is a serious indictment of the racism in our culture. To say something matters is the most basic assertion of physicality and humanity: we exist, we have mass and volume, we take up space.[10]

In this way, Black Lives Matter has to be among the most unalarming and nonthreatening slogans in the history of civil rights. Yet, it has inspired immense white fear, backlash, and police violence. Black Lives Matter has been called racist, militant, and a "terrorist organization."[11] Not only is this indicative of our culture's racism, but it shows how far backward the culture has moved in this "post-racial" time.[12] Now, the simple assertion that Black lives mean something, mean anything, is threatening to white fragility.

The use of the word *matter* shows that the current fight is about whether Black people, and their lives, have any meaning at all. It is a basic assertion of Black humanity, not an assertion of value or importance: it isn't "Black Lives Are Valuable" or "Black Lives Are Important." But even with this gentle and benign slogan, the backlash has been remarkable, from all corners, including, as Bridget mentioned, from members of the Black community, such as

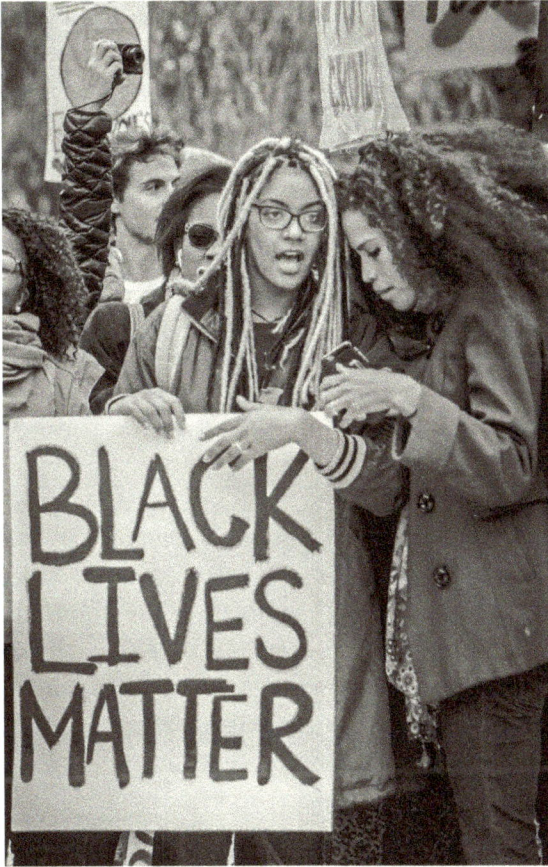

Figure 3. Black Lives Matter protesters in Washington, DC, 2015. Photo by Johnny Silvercloud.

Marcellus Wiley's calling out the organization for its alleged lack of family values.

In contrast, we have #MeToo's largely quantitative name. Why is sexual harassment something that can gain momentum simply from counting all the women who have experienced it, but Black Lives Matter must be substantive? Certainly, the numbers of Black people stopped, searched, beaten, and killed by the police is staggering enough that a #MeToo-type hashtag would be quantitatively meaningful. But the language difference in the two movements suggests that the problem of violence against Black people is not a problem of awareness of the scope of the problem; instead, it is a problem of white people knowing but not caring.

Assumptions

Mehrsa Baradaran: So, that's a good place to pick up, Kathy. I think one assumption shared by both movements is that the traditional avenues of seeking justice and social reform have broken down or perhaps never worked.

Keisha Lindsay: Right off the bat, I think it's worthwhile to acknowledge that both movements believe that the power of ordinary people can effect social change. In other words, both movements take it for granted that regular people can and should raise their voices to protest what they regard as injustices in their lives—be it in their personal lives, their professional lives, or both. In practice, this means that participants in Black Lives Matter and #MeToo include everyone from celebrities, to administrative assistants, to community-based activists. That kind of broad base is powerful.

Osamudia James: That's an interesting point, Keisha. The fact—as Mehrsa said—that both movements arise out of a perception that previous modes of change and progress are broken, Black Lives Matter and #MeToo both reject the politics of respectability. People are coming together to say that neither Black people nor women have to don the "appropriate" dress, speak the "right" language, or move in the "correct" spaces to deserve justice and humane treatment from the government, from the police, or from others in their community. No amount of bootstrapping or leaning-in will end sexual violence or racial subordination as long as we maintain societal hierarchies that place these two groups at the bottom and attempt to justify the physical and psychic harm to which they are regularly subjected.

Mehrsa Baradaran: I think that's right, Osamudia. With #MeToo, there was a sense, I think, of resignation that a lot of women had in thinking that this is just how things are, and you deal with it and protect yourself or you go to HR, and then you can move up the corporate ladder and gain power. When I was working on Wall Street, the type of behavior highlighted by #MeToo was rampant, but none of us women blew the whistle on anybody because it seemed like this was just how it was. But we also believed that you could just rise above it.

I think that's why Hillary Clinton's defeat in the 2016 presidential election, especially to an archetype misogynist who bragged about sexual harassment, just blew open the door. I think the assumption many women had that institutional advancement was possible by playing along and being nice just stopped. I think that wave was immediate. I felt it suddenly, too, and just as suddenly realized there was no way that anything would change without a revolution.

Aya Gruber: The political alliance of women was definitely activated by the election of a "pussy grabber in chief." #MeToo efficiently and effectively conveyed the message—albeit one couched in terms entirely too sex-regulatory for my taste—that women live within a patriarchy, and with enough political activism and coalition building, that patriarchy can be dismantled. In addition, #MeToo meaningfully improved the lives of innumerable sexual assault survivors. It pushed the culture far toward destigmatizing sexual assault victimization. Women could start the process of shedding the shame, pain, and guilt of being sexually victimized by uttering two simple words: me too.[13]

Bennett Capers: When we talk about the assumptions of the movements, I think it is interesting to see that sometimes Black Lives Matter and #MeToo may seem simpatico, but they can differ when it comes to actual cases. For me, Harvard University's decision to not renew the contracts of two of its first African American faculty deans, largely because of student protests over their representation of Harvey Weinstein on sexual assault and predation charges, is illustrative of this conflict.[14] For student protesters and many in the #MeToo movement, the deans' representation of Weinstein likely feels like a betrayal of sexual assault victims. It's certainly consistent with the demand, made by some, that we should just "believe women."[15] I suspect many of us who also support Black Lives Matter see the representation of Weinstein differently, given (a) the long history associating Black men with rape and (b) the equally long history of denying those men equal protection.

Weinstein is definitely not a brother, even an honorary one, but if we were playing a game of word association, the line from Weinstein to Bill Cosby would be a short one indeed. And that in turn would trigger not just the Cosbys of the world, but also the Emmet Tills and, since we're talking about the right to counsel, even Tom Robinson in *To Kill a Mockingbird*. The idea that a defendant accused of rape, regardless of actual guilt or innocence, is undeserving of defense or due process, is anathema to many of us who recognize this country's long history of denying defenses to Black men accused of that crime, and instead letting the mob function as the jury and executioner. I suspect this is something people of color, including women of color, "get" intuitively, but which might not be as obvious (or important?) to more privileged women. I'd love to know what my co-authors think about this.

Lolita Buckner Inniss: Bennett mentioned the complexities of having a prominent Black male lawyer like Harvard law professor Ronald Sullivan representing a serial sexual assault defendant like Harvey Weinstein. Generally speaking, false accusations of sexual assault are rare.[16] However, the Black community in the United States, both historically and in modern times, has lived with the trauma of false claims of sexual assault against Black men, which are

Figure 4. Anita Hill testifying before Congress at the Senate confirmation hearing for Supreme Court Justice Clarence Thomas, 1991. Photo by Michael R. Jenkins.

frequently made by white women. This reality makes the phrase "believe women" one that, while stating a generally accepted and acceptable premise, is mingled with skepticism, pain, and even grief for many Black Americans. Also, note the further complexity, given that Harvey Weinstein's New York conviction was overturned, although the California conviction still stands.[17]

Sadly, some women are complicit in this culture of silence around sexual assault and harassment. Such grief is all the more compounded when the accuser and the alleged assailant are Black, as in the case of Justice Clarence Thomas and Professor Anita Hill. Professor Hill accused Thomas of sexually harassing her when the two had worked together at the Equal Employment Opportunity Commission.[18]

I have seen and experienced having men's sexual harassment used as a weapon by women who perfectly well know that it happens but choose to ignore it—not out of fear, nor out of not knowing what to do, and not out of lacking the power to act. Rather, some women use sexual harassment as a way of hurting or marginalizing other women. For some women, there is a grim satisfaction when the monster with the potential to harm us all catches one of us who is disliked or devalued by others.

Mehrsa Baradaran: Bennett and Lolita are spot on. Historically speaking, Black men have never received their full due process rights. Fabricated allegations of sexual abuse were often used to justify the lynching of Black men, or even their discreditation. So Lolita is absolutely right that the charge to always "believe women" may be different for some people of color than for some white people. It's a slogan that I've never been comfortable with. I mean, given the fact that the majority of white women voted for Trump, you might even say that there are many women who actively choose to uphold the patriarchal order and white supremacy, rather than fight for other women and people of color.

Methods

Aya Gruber: Both movements were born on social media, and their popularity has much to do with the simplicity and catchiness of their hashtags, although as Kathy points out above, there is a difference between Black Lives Matter's *qualitative* claim and #MeToo's *quantitative* claim. Both movements harnessed social media in responding to specific instances of private criminal conduct: Harvey Weinstein's sexual assaults and George Zimmerman's killing of Trayvon Martin.

In the case of #MeToo, shortly after the hashtag first went viral, women of color advanced a trenchant critique that their voices were being silenced. In 2006, Tarana Burke had quietly started the "me too Movement" as part of her social service program Just Be, Inc., which "focused on the health, well-being and wholeness of young women of color."[19] But during the maelstrom of Weinstein news, it was Alyssa Milano who was credited for creating the "me too" catchphrase. Upset women of color on Twitter, now known as X, had to

Figure 5. Tarana Burke, 2018.

"out" Burke as the originator. Burke eventually responded: "In this instance, the celebrities who popularized the hashtag didn't take a moment to see if there was work already being done [and] sisters still managed to get diminished or erased."[20] Since that time, Burke has been a prominent figure in the movement and credited as its founder.

Keisha Lindsay: I think this is a good time to remind ourselves that corporate-owned social media is not necessarily a progressive, liberating means of organizing against race- and/or gender-based oppression. Until quite recently, many participants in both movements seem to have taken it for granted that X (formerly Twitter), Facebook, and other forms of social media are, at the very least, value-neutral spaces that won't harm their objectives.

Part of the issue here, I think, is the failure of some participants, in both movements, to pay enough attention to the relationship between capitalist exploitation, racism, and patriarchy. At the same time, I also think that, as is the case across the nation, there is a growing critique of social media companies among Black Lives Matter and #MeToo supporters. And, of course, the 2015 revelation that the FBI had been using Facebook and other social media platforms to track the movements of participants in the Black Lives Matter movement also helped to raise awareness of this issue among a wide range of activists.[21]

Bridget Crawford: I am interested in how powerful messages delivered primarily via social media (through hashtags like #BlackLivesMatter and #MeToo) have translated into real-life, formalized legal structures. Status as a formally incorporated non-profit is important because it allows an organization to receive tax-deductible charitable contributions. For the Black Lives Matter movement to mount (and fund) legal challenges, being able to receive tax-deductible donations is a boost.

Organizationally speaking, Black Lives Matter is grassroots in nature. Initially, there had been a loose promise by Patrisse Cullors, Alicia Garza, and Opal Tometi to "build a decentralized organization governed by the consensus of Black Lives Matter chapters."[22] In fact, there is an organization called "Black Lives Matter" with a decentralized global structure and chapters organized by city.[23] As of September 2023, there were over forty organizations using the words "Black Lives Matter" in their legal names that had received formal recognition from the Internal Revenue Service as tax-exempt organizations.[24] However, the Black Lives Matter Global Network Foundation Inc. has emerged as the primary recipient of charitable gifts. It received $90 million in donations in 2020 alone.[25]

With money comes responsibility, publicity, and—too often—predictable missteps. The publicly available tax returns of the Black Lives Matter Global Network Foundation Inc. show that the organization purchased a $6 million home, allegedly a "campus for a Black artists fellowship"; made almost a million dollars in payments to a company founded by the father of Cullors' child, supposedly to "produce live events and provide other creative services"; and paid more than $840,000 to a security firm run by Cullors' brother. At least two states are or were investigating the organization for its financial dealings.[26]

The relationship between the "national" Black Lives Matter foundation and local chapters has been the subject of some debate. One of the leaders of the Philadelphia chapter of Black Lives Matter confronted Cullors over the organization's lack of transparency and its failure to transfer control to local organizers.[27] However, according to the publicly filed tax return of Black Lives Matter Global Network Foundation Inc., which is linked from the organization's website, the group made $26 million in grants to organizations and families.

The names of those who have donated to the Black Lives Matter Global Network Foundation Inc. are closely guarded. It is not clear how important the availability of a tax deduction, or fiscal transparency, is for some donors. Celebrities such as The Weeknd have made cash donations. Jay Z's Tidal streaming music service has held fundraising concerts.[28] That said, everyday citizens also make donations and provide material support. There are plenty of celebrities and non-celebrities alike who literally marched with their feet in the 2020 protests against police brutality in the wake of the killing of George Floyd.

It is important to note that there are other tax-exempt organizations, such as the NAACP Legal Defense and Educational Fund Inc., that are deeply engaged in the same issues as the Black Lives Matter movement. Even if the legal structures and principal activities of the Black Lives Matter movement and, say, the American Civil Liberties Union (to give another example of a well-known impact litigation organization) are different, many people who are affiliated with one organization or movement also support other organizations and movements doing the same or similar work. Separate legal existence does not necessarily mean separate legal interests (although I'm not under some naive impression that the members of the non-profit sector, including legal advocacy organizations, speak with a singular voice on any issue).

It seems to me that there is considerable movement of people, ideas, and vocabulary across historically more rigid lines between social advocacy and commercially oriented activities. For example, in 2019 the actors in a New York off-Broadway biographical play about Gloria Steinem, *Gloria: A Life*, led a pre-planned audience "talk back" after the performance. In setting the tone for the conversation, the talk-back leaders quoted Alicia Garza, Patrisse Cullors, and Opal Tometi as proponents of four conversation guidelines that "Gloria says . . . are the best conversation guidelines she's ever known."[29] Those guidelines are (1) "lead with love," (2) "low ego," (3) "high impact," and (4) "move at the speed of trust." To my ear, it is no coincidence that *The Speed of Trust* is also the title of a popular business book by Steven M. R. Covey.[30]

Consider also the corporate structure of the #MeToo movement. A group of celebrities founded and funded the Time's Up Legal Defense Fund, along with attorney Roberta Kaplan (who argued on behalf of Edith Windsor in the landmark gay rights case of *United States v. Windsor*[31]) and Fatima Goss Graves, a Black woman who is the president and CEO of the National Women's Law Center. Fundraising for the organization began in earnest on January 1, 2018, when a group of over four hundred women, many of whom were leaders in the entertainment industry, including Alfre Woodard, Alyssa Milano, America Ferrera, Amy Poehler, Anjelica Huston, Anna Deveare Smith, Cate Blanchett, Charlize Theron, Jennifer Lopez, Kerry Washington, Rashida Jones, Sandra Bullock, Taraji P. Henson, Taylor Swift, and Shonda Rhimes, bought a full-page advertisement in national newspapers that began with the words, "Dear Sisters."[32]

The Time's Up Legal Defense Fund raised well over $22 million and includes a network of more than eight hundred attorneys.[33] But all has not run completely smoothly for this organization either. In 2021, Time's Up co-founder Roberta Kaplan and CEO Tina Tchen were forced to resign from their leadership roles after revelations that they had been involved with efforts to discredit one of the women who had brought a sexual harassment claim against New York Governor Andrew Cuomo.[34]

From the beginning, organizers conceived of the Time's Up "movement" as having distinct programs: legislation, litigation, industry-specific parity efforts, and public awareness.[35] Accordingly, the organization comprised various entities, including Time's Up Now, a 501(c)(4) organization that engaged in political lobbying; the Time's Up Foundation, a 501(c)(3) public charity that funded the Time's Up Legal Defense Fund and other charitable work; and affiliate industry-specific groups, such as Time's Up Advertising, Time's Up Tech, Time's Up Health Care, Time's Up Entertainment, and Time's Up UK.[36] In 2023, the organization decided to stop all operations other than the Time's Up Legal Defense Fund.[37]

Bennett Capers: Bridget, I love that you brought up the tax-exempt structure and corporate forms of the two movements because it brings up another issue: access to money. Can you talk a little about that?

Bridget Crawford: Starting or maintaining a successful social justice campaign does not require money, of course. Just four days after the shooting at Marjory Stoneman Douglas High School, students in Parkland, Florida, organized the national March for Our Lives, gave the name "Never Again" to their activist movement, and took to Facebook and other social media platforms to advocate for strict background checks for gun purchasers.[38] No one paid them to do that.

But it is also true that well-funded non-profit organizations have access to and wield a different kind of power than all-volunteer organizations that operate on a shoestring budget. One example that comes to mind is the Southern Poverty Law Center. Morris Dees and Joseph Levin Jr. began their work as a small civil rights law firm in 1971.[39] It eventually grew, according to the first Black federal judge in Alabama, to become known as "the single most responsive and reliable civil rights institution in the South."[40] According to its audited financial statement of October 31, 2021, the Southern Poverty Law Center has annual revenue of over $100 million and an endowment of over $730 million.[41] It uses these resources to fund successful litigation against the Ku Klux Klan and other hate groups in the United States.[42]

But the experience of the Southern Poverty Law Center also illustrates that the bias and discrimination which exists in the larger world can take root in "good" organizations too. Former and current employees of the organization have complained of years of workplace discrimination and sexual misconduct. In 2019, founder Morris Dees was fired after being disciplined twice for "inappropriate conduct," with at least one of those incidents involving a female employee who felt uncomfortable because of Dees' behavior. Other leaders have left the organization in the wake of claims of racial bias.[43]

Mehrsa Baradaran: Fascinating observation, Bridget, on the corporate co-option of the #MeToo movement. I think that's right—in a way, even the most radical movements can turn mainstream. I was also really struck by the Nike ad involving Colin Kaepernick, which was, in a way, the commodification of a Black Lives Matter activist. I think you can see it as a hopeful sign that Nike did the math and realized they would sell more products by embracing this movement, but I think some people saw it as a troubling development.

Similarities

Keisha Lindsay: Both Black Lives Matter and #MeToo were founded by Black feminists who embraced an intersectional analytical framework. However, there is a case to be made, as several of us do in this discussion, that many participants in both movements are increasingly gravitating toward the same single-axis orientation that

COLIN KAEPERNICK TAKES A KNEE

Colin Kaepernick played as a quarterback for the San Francisco 49ers at the time he began his peaceful protests against police brutality and racial inequality in America by refusing to stand up during the national anthem at the start of each game. Rather, he chose to kneel in an effort to support his cause while still displaying respect. He began his protests during the 2016 preseason and continued until he opted out of his contract with the San Francisco 49ers in March 2017 and became a free agent. Kaepernick's protests were in response to the unjust deaths of Blacks by police officers and systemic racial oppression in the United States. Kaepernick explained, "I am not going to stand up to show pride in a flag for a country that oppresses Black people and people of color."

[In 2019, Kaepernick settled a grievance with the National Football League] alleging that team owners were plotting to prevent him from playing in the NFL.

Nike's deliberate decision to feature Colin Kaepernick in its thirtieth anniversary of "Just Do It" campaign [in 2018] demonstrates the expected economic return sought from applying the nonracist and Black cultural competence signal. After featuring the Kaepernick advertisement Nike's overall sales increased contributing to "a [ten] percent jump in income to $847 million."

Excerpt from Natè Simmons, "Racial Capitalism: Complexities with Enforcing Corporate Commitments to End Racial Injustice," *University of Illinois Chicago Law Review* 519, no. 3 (2022): 534.

has defined earlier movements, based on the notion that activists can and should focus on one oppression at a time. Hence, there has been an increased focus among Black Lives Matter activists on racism, and among #MeToo activists on sexism, with a decreased focus, in both groups, on the relationship between race and gender-based oppression.

Noa Ben-Asher: Recognizing the importance of social media and adoption of corporate structures, I want to pivot to talking about a rhetorical trajectory that seems to have been taken up enthusiastically by both movements: that of trauma. The assumption is that trauma is an important and prevalent injury which many individuals and communities suffer as a result of racial and sex discrimination.

This played out, for instance, in Brett Kavanaugh's Supreme Court nomination hearing, particularly regarding the testimony of Christine Blasey Ford. Democratic senators, commentators, and Ford herself emphasized her trauma as the primary injury from being sexually assaulted. By contrast, in the 1990s, Anita Hill's trauma went unnoticed when she raised a similar accusation against Clarence Thomas under the same circumstances. The discursive and generative power of trauma is fascinating, and its role in shaping social justice movements calls for further exploration.

Mehrsa Baradaran: Noa is so right that both of the movements hinge on the public airing of tragedy and trauma. There's Michael Brown's body being left out on the street, Trayvon Martin's last moments, George Floyd's death with the police officer kneeling on his neck, and so many Black men who have had to recount or provide evidence their confrontations with police. And the women who had to tell their stories of rape, assault, and molestation. It was awful for them, and awful for us to watch, but all necessary to fuel the movement. I know many of us stayed up late watching the Ferguson protests, watched and re-watched the video of Eric Garner's death, Sandra Bland's encounter with the police, George Floyd's killing—

Figure 6. Dr. Christine Blasey Ford testifying before the U.S. Senate Committee on the Judiciary, 2018.

we watched the U.S. Gymnastics team testify in court during the criminal trial of team doctor Larry Nassar, we watched Christine Blasey Ford's testimony in the Kavanaugh hearings.[44]

These were difficult moments of shared trauma and tragedy. They were awful to watch, and yet many of us felt like it was our duty to watch, to witness, and to do something about it. So these are both movements that built solidarity based on empathy. The very name "MeToo" illustrates that. And Black Lives Matter is also a demand.

Noa Ben-Asher: Thinking about the names of the movements in this context may be worthwhile. "MeToo," as Mehrsa writes, is a message of seeing through similarity. It is also, as Kathy explains, a message that expresses quantity. It is the message: "I see you because I've suffered, like you."

"Black Lives Matter," on the other hand, is an altogether different kind of speech act. It is primarily an ethical demand—not a description of how our world works. The demand is that Black lives *should* matter. The fact that the police act as though those lives don't matter is an ethical problem. It is a problem of social justice. So, in that sense, the names of these movements perhaps reflect different orientations toward social action and justice: one of individual empathy; the other, of explicit ethical demands.

Kathy Stanchi: I agree, Noa. The ethical rhetoric of Black Lives Matter (as a slogan) is very different, than, for example, the Black Panthers' slogan "All Power to the People" with the iconic raised fist, or "Black Power," or even the "Black Is Beautiful" slogan of the 1960s. Power and beauty are valuative, qualitative judgments; they are more than assertions of basic Black humanity. They are statements of Black strength or excellence. The use of the word *matter*, by contrast, shows that the current fight is about whether Black people, and their lives, have *any* meaning.

Lolita Buckner Inniss: This focus on rhetoric also invites us to consider who is centered in each discourse. The phrase "#MeToo" expresses solidarity, but it does that by centering the speaker as victim; the heart of the expression is "me." Much has been written about the social and psychological significance of the first-person referents "I" and "me." On the one hand, they seem to connote complete individuality. At other times, "I" and "me" serve as collective references that obscure the speaker's individuality.[45]

In contrast, Black Lives Matter as an expression—as an ethical claim, as Noa explains—is powerful in itself. There is tremendous strength and dignity in saying "Black lives matter" as a way to make an ethical claim that asserts that the lives of Black individuals have equal value and should be treated with the same respect, dignity, and rights as those of any other person. From an ethical standpoint, the #MeToo movement is also rooted in the idea that all individuals have the right to be treated with respect and dignity, and that sexual misconduct is a violation of that right. That said, #MeToo also highlights the importance of consent—that is, fully informed consent and the right to change one's mind.

This ethical perspective differs from qualitative framing. As Kathy notes, Black Lives Matter, as a qualitative claim, asserts a truth about an entire group of people that may be taken up by anyone, Black or not, rather than centering the experience of a particular speaker. Similarly, #MeToo not only encourages survivors to speak out about their experiences—it also demands that we all seek to hold perpetrators accountable for their actions.

Differences

Keisha Lindsay: I want to jump back to Mehrsa's point about television. When we are talking about why the mainstream media is now paying more attention #MeToo, we should consider another factor—the reality that the white women who increasingly dominate the #MeToo movement are better positioned to command media attention than the Black men whose voices now dominate the Black Lives Matter movement. I say this because whites, including white women, are far better represented in the nation's newsrooms than are Black people—be they Black men or Black women. For instance, the proportion of all print and online journalists who are white men and white women is 47.19 percent and 31.05 percent, respectively. The comparable figure for Black men and Black women, respectively, is 3.7 percent and 3.62 percent.[46]

Mehrsa Baradaran: But also, Keisha, Black Lives Matter only deals with a small subset of Americans as direct victims. Many of us have no experiences at all with which to relate to this movement. While most of us have some personal experience with consent and sexual harassment, most of us have never feared being killed by the police due to our character. Those who have had these experiences have had to share their stories with the rest of us to make us aware. The cell phone videos have helped the unbelieving to see for themselves. In that way, both these movements have required a lot from the victims and potential victims.

Keisha Lindsay: Regardless, as Bridget and several other folks have already mentioned, remember that the corporate-controlled media seeks to maximize its profits by foregrounding news stories about reforming, rather than radically redefining, existing socioeconomic structures.[47]

Key tenets of the #MeToo movement are amenable to exactly this kind of "reformist" coverage. A prime example is that many #MeToo activists demand that women be given a chance to compete, without the threat of sexual harassment and assault, for leadership positions in corporate boardrooms, law firms, and other decidedly middle- and upper-class workspaces. While this demand is clearly a valid one, it is also premised more on women getting a seat at the table where racial, gendered, and class-based hierarchies of power are sustained, and less about radically dismantling these same hierarchies.

Of course, when many of the Black male voices that now dominate Black Lives Matter posit Black men as both the principal victims of and resistors against racism, they also posit a patriarchal message that reinscribes rather than challenges gendered inequalities of power. However, what ultimately distinguishes the present incarnation of the Black Lives Matter movement from the #MeToo movement is that the former also offers a structural critique of oppression—namely, racial oppression—that is not merely about getting middle-class Black men into positions of power. This critique is also about identifying and dismantling racism's harmful effects on Black men, and sometimes Black women, from a variety of class backgrounds. These harmful effects take place in many settings, including the criminal justice system and the classroom. As such, Black Lives Matter arguably threatens structural relations of power in ways that #MeToo does not, *and* does so in ways that, consequently, make it a less than palatable topic for the mainstream media.

Lolita Buckner Inniss: We have to acknowledge that, at least until 2020, Black Lives Matter did not seem to garner the sort of concern or acclaim of #MeToo. This changed in the maelstrom triggered by the COVID-19 pandemic and the record-setting multiracial protests in 2020. But even despite the new attention to Black matters, speaking out about Black injustice has frequently found less sympathetic audiences, and less willingness to craft policies that would help to diminish anti-Black racism.[48]

That said, anti-Black racism has especially gained greater visibility in the wake of Black Lives Matter. While more potent forms of discrimination against Black people often garner attention, anti-Black racism can manifest in less immediate or obvious ways, such as in societal stereotypes and cultural representations that depict Black people in a negative or dehumanizing light. Anti-Black racism is also seen in economic, political, and social disparities and discrimination that Black people face in the society.

Osamudia James: I think what you are talking about, Lolita, and what you described, Mehrsa, are issues of proximity. Most men have women in their lives to whom they're close. This obviously does not prevent sexual violence, but it does facilitate the prerequisite intimacy necessary for the development of empathy, and for the suspension of belief that allows men to accept that a woman's experience could be radically different from their own.

In contrast, due to both institutional forces and the choices of white people (e.g., white flight), Blacks and whites still live intensely segregated lives. And even as multiracial relationships are on the rise, many white people, including those in power, are not at all proximate to either Black people or their experiences. That distance renders the stories of blue on Black violence, even when caught on tape, incomprehensible and unbelievable.

Bridget Crawford: Ultimately, 2020 may have been a watershed moment that finally brought some (but not enough) change to policing in the United States. Many people still find themselves asking whether our government is really of the people, for the people, and by the people. The COVID-19 crisis made people at every point on the political spectrum ask big-picture questions about how well government systems function.

I am not the first person to say that the exhortation to vote seems woefully inadequate in times of great turmoil. But I remain a true believer in the fragile democracy we have in this country. We must exercise our constitutional rights and elect leaders who we believe will preserve rights and increase the well-being of the entire country. Our collective obligation as citizens includes advocating for those whose rights to vote are under attack or made more difficult by entrenched interests. Democracy needs the participation of all, not the few.

DISCUSSION QUESTIONS

1. Look at the list of "What We Believe" in Bennett Capers's contribution at the beginning of the chapter. On which of these items would there be strong consensus in the United States? On which of these items would there be less consensus?

2. Kathy Stanchi talks about Black Lives Matter as having *qualitative* claims and #MeToo as having *quantitative* claims. Do you believe that both slogans inspire fear? Hope? Something else?

3. In the 2016 presidential election, Hillary Clinton won the popular vote but lost the Electoral College vote and Donald Trump was elected president. What does Mehrsa Baradaran mean when she says that Clinton's defeat was a watershed moment in the #MeToo movement?

4. Consider the role of social media in publicizing events, gathering support, and simply sharing information. Are there reasons that organizers should take a skeptical or critical approach to social media? What would that look like?

5. Can you think of examples of the ways corporations try to "cash in" on social justice issues or awareness? What is the relationship between successful social justice movements and corporations in the United States?

6. Do you understand Black Lives Matter and #MeToo to be reformist organizations or ones that seek to redefine current socio-political structures and operations? Does a movement have to be one or the other, or can it pursue both reformist and transformational ends?

NOTES

1. "Black Lives Matter . . . What We Believe," University of Central Arkansas, accessed February 6, 2023, https://perma.cc/4SD8-Z8A6.

2. Anthony Leonardi, "Black Lives Matter 'What We Believe' Page That Includes Disrupting 'Nuclear Family Structure' Removed From Website," *Washington Examiner*, September 21, 2020, https://www.washingtonexaminer.com/news/black-lives-matter-what-we-believe-page-that-includes-disrupting-nuclear-family-structure-removed-from-website [https://perma.cc/Q7AR-EPHS].

3. See Daniel Canova, "Former NFL Player Marcellus Wiley Rips Black Lives Matter after It Removes Page on Disrupting 'Nuclear Family Structure,'" *Fox News*, September 23, 2021, https://www.foxnews.com/sports/former-nfl-player-marcellus-wiley-rips-black-lives-matter-after-it-removes-page-on-disrupting-nuclear-family-structure [https://perma.cc/Q986-7QLY].

4. See, for example, Camille Wilson Cooper and Shuntay Z. McCoy, "Poverty and African American Mothers: Countering Biased Ideologies, Representations and the Politics of Containment," *Journal of the Association for Research on Mothering* 11, no. 2 (2009): 45–55.

5. Black Lives Matter, "About," accessed January 10, 2023, https://blacklivesmatter.com/about/ [https://perma.cc/NRJ3–67Y7].

6. See Opal Tometi at Black Lives Matter, "Our Co-Founders," accessed June 19, 2021, https://perma.cc/V2DH-UT58.

7. See Alix Langone, "#MeToo and Time's Up Founders Explain the Difference between the 2 Movements—And How They're Alike," *Time*, updated March 22, 2018, https://time.com/5189945/whats-the-difference

-between-the-metoo-and-times-up-movements/ [https://perma.cc
/57H5-NLV3].

8. Rick Rojas and Jessica Jaglois, "Five Officers Charged with Murder in Memphis Police Killing," *New York Times*, updated February 1, 2023, https://www.nytimes.com/2023/01/26/us/tyre-nichols-memphis-police .html [https://perma.cc/H696-RYSH].

9. Black Lives Matter, "About."

10. The Oxford English Dictionary cites the derivation of the word *matter* as the French word for *wood*, suggesting that the word derives from this notion of physical presence or materiality. *Oxford English Dictionary Online*, s.v. "matter (*n.*)," accessed February 7, 2023, https://www.oed.com /view/Entry/115083 [https://perma.cc/CP3Q-RNRD].

11. See, for example, Emily Cureton, "In Rural Oregon, Threats and Backlash Follow Racial Justice Protests," NPR, September 3, 2020, https:// www.npr.org/2020/09/03/906809148/in-rural-oregon-threats-and-back-lash-follow-racial-justice-protests [https://perma.cc/3MHP-4Y6G] (reporting a poster at a counter-Black Lives Matter protest reading "BLM is a RACIST movement . . . PROVE ME WRONG"); Vince Grzegorek, "'Black Lives Matter is a Terrorist Organization'—The Cleveland Police Union's Ugly History with BLM," *Cleveland Scene*, July 2, 2020, https://www .clevescene.com/news/black-lives-matter-is-a-terrorist-organization-the -cleveland-police-unions-ugly-history-with-blm-33288734 [https://perma .cc/T45M-CWDK] (quoting statements by the president of the Cleveland Police Patrolmen's Association calling Black Lives Matter a "terrorist" organization). Linda Greene notes that Black Lives Matter has been blamed for the "collapse of social order." Linda S. Greene et al., "Talking about Black Lives Matter and #Metoo," *Wisconsin Journal of Law, Gender, and Society* 34, no. 2 (2019): 139.

12. See, for example, Ian Haney Lopez, "Is the 'Post' in Post-Racial the 'Blind' in Colorblind?," *Cardozo Law Review* 32, no. 3 (2011): 807–32; Sumi Cho, "Post-Racialism," *Iowa Law Review* 94, no. 5 (2009): 1589–650.

13. Of course, as noted above, the notion of sisterhood through victimhood can ultimately be harmful, as can any power derived from a traumatized status. Nevertheless, feeling perhaps too empowered by one's victimized status is better than feeling mortified and stigmatized by it.

14. For more on the decision, see Kate Taylor, "Harvard's First Black Faculty Deans Let Go Amid Uproar over Harvey Weinstein Defense," *New York Times*, May 11, 2019, https://www.nytimes.com/2019/05/11/us/ronald -sullivan-harvard.html   [https://perma.cc/9H98-WZMJ];   Randall

Kennedy, "Opinion: Harvard Betrays a Law Professor—and Itself," *New York Times*, May 15, 2019, https://www.nytimes.com/2019/05/15/opinion /race-identity/harvard-law-harvey-weinstein.html [https://perma.cc /9E62-ZMP6].

15. See Marie Solis, "When Believing Women Isn't Enough to Help Them," *Vice.com*, October 9, 2019, https://www.vice.com/en_us/article /gyemm3/when-believing-women-isnt-enough-to-help-them [https:// perma.cc/7YJU-A2KY].

16. See, for example, Lolita Buckner Inniss, "The Absent Racial #MeToo and Rekindling Intersectional Identity," *Ain't I a Feminist Legal Scholar Too?* (blog), September 23, 2018, http://innissfls.blogspot.com/2018/09 /the-absent-racial-metoo.html [https://perma.cc/77NV-Z8LK].

17. Jan Ransom, "Mr. Weinstein's Criminal Convictions in California Still Stand," *New York Times*, April 25, 2024, https://www.nytimes.com /live/2024/04/25/nyregion/harvey-weinstein-appeal [https://perma.cc /D3R2-K95V].

18. Lolita Buckner Inniss, "'From Space-Off to Represented Space.' Review of *Reimagining Equality: Stories of Gender, Race, and Finding Home* by Anita Hill," *Berkeley Journal of Gender Law and Justice* 28, no. 1 (2013): 1101–32.

19. Tarana Burke, "Purpose," Just Be, Inc., accessed February 7, 2023, https://justbeinc.wixsite.com/justbeinc/purpose-mission-and-vision [https://perma.cc/PTX9-PFSE].

20. Zahara Hill, "A Black Woman Created the 'Me Too' Campaign against Sexual Assault 10 Years Ago," *Ebony*, October 18, 2017, https://www.ebony .com/black-woman-me-too-movement-tarana-burke-alyssa-milano / [https://perma.cc/CJP2-CE89].

21. See, for example, Nusrat Choudhury, "The Government Is Watching #BlackLivesMatter, and It's Not Okay," ACLU, August 4, 2015, https://www .aclu.org/news/racial-justice/government-watching-blacklivesmatter-and -its-not-okay [https://perma.cc/256M-X7P3].

22. Aaron Morrison, "Black Lives Matter Has $42 Million in Assets," *Associated Press*, May 17, 2022, https://apnews.com/article/government -and-politics-race-ethnicity-philanthropy-black-lives-matter -5bc4772e029da522036f8ad2a02990aa [https://perma.cc/KDC6-3CK7].

23. Black Lives Matter, "Herstory," accessed February 6, 2023, https:// blacklivesmatter.com/herstory/ [https://perma.cc/3N5H-VH57].

24. See "Tax Exempt Organizations Search," United States Internal Revenue Service, https://apps.irs.gov/app/eos/ (in the "Search By" box,

choose "Organization Name" and enter *black lives matter*, no quotation marks and no Boolean "AND" operators).

25. Morrison, "Black Lives Matter Has $42 Million."

26. Morrison, "Black Lives Matter Has $42 Million"

27. Morrison, "Black Lives Matter Has $42 Million."

28. See, for example, Lydia Price, "How The Weeknd, Kim Kardashian West and More Stars Have Supported Black Lives Matter," *People.com*, August 12, 2016, https://people.com/celebrity/how-celebrities-have-supported-black-lives-matter/ [https://perma.cc/2VTR-CDZH].

29. See, for example, Leah Fessler, "Gloria Steinem Says These are the Best Guidelines for Difficult Conversations," *QZ.com*, November 18, 2018, https://qz.com/work/1467935/gloria-steinem-says-these-are-the-best-guidelines-for-difficult-conversations [https://perma.cc/FHQ6-M5Z4].

30. See Steven M. R. Covey and Rebecca R. Merrill, *The Speed of Trust: The One Thing That Changes Everything* (New York: Free Press, 2008), xxiv.

31. United States v. Windsor, 570 U.S. 744 (2013).

32. See Cara Buckley, "Powerful Hollywood Women Unveil Anti-Harassment Action Plan," *New York Times*, January 1, 2018, https://www.nytimes.com/2018/01/01/movies/times-up-hollywood-women-sexual-harassment.html [https://perma.cc/F5T3-54M8].

33. See, for example, Joanna Walters, "#MeToo a Revolution That Can't be Stopped, Says Time's Up Co-founder," *The Guardian*, October Oct. 21, 2018, https://www.theguardian.com/world/2018/oct/21/metoo-revolution-times-up-roberta-kaplan [https://perma.cc/G49V-UET5].

34. See Jodi Kantor and Michael Gold, "Roberta Kaplan, Who Aided Cuomo, Resigns from Time's Up," *New York Times*, August 9, 2011, https://www.nytimes.com/2021/08/09/nyregion/roberta-kaplan-times-up-cuomo.html [https://perma.cc/KNP3-EN4K]; Mandalit del Barco, "Time's Up CEO Resigns over Cuomo Fallout," *NPR*, August 26, 2021, https://www.npr.org/2021/08/26/1031521703/tina-tchen-times-up-ceo-resigns-cuomo [https://perma.cc/C327-AATZ].

35. Buckley, "Powerful Hollywood Women."

36. See Time's Up, "We're Here to Accomplish Three Goals," accessed April 24, 2024, https://perma.cc/JP57-FQNA.

37. Jocelyn Noveck, "Time's Up to Halt Operations, Shift Resources to Legal Fund," *AP News*, January 22, 2023, https://apnews.com/article/times-up-metoo-1ac800e48a96357d7fb29c18848c50d2 [https://perma.cc/DRN3-7JWR].

38. See, for example, Emily Witt, "How the Survivors of Parkland Began the Never Again Movement," *New Yorker*, February 19, 2018, https://www .newyorker.com/news/news-desk/how-the-survivors-of-parkland-began -the-never-again-movement [https://perma.cc/VH9A-69R4].

39. See Southern Poverty Law Center, "About Us," accessed February 8, 2023, https://www.splcenter.org/about [https://perma.cc/V29P-SKLJ].

40. Audra D. S. Burch, Alan Blinder, and John Eligon, "Roiled by Staff Uproar, Civil Rights Group Looks at Intolerance Within," *New York Times*, March 25, 2019, *New York Times*, March 25, 2019, https://www.nytimes .com/2019/03/25/us/morris-dees-leaves-splc.html   [https://perma.cc /B3RY-Z2RM] (quoting Judge U. W. Clemon).

41. Southern Poverty Law Center, *Southern Poverty Law Center, Inc. and SPLC Action Fund Consolidated Financial Statements: October 31, 2021,* accessed February 8, 2023, https://www.splcenter.org/sites/default/files /audited_financial_statements_103121.pdf [https://perma.cc/9TV9-7GU3].

42. Burch, Blinder, and Eligon, "Roiled by Staff Uproar."

43. Burch, Blinder, and Eligon, "Roiled by Staff Uproar."

44. Marc Edelman and Jennifer M. Pacella, "Vaulted into Victims: Preventing Further Sexual Abuse in U.S. Olympic Sports through Unionization and Improved Governance," *Arizona Law Review* 61, no. 3 (2019): 463–65.

45. See Lolita Buckner Inniss, "Bicentennial Man—The New Millennium Assimilationism and the Foreigner among Us," *Rutgers Law Review* 54, no. 4 (2002): 1124.

46. Women's Media Center, *The Status of Women of Color in the U.S. News Media* 2018, accessed February 8, 2023, https://womensmediacenter .com/assets/site/reports/the-status-of-women-of-color-in-the-u-s-media- 2018-full-report/Women-of-Color-Report-FINAL-WEB.pdf   [https:// perma.cc/U2ZY-C6B6].

47. Michael F. Jacobson and Laurie Ann Mazur, *Marketing Madness: A Survival Guide for a Consumer Society* (Abingdon, UK: Routledge, 1995).

48. See Lolita Buckner Inniss, "A 'Ho New World: Raced and Gendered Insult as Ersatz Carnival and the Corruption of Freedom of Expression Norms," *New York University Review of Law and Social Change* 33, no. 1 (2009): 76.

BIBLIOGRAPHY

Akbar, Amna A. "Toward a Radical Imagination of Law." *New York University Law Review* 93, no. 3 (2018): 405–79.

Arnow-Richman, Rachel, James Hicks, and Steven Davidoff Solomon. "Do Social Movements Spur Corporate Change? The Rise of 'MeToo Termination Rights' in CEO Contracts." *Indiana Law Journal* 98, no. 1 (2022): 125–76.

Black Lives Matter. "About." Accessed January 10, 2023. https://black-livesmatter.com/about/ [https://perma.cc/NRJ3–67Y7].

———. "Herstory." Accessed February 6, 2023. https://blacklivesmatter .com/herstory/ [https://perma.cc/3N5H-VH57].

———. "Our Co-Founders." Accessed June 19, 2021. https://perma.cc /V2DH-UT58.

"Black Lives Matter . . . What We Believe." University of Central Arkansas. Accessed February 6, 2023. https://perma.cc/4SD8-Z8A6.

Buckley, Cara. "Powerful Hollywood Women Unveil Anti-Harassment Action Plan." *New York Times*, January 1, 2018. https://www.nytimes .com/2018/01/01/movies/times-up-hollywood-women-sexual-harassment .html [https://perma.cc/F5T3–54M8].

Burch, Audra D. S., Alan Blinder, and John Eligon. "Roiled by Staff Uproar, Civil Rights Group Looks at Intolerance Within." *New York Times*, March 25, 2019. https://www.nytimes.com/2019/03/25/us /morris-dees-leaves-splc.html [https://perma.cc/B3RY-Z2RM].

Burke, Tarana. "Purpose." Just Be, Inc. Accessed February 7, 2023. https://justbeinc.wixsite.com/justbeinc/purpose-mission-and-vision [https://perma.cc/PTX9-PFSE].

Canova, Daniel. "Former NFL Player Marcellus Wiley Rips Black Lives Matter after It Removes Page on Disrupting 'Nuclear Family Structure.'" *Fox News*, September 23, 2021. https://www.foxnews.com/sports /former-nfl-player-marcellus-wiley-rips-black-lives-matter-after-it -removes-page-on-disrupting-nuclear-family-structure [https://perma .cc/Q986–7QLY].

Chira, Susan. "Why Did Hillary Clinton Let This Happen?" *New York Times*, January 26, 2018. https://www.nytimes.com/2018/01/26/opinion/hillary -clinton-sexual-harassment.html [https://perma.cc/73YA-YNEY].

Cho, Sumi. "Post-Racialism." *Iowa Law Review* 94, no. 5 (2009): 1589–650.

Choudhury, Nusrat. "The Government Is Watching #BlackLivesMatter, and It's Not Okay." ACLU, August 4, 2015. https://www.aclu.org/news /racial-justice/government-watching-blacklivesmatter-and-its-not-okay [https://perma.cc/256M-X7P3].

Covey, Steven M. R., and Rebecca R. Merrill. *The Speed of Trust: The One Thing That Changes Everything.* New York: Free Press, 2008.

Cureton, Emily. "In Rural Oregon, Threats and Backlash Follow Racial Justice Protests." *NPR*, September 3, 2020. https://www.npr.org/2020 /09/03/906809148/in-rural-oregon-threats-and-backlash-follow-racial -justice-protests [https://perma.cc/3MHP-4Y6G].

del Barco, Mandalit. "Time's Up CEO Resigns over Cuomo Fallout." *NPR*, August 26, 2021. https://www.npr.org/2021/08/26/1031521703/tina-tchen-times-up-ceo-resigns-cuomo [https://perma.cc/C327-AATZ].

Edelman, Marc, and Jennifer M. Pacella. "Vaulted into Victims: Preventing Further Sexual Abuse in U.S. Olympic Sports through Unionization and Improved Governance." *Arizona Law Review* 61, no. 3 (2019): 463–503.

Fessler, Leah. "Gloria Steinem Says These are the Best Guidelines for Difficult Conversations." *QZ.com*, November 18, 2018. https://qz.com /work/1467935/gloria-steinem-says-these-are-the-best-guidelines-for -difficult-conversations [https://perma.cc/FHQ6-M5Z4].

Greene, Linda S., Lolita Buckner Inniss, Bridget J. Crawford, Mehrsa Baradaran, Noa Ben-Asher, I. Bennett Capers, Osamudia R. James, and Keisha Lindsay. "Talking about Black Lives Matter and #Metoo." *Wisconsin Journal of Law, Gender, and Society* 34, no. 2 (2019): 109–78.

Grzegorek, Vince. "'Black Lives Matter Is a Terrorist Organization'—The Cleveland Police Union's Ugly History with BLM." *Cleveland Scene*, July 2, 2020. https://www.clevescene.com/news/black-lives-matter-is -a-terrorist-organization-the-cleveland-police-unions-ugly-history-with-blm-33288734 [https://perma.cc/T45M-CWDK].

Hill, Zahara. "A Black Woman Created the 'Me Too' Campaign against Sexual Assault 10 Years Ago." *Ebony*, October 18, 2017. https://www .ebony.com/black-woman-me-too-movement-tarana-burke-alyssa -milano/ [https://perma.cc/CJP2-CE89].

Inniss, Lolita Buckner. "The Absent Racial #MeToo and Rekindling Intersectional Identity." *Ain't I a Feminist Legal Scholar Too?* (blog). September 23, 2018. http://innissfls.blogspot.com/2018/09/the-absent -racial-metoo.html [https://perma.cc/77NV-Z8LK].

———. "Bicentennial Man—The New Millennium Assimilationism and the Foreigner among Us." *Rutgers Law Review* 54, no. 4 (2002): 1101–32.

———. "'From Space-Off to Represented Space.' Review of *Reimagining Equality: Stories of Gender, Race, and Finding Home* by Anita Hill." *Berkeley Journal of Gender Law and Justice* 28, no. 1 (2013): 138–51.

————. "A 'Ho New World: Raced and Gendered Insult as Ersatz Carnival and the Corruption of Freedom of Expression Norms." *New York University Review of Law and Social Change* 33, no. 1 (2009): 43–86.

Jacobson, Michael F., and Laurie Ann Mazur. *Marketing Madness: A Survival Guide for a Consumer Society*. Abingdon, UK: Routledge, 1995.

Kantor, Jodi, and Michael Gold. "Roberta Kaplan, Who Aided Cuomo, Resigns from Time's Up." *New York Times*, August 9, 2011. https://www.nytimes.com/2021/08/09/nyregion/roberta-kaplan-times-up-cuomo.html [https://perma.cc/KNP3-EN4K].

Kennedy, Randall. "Harvard Betrays a Law Professor—and Itself." *New York Times*, May 15, 2019. https://www.nytimes.com/2019/05/15/opinion/race-identity/harvard-law-harvey-weinstein.html [https://perma.cc/9E62-ZMP6].

Kurtzleben, Danielle. "The Trailblazers and Turning Points on the Road to #MeToo." *Washington Post*, July 5, 2019. https://perma.cc/DGS7-B6MZ.

Langone, Alix. "#MeToo and Time's Up Founders Explain the Difference between the 2 Movements—And How They're Alike." *Time*, updated March 8, 2018. https://time.com/5189945/whats-the-difference-between-the-metoo-and-times-up-movements/ [https://perma.cc/57H5-NLV3].

Leonardi, Anthony. "Black Lives Matter 'What We Believe' Page That Includes Disrupting 'Nuclear Family Structure' Removed from Website." *Washington Examiner*, September 21, 2020. https://www.washingtonexaminer.com/news/black-lives-matter-what-we-believe-page-that-includes-disrupting-nuclear-family-structure-removed-from-website [https://perma.cc/Q7AR-EPHS].

Lopez, Ian Haney. "Is the 'Post' in Post-Racial the 'Blind' in Colorblind?" *Cardozo Law Review* 32, no. 3 (2011): 807–32.

Martinez, Veronica Root, and Gina-Gail S. Fletcher. "Equality Metrics." *Yale Law Journal Forum* 130 (June 2021). https://www.yalelawjournal.org/forum/equality-metrics [https://perma.cc/79GB-AEEU].

Morrison, Aaron. "Black Lives Matter Has $42 Million in Assets." *AP News*, May 17, 2022. https://apnews.com/article/government-and-politics-race-ethnicity-philanthropy-black-lives-matter-5bc4772e029da522036f8ad2a02990aa [https://perma.cc/KDC6-3CK7].

Noveck, Jocelyn. "Time's Up to Halt Operations, Shift Resources to Legal Fund." *AP News*, January 22, 2023. https://apnews.com/article

/times-up-metoo-1ac800e48a96357d7fb29c18848c50d2 [https://
perma.cc/DRN3-7JWR].

Oxford English Dictionary Online. S.v. "matter (*n.*)." Accessed February 7,
2023. https://www.oed.com/view/Entry/115083 [https://perma.cc
/CP3Q-RNRD].

Price, Lydia. "How The Weeknd, Kim Kardashian West and More Stars
Have Supported Black Lives Matter." *People.com*, August 12, 2016.
https://people.com/celebrity/how-celebrities-have-supported-black
-lives-matter/ [https://perma.cc/2VTR-CDZH].

Ransom, Jan. "Mr. Weinstein's Criminal Convictions in California Still
Stand." *New York Times*, April 25, 2024. https://www.nytimes.com
/live/2024/04/25/nyregion/harvey-weinstein-appeal [https://perma
.cc/D3R2-K95V].

Rojas, Rick, and Jessica Jaglois. "Five Officers Charged with Murder in
Memphis Police Killing." *New York Times*, updated February 1, 2023.
https://www.nytimes.com/2023/01/26/us/tyre-nichols-memphis
-police.html [https://perma.cc/H696-RYSH].

Solis, Marie. "When Believing Women Isn't Enough to Help Them." *Vice.
com*, October 9, 2019. https://www.vice.com/en_us/article/gyemm3
/when-believing-women-isnt-enough-to-help-them [https://perma
.cc/7YJU-A2KY].

Southern Poverty Law Center. "About Us." Accessed February 8,
2023. https://www.splcenter.org/about [https://perma.cc/
V29P-SKLJ].

———. *Southern Poverty Law Center, Inc. and SPLC Action Fund Consolidated Financial Statements: October* 31, 2021. Accessed February 8,
2023. https://www.splcenter.org/sites/default/files/audited_financial_
statements_103121.pdf [https://perma.cc/9TV9-7GU3].

Taylor, Kate. "Harvard's First Black Faculty Deans Let Go Amid Uproar
over Harvey Weinstein Defense." *New York Times*, May 11, 2019.
https://www.nytimes.com/2019/05/11/us/ronald-sullivan-harvard.html
[https://perma.cc/9H98-WZMJ].

Time's Up. "We're Here to Accomplish Three Goals." Accessed April 24,
2024. https://perma.cc/JP57-FQNA.

Traister, Rebecca. "The Toll of Me Too: Assessing the Costs for Those
Who Came Forward." *The Cut*, September 30, 2019. https://www
.thecut.com/2019/09/the-toll-of-me-too.html [https://perma.cc
/B7T8-3W28].

United States v. Windsor, 570 U.S. 744 (2013).

Walsh, Colleen. "Must We Allow Symbols of Racism on Public Land?" *Harvard Gazette*, June 19, 2020. https://news.harvard.edu/gazette /story/2020/06/historian-puts-the-push-to-remove-confederate -statues-in-context/ [https://perma.cc/3PUC-XHUX].

Walters, Joanna. "#MeToo a Revolution That Can't Be Stopped, Says Time's Up Co-founder." *The Guardian*, October 21, 2018. https://www .theguardian.com/world/2018/oct/21/metoo-revolution-times-up -roberta-kaplan [https://perma.cc/G49V-UET5].

Wexler, Lesley. "#MeToo and Law Talk." *University of Chicago Legal Forum* 2019 (2019): Article 21. https://chicagounbound.uchicago.edu /uclf/vol2019/iss1/21/ [https://perma.cc/XG4V-U5Z6].

Wilkins, Denise J., Andrew G. Livingstone, and Mark Levine. "Whose Tweets? The Rhetorical Functions of Social Media Use in Developing the Black Lives Matter Movement." *British Journal of Social Psychology* 58, no. 4 (2019): 786–805.

Wilson Cooper, Camille, and Shuntay Z. McCoy. "Poverty and African American Mothers: Countering Biased Ideologies, Representations and the Politics of Containment." *Journal of the Association for Research on Mothering* 11, no. 2 (2009): 45–55.

Witt, Emily. "How the Survivors of Parkland Began the Never Again Movement." *New Yorker*, February 19, 2018. https://www.newyorker .com/news/news-desk/how-the-survivors-of-parkland-began-the -never-again-movement [https://perma.cc/VH9A-69R4].

Women's Media Center. *The Status of Women of Color in the U.S. News Media* 2018. Accessed February 8, 2023. https://womensmediacenter .com/assets/site/reports/the-status-of-women-of-color-in-the-u-s- media-2018-full-report/Women-of-Color-Report-FINAL-WEB.pdf [https://perma.cc/U2ZY-C6B6].

Intersectionality, Identity Politics, and Transformation

WITH CONTRIBUTIONS BY

Bridget J. Crawford   Keisha Lindsay

Linda S. Greene   Ruthann Robson

Aya Gruber   Kathryn M. Stanchi

Lolita Buckner Inniss   Lua Kamál Yuille

Osamudia James

BACKGROUND

From a practical and theoretical perspective, both the Black Lives Matter movement and the #MeToo movement are grounded in claims about group identity and group-based rights. Black Lives Matter asserts the fundamental dignity and humanity of all Black people in working toward "a world where Black lives are no longer systematically targeted for demise."[1] The #MeToo movement seeks "to address both the dearth of resources for survivors of sexual violence and to build a robust community of advocates and allies."[2] Black Lives Matter understands Black people as being dehumanized and victimized because of their race. Women are sexually harassed at work, disproportionately compared to men, because they are women. Both movements posit identity at the core of the problems they have identified.

Simultaneously with the understanding of race-based and gender-based harms, both Black Lives Matter and #MeToo are informed by intersectional analysis. Because intersectionality is territory that is well-trodden elsewhere, as well as by our dialogue participants in this chapter, we will be brief in our description. Intersectionality is a mode of inquiry that understands that identity is complex and multifaceted. One's full experience or identity can never be adequately explained by a single descriptor; one is never "just" one identity category. That is, a friend may describe himself as a Black trans man. Another is a Chinese American cisgender lesbian woman. Furthermore, identity categories are not cumulative (i.e., "race plus gender"). Rather identities reside, join, "meet," or intersect in one person, just as streets do at a corner.

Intersectionality, as a term and as a mode of analysis, is strongly associated with Black feminist theory. The Combahee River Collective, a Black lesbian feminist organization active in the late 1970s, published a statement that is typically thought to be an early articulation of intersectional thought. The group explained that it was "struggling against racial, sexual, heterosexual, and class oppression," and defined its task as "the development of integrated analysis and practice based upon the fact that the major systems of oppression are interlocking."[3] Legal scholar Kimberlé Crenshaw was the first to employ the metaphor of a traffic intersection. In a 1989 essay, she explained:

> Discrimination, like traffic through an intersection, may flow in one direction, and it may flow in another. If an accident happens in an intersection, it can be caused by cars traveling from any number of directions and, sometimes, from all of them. Similarly, if a Black woman is harmed because she is in the intersection, her injury could result from sex discrimination or race discrimination.[4]

Intersectional analysis has deep roots in Black feminist thought, and Black feminist legal theory in particular.

As a mode of inquiry and analysis, intersectionality pushes against the "flattening" of identity into a single axis like race or sex. One sees the influence of intersectional thought in the Black Lives Matter statement that the movement affirms "all Black lives along the gender spectrum," and seeks to center those who have been "marginalized within Black liberation movements."[5] Similarly, the recent joint report of Time's Up Legal Defense Fund and the National Women's Law Center emphasizes the movement's work on behalf of "those who face multiple forms of discrimination, including women of color, LGBTQIA+ people, and low-income women and families."[6] In this way, both Black Lives Matter and #MeToo are building on the work of earlier Black feminist thought.

Intersectional feminist thought is now pervasive in both grass-roots thinking and feminist academic scholarship. Consider, for example, the title of a 2011 essay by author Favia Dzodan, "My Feminism Will Be Intersectional or It Will Be Bullshit," since replicated (without any apparent remuneration to Dzodan) on a variety of Etsy products.[7] Consider also that the *Berkeley Journal of Gender, Law and Justice*, which is the specialty law journal at the University of California, Berkeley, devoted to gender issues, publishes only pieces that "critically examine . . . the intersection of gender with one or more axes of subordination, including, but not limited to, race, class, sexual orientation, and disability."[8] As these examples show, understanding gender as one of many identity axes is a hallmark of intersectional analysis.

As much as intersectionality may be common or expected in some spaces, the law is notoriously hostile to intersectional claims. When Kimberlé Crenshaw introduced the concept of intersectionality to a larger academic audience in 1989, she did so in a law review article devoted to a discussion of three lawsuits involving allegations of employment discrimination. In all three cases, the plaintiffs were Black women. Further, in all three cases, federal courts failed to treat the claims as involving combined race and sex discrimination, showing how unreceptive the anti-discrimination law is to intersectional claims.[9] Instead, as Crenshaw showed, law is best equipped to respond to allegations of specific harm on the basis of race *or* sex.

Notwithstanding the challenges of using law as a tool to address complex injustice, both the Black Lives Matter and the #MeToo movements seek law-based solutions, at least in part. Indeed, in the quest for racial justice, larger demands, such as the end to systemic racism, remain unmet. But there have been some concrete reforms. For example, since the killing of George Floyd by a Minneapolis police officer, at least thirty states and Washington, DC, have enacted some police reform, generally clustered in one of three areas: (1) use of force by officers, (2) duty of officers to intervene in misconduct by others, and (3) how police misconduct gets reported and taken into account for personnel purposes.[10]

Likewise, the #MeToo movement's goal of harassment-free workplaces likely will be impossible to achieve. That said, at least twenty-two states and Washington, DC, have passed a variety of supportive legislation, in four broad categories, as identified by the National Women's Law Center: "ensuring all working people are covered by harassment protections; restoring worker power and increasing employer transparency and accountability; expanding access to justice; and promoting prevention strategies."[11]

With a curiosity about intersectionality's influence on the Black Lives Matter and #MeToo movements, and the law's potential and limitations to bring about the reforms the groups demand, we invited our participants to consider these questions:

> How does the lens of intersectionality help us to
> understand the interior characteristics and influence
> of the Black Lives Matter and/or #MeToo movements?
> Does law have the potential to produce meaningful
> and transformative solutions to the phenomena that
> led to either or both movements? Does law pose an
> obstacle to transformative change? What role should

law play in achieving a society that is race conscious and gender conscious? Should we view race consciousness and gender consciousness with skepticism?

DIALOGUE

Intersectionality

Linda Greene: When I think of intersectionality, I think of Marcia Gillespie's "We Speak in Tongues," published in *Ms. Magazine.* She really explained the indivisibility of intersectional identity:

> We say, I am a Black Woman, I cannot separate my race from my sex, cannot separate racism from sexism. They are rarely separate, never indivisible. So, don't ask me to choose, I cannot; I am myself, I am not you. Nor will I let you choose for me. And I will not let you pretend that racism and sexism are not inseparable issues in all of our lives.[12]

Black women have played crucial role in raising the issues of sexual violence and sexual harassment, and they were doing so long before Tarana Burke started #MeToo and before any celebrities used the hash tag.[13] For example, in 1974, in a much publicized North Carolina trial, Joan Little was acquitted in the death of her white jailer, Clarence Allgood, whom Little said she stabbed when he tried rape her.[14] Another early, and prominent, case involved Carmita Wood, an administrative assistant at Cornell University, who brought the first sexual harassment claim under New York state law when she sued her boss, nuclear physicist Boyce McDaniel, in 1975.[15] When, in 1986, the Supreme Court finally recognized sexual harassment as a form of discrimination prohibited by Title VII of the Civil Rights Act of 1964, it did so in *Meritor Savings Bank v. Vinson,* a case in which a Black woman claimed that her boss harassed and raped her repeatedly during work hours for three years, occasionally in the bank vault at work.[16] Anita Hill's testimony during the confirmation hearings for Clarence Thomas in 1991, which was viewed by twenty million people, put the issue of sexual harassment against Black women before the public in high-stakes proceedings with a Supreme Court appointment at stake.[17]

Keisha Lindsay: Linda is certainly right, and we can take it back even further. The concept of intersecting or interlocking oppressions has long been evident in the work of Anna Julia Cooper and other historical Black women thinkers and writers.[18] What we think of as contemporary intersectionality emerged during the very period—the late 1970s and the 1980s—when Black women began to enter the academy in greater numbers.[19] To embrace an intersectional framework is to understand, for instance, that Black women's experience of racism is informed by their experience of sexism. Put more concretely, racist whites routinely assume that Black women are racially inferior *because* they are failed women—meaning, for example, welfare queens and jezebels—rather than "real" women who are sexually monogamous wives in patriarchal, nuclear family households. To embrace intersectionality is also to reject a binary approach in which race, gender, and other hierarchies of power are taken as "distinct and isolated realms of experience" operating along "independent axes."[20] I will say more later about how the logic of intersectionality enables us to understand the interior characteristics and influence of both movements.

Osamudia James: I'd like to add something I learned from a colleague of mine at the University of Miami, Professor Donnette Francis. She has reminded me in the past to think about intersectionality as a series of questions, and not a foregone conclusion. That is, what group are we talking about, and what are the historical conditions that have subordinated or marginalized that group in intersecting and overlapping ways? The cultural and colonial imperialism of the United States has traveled such that Black Lives Matter has importance as far away as the United Kingdom, France, Italy, and Australia.[21] The overlapping systems of oppression there, however, differ from those in the United States, and merit interrogation of their own.

Lolita Buckner Inniss: Let's add to the mix that, while viewing people through intersectional lenses helps to paint a more detailed and nuanced picture, intersectionality sometimes fails because it is viewed as possibly too over-inclusive or too under-inclusive, thereby obscuring complex forms of bias.

Bridget Crawford: Let's also add the way that many people use the term *intersectional* when what they really want to convey is a race-conscious recognition of the experiences of people of color.[22]

Lua Yuille: Like Lolita, I see intersectionality (which it may well be time to replace with *cross-dimensionality*) as, first and foremost, a descriptive tool. And, like Osamudia, I appreciate that it does not give answers so much as make a demand that justice be multivalent. But I worry that the moniker has become a form of "legitimacy branding," instead of the heuristic it was intended to be. Even though Black Lives Matter was founding by Black women, I struggle to see Black Lives Matter, as it operates in the world, as robustly intersectional. It centers the experience of Black men. In the same way, #MeToo resonates in the key of "white woman."

Bridget Crawford: At least when it comes to #MeToo, it's certainly the victories in cases involving high-profile white women that tend to get the most press coverage. In 2020, film producer Harvey Weinstein was sentenced to twenty-three years in prison for rape and a criminal sexual offense. Yes, his New York conviction was overturned due to judicial errors, but as of this writing, his sixteen-year sentence in California still stands.[23]

Aya Gruber: Remember that when the Weinstein verdict first came down in 2020, *New York Times* reporters Jodi Kantor and Megan

ABOUT HARVEY WEINSTEIN

In the fall of 2017, the world watched in shock, awe, dismay, and vindication as famed producer and movie mogul Harvey Weinstein faced an onslaught of allegations detailing decades of sexual and other misconduct toward dozens of women. Combined with the astonishment and concern, however, was a sense of resignation: Weinstein's misbehavior had been an open secret in Hollywood for years, seen yet largely ignored by dozens—if not hundreds—of individuals both inside and outside of the entertainment industry. Women had warned each other behind the scenes to avoid vulnerable interactions with the producer; media outlets had been persuaded to suppress stories of Weinstein's indiscretions. Allegations regarding Weinstein's sexual misconduct even found their way into the opening monologue of the 2013 Academy Awards. Yet despite the swirls of allegations against him, Weinstein for years operated almost completely unchecked.

In many ways, the eventual public airing of the charges against Weinstein opened the floodgates for countless women to come forward, not only corroborating stories of Weinstein's misdeeds, but also alleging similar misbehavior by scores of other men, some well-known and some not. From radio hosts to college professors to businesspeople, men across various industries found themselves accused of a broad range of sexual misbehavior in the workplace. Women turned to social media to express their collective outrage, with millions of people engaging with the #MeToo movement, further exposing the breadth of this problem across society.

Amidst the outrage and disbelief, however, another reaction has emerged—a sort of desperate handwringing, as academics and members of the media and the public brood about what can be done to prevent this type of misconduct from continuing to occur. Even the Equal Employment Opportunity Commission (EEOC), a purported expert on fostering fair and unbiased workplace relations, has expressed befuddlement regarding this issue.

Excerpt from Jessica Fink, "Disgorging Harvey Weinstein's Salary," *Berkeley Journal of Employment and Labor Law* 41, no. 2 (2020): 286–88.

Twohey published an article in which different stakeholders in the movement provided their immediate reactions. Of course, many indicated that the verdict was a crowning achievement of the movement.[24]

Bridget Crawford: It will be interesting to see whether the over-turning of the conviction is seen as a low point for the movement.

Aya Gruber: Possibly. To me, it was striking that the very reporters who, along with Ronan Farrow, initially broke the Weinstein story and whose investigative reporting prompted the #MeToo movement, regarded the conviction as a fitting end to the story. When the judge sentenced the disgraced mogul to twenty-three years in prison, a vir-tual life sentence at his age, there were near universal expressions of satisfaction, although those were mixed with some cautions that "no amount of jail time" is enough.[25] Voices on Twitter (now known as X) even expressed joy at the thought that he would be raped in prison. Just as COVID-19 began to tear through New York's overcrowded and unsanitary penal institutions, news broke that Weinstein con-tracted the deadly disease. This, too, was celebrated on social media, albeit in combination with some criticism that the prison system was yet "too easy" on Weinstein because he received a COVID-19 test (when many on the "outside" could not).[26] Such "victories," to me, feel like a sad simulacrum of success for a social justice movement.

But if we're talking about #MeToo's achievements, we recognize that they have come not in one spectacular conviction, but more subtly and over time. They have been monumental. They are enough to make me think that #MeToo will ultimately bend the arc toward justice, despite my abjuration of its carcerality.

Bridget Crawford: And, of course it is not a distaste for carcerality that led to the overturning of Weinstein's conviction, but rather what was deemed to be an error allowing certain evidence into trial.

HARVEY WEINSTEIN'S TWENTY-THREE-YEAR SENTENCE

At the sentencing after his convictions for rape and sexual assault, Mr. Harvey Weinstein's attorneys requested a sentence of five years, in light of his failing health and his age (he was then sixty-seven years old). The judge sentenced Mr. Weinstein to twenty-three years in prison, noting that although this was Weinstein's first conviction, it was not his first offense. Weinstein's attorney denounced the sentence as "obscene," "obnoxious," and "cowardly."

According to the United States Sentencing Commission, the average sentence for rape is 178 months (almost fifteen years). The average sentence for "abusive sexual contact" is twenty-seven months (over two years).

Sources: Eric Levenson, Lauren del Valle, and Sonia Moghe, "Harvey Weinstein Sentenced to 23 Years in Prison after Addressing His Accusers in Court," *CNN*, March 11, 2020, https://www.cnn.com/2020/03/11/us/harvey -weinstein-sentence/index.html (quoting Weinstein attorney Donna Rotunno); and United States Sentencing Commission, *Quick Facts on Sexual Abuse Offenders* (2018): 2, https://www.ussc.gov/sites/default/files/pdf /research-and-publications/quick-facts/Sexual_Abuse_FY18.pdf [https:// perma.cc/QL64-EJ8D].

Law

Lolita Buckner Inniss: Aya, you raise a good point about how we should evaluate the so-called legal victories of social justice movements. I think it is worth talking about where and how law produces solutions, and when it is an obstacle.

Lua Yuille: To me, the law both has the potential to produce meaningful change and transformative solutions *and* poses an obstacle to transformative change. But I want to distinguish "The Law" from law. What I am calling "The Law" (which includes progressive civil rights law) was not designed to do the work Black Lives Matter and #MeToo want it to do. In a broad sense, both movements demand that law deftly and organically change to respond to the technology of oppression.[27]

The Law was set up to do the opposite; it protects an elemental status quo. Even if activists, politicians, and jurists genuinely aim to dismantle the types of systemic, institutionalized problems that motivate Black Lives Matter or #MeToo, it is clear that, if they work within existing structures, the result will be necessarily limited within the definitional scope of the status quo. This observation is not new, though in my own work I have attempted to demonstrate why this is the case.[28] John Marshall bound himself to this idea when he explained that "the Courts of the conqueror cannot deny" the supremacy of the conqueror.[29] And, of course, it is Audre Lorde's curse: "For the master's tools will never dismantle the master's house. They may allow us temporarily to beat him at his own game, but they will never enable us to bring about genuine change."[30]

Ruthann Robson: This is not to say that it is wrong to demand legal solutions. The law is one tool to dismantle white supremacist patriarchy because white supremacist patriarchy uses the tool of the law to maintain itself. As Lorde continued after the quote Lua gave, these master's tools "may allow us temporarily to beat him at his own game, but they will never enable us to bring about genuine change. And this fact is only threatening to those women who still define the master's house as their only source of support."[31]

So even if it is temporary, we can use the same hammer—for example, the hammer of law—that the master used to build the house to also break the boards that the master nailed together. If I thought that this was not possible, I would not be a lawyer and I would not teach law! But we need more than the simple "hammer" of law. And it is also important to focus on who wields those hammers.

Lua Yuille: That is fair. I remain convinced that law—in the sense of compulsory and enforceable norms—is the most powerful mechanism for transformative social change. Law teaches and trains people how to think and how to behave. Like students in school, not every person assimilates the lessons, and some people reject them outright. But the right curriculum and the right teaching strategies get most students to where they need to be. The challenge is to find a liberatory curriculum for the law. How do we make law that is not "the master's tool"? How do we make law that builds into its structure a response to the evolving nature of injustice?

Ruthann Robson: The obstacle of the law that I think we don't stress enough is this: we are changed when we express our demands in the legal arena and begin to think of the problems as legal ones. So that, for example, when queer liberation was funneled into "marriage equality," much was changed and, to my mind, much was lost. When I think of other movements working for what we might call "liberation," including Black Lives Matter and #MeToo, I think of how the discipline of law should not discipline our aspirations. Decades ago, in trying to conceptualize a lesbian legal theory, I was preoccupied by the question "how do we [lesbians] use the law rather than be used by it" and posited that the law (and legal notions) "domesticated" lesbian existence and relations, since lesbians aspired to be "assimilated" as the definition of success.[32]

USING THE LAW VS. BEING USED BY LAW

While marriage and the quasi-marriage relationships contemplated by adoption and domestic partnership have many practical benefits, as well as practical disadvantages, marriage and quasi-marriage are suspect in lesbian legal theory. Underlying the lesbian critique of marriage is the gendered perspective on marriage developed by feminists.

Excerpt from Ruthann Robson and S. E. Valentine, "Lov(h)ers: Lesbians as Intimate Partners and Lesbian Legal Theory," *Temple Law Review* 63, no. 3 (1990): 536.

Osamudia James: To me, the law is only one part of larger movements for change. It works better in some circumstances than others. Legal challenges can sap movements of their emotional and rhetorical energy—having to boil down a movement into a specific right that the law recognizes, against a party over which a court has jurisdiction, in pursuit of a remedy that the law can provide, can be sterile, draining, and ultimately unsuccessful. Although critical race theorists have taught us that rights can be important for minority groups and that rights provide crucial prohibitions on discrimination, critical legal studies has also taught us that rights can be illusory, giving citizens just enough of a sense of equality such that a fundamentally unfair system is legitimized, to say nothing of what it takes to actually vindicate rights.[33] The latter takes resources, and representation, and access to the direct services that do not necessarily follow from the big wins of impact litigation in which a legal right has been secured. In the wake of the *Brown v. Board* victory,[34] leaders like Martin Luther King Jr. insisted that litigation could never be a replacement for participatory democracy, and that, in the end, it was up to Black people to stand up nonviolently to segregation that, thus far, had suffered a "legal death" but not a factual one.[35]

WHAT IS CRITICAL RACE THEORY?

Critical race theory is a body of legal scholarship, now about a decade old [as of 1995], a majority of whose members are both existentially people of color and ideologically committed to the struggle against racism, particularly as institutionalized in and by law.

Critical race theory writing and lecturing is characterized by frequent use of the first person, storytelling, narrative, allegory, interdisciplinary treatment of law, and the unapologetic use of creativity. The work is often disruptive because its commitment to anti-racism goes well beyond civil rights, integration, affirmative action, and other liberal measures. This is not to say that critical race theory adherents automatically or uniformly "trash" liberal ideology and method (as many adherents of critical legal studies do). Rather, they are highly suspicious of the liberal agenda, distrust its method, and want to retain what they see as a valuable strain of egalitarianism which may exist despite, and not because of, liberalism.

Excerpt from Derrick A. Bell, "Who's Afraid of Critical Race Theory?," *University of Illinois Law Review* 1995, no. 4 (1995): 898–99.

Laws also cannot prevent people from simply abandoning the sites of legal victories. I might not really care, for example, if my neighbor believes that Black lives matter; I only care that laws make it so that my neighbor can't legally exclude me from buying the house next to hers. At the same time, even as *Shelley v. Kraemer* struck down racially restrictive covenants,[36] the law did not prevent the widespread flight that enabled whites to avoid integration, thus keeping Black people socially and economically isolated despite having won a legal victory against covenants. Ultimately, then, laws must work in conjunction with social movements, policy commitments, and market incentives to produce substantive and lasting change.

Lua Yuille: Law, writ large to encompass customary norms that are seen as obligatory,[37] should be the chief tool for advancing a society that is race and gender conscious. So long as race and gender remain salient and operational categories of de jure and de facto oppression (or even just disadvantage), consciousness of and responsiveness to their function cannot be left to any noncompulsory institution. This issue is so important that rather than view race or gender consciousness with skepticism, that is how we should view "blindness" or "neutrality" or "equality."

What does intersectionality do if not demonstrate that sameness is an empty pursuit? Race and gender (along with sexual orientation, religion, class, and so forth) interact to allocate power and position to a person in society. If you are blind to these factors, then you have not seen the person at all. The results of blind, neutral, equal allocations and positioning cannot be said to be just or equitable. Justice and equity are not about "hearts and minds." They are about institutions. So the pursuit of justice and equity must travel with institutional currency, and that is law.

Linda Greene: It is an American paradox that, as our society becomes more conscious of the complexity of gender identity and sexual orientation, and embraces the consumption of the athletic and artistic contributions of Blacks, the call for colorblindness has both deep resonance and constitutional legitimacy.[38]

Ruthann Robson: Under different labels—identity politics, essentialism—we have struggled with the conundrums of how difference is deployed and how we should deploy it. As Linda says, it is a paradox. In looking closer at the so-called affirmative action cases for example, we see in *Adarand*, decided in 1995, that Justice O'Connor, who wrote for a majority of the Court, used the word that word *skepticism* to describe the principle that must be applied to all racial classifications employed by government, meaning that they merit strict scrutiny.[39] As Justice Stevens made clear in his dissent in that case, this produces the "anomalous result that the Government can more easily enact affirmative-action programs to remedy discrimination against women than it can enact affirmative-action programs to remedy discrimination against African-Americans—even though the primary purpose of the Equal Protection Clause was to end discrimination against the former slaves."[40] Stevens goes on to write that the Court's conclusion would "disregard the difference between a 'No Trespassing' sign and a welcome mat. It would treat a Dixiecrat Senator's decision to vote against Thurgood Marshall's confirmation in order to keep African-Americans off the Supreme Court as on a par with President Johnson's evaluation of his nominee's race as a positive factor," and would "equate a law that made black citizens ineligible for military service with a program aimed at recruiting black soldiers."[41]

Yet arguing against race consciousness by government, Justice Clarence Thomas—the only Black justice on the 2020 U.S. Supreme Court (before the appointment of Ketanji Brown Jackson in 2022) and, having succeeded Justice Thurgood Marshall, only the second in its history—has contended essentially that we fool ourselves if we think we can distinguish between exclusion and inclusion. Justice Thomas noted that slaveholders expressed the belief that they were essentially welcoming of Black people by "elevating" them through slavery, and that racial segregationists expressed the belief that segregation usefully protected Blacks from the violence of racist whites.[42]

The bottom line, I think, is that racial and gender consciousness must be treated with skepticism, just as the law and our politics must be treated with skepticism.

Kathy Stanchi: I'm not sure I like the terms *race conscious* and *gender conscious*. Depending on what we mean by "conscious," you could view, for example, the obsession of the religious right with policing gender as eminently "gender conscious." My ideal would be for law to be antiracist, in the way that Ibram X. Kendi uses the word—you are either antiracist, or you are racist, and there is no "neutral" in between.[43] I would also like the law to be instrumental in creating and supporting gender equity and justice.

Although all the branches of government play a role in making the law support racial and gender justice, I want to comment here on the role of the Supreme Court, which has rarely acknowledged its complicity in upholding white dominance and male dominance. And, yet, from *Plessy v. Ferguson* to *The Slaughterhouse Cases* to

HOW DOES THE UNITED STATES SUPREME COURT TALK ABOUT "RACISM"?

The Court's use of "racist" and "racism" in its jurisprudence makes clear that it accepts little responsibility for racism and white supremacy in America. The Court certainly never apologizes for its upholding and constructing racism in the law. Although some Justices have called out the Court's complicity in racism or white supremacy in separate opinions, these instances are rare.

When the Court takes responsibility for its role in perpetuating racism, it opens up rhetorical space for the law to become part of the solution. Calling out racism also provides a foothold (and a citation) for advocates trying to achieve racial justice. Finally, for the victims of racism, calling out the law's complicity in racism is of great significance, not just as a matter of law but as a matter of cultural and social importance.

Excerpt from Kathryn M. Stanchi, "The Rhetoric of Racism in the United States Supreme Court," *Boston College Law Review* 62, no. 4 (2021): 1319, 1320.

Bradwell v. Illinois, the Supreme Court has been instrumental in constructing the racial and gender injustices in our society. The first step must be for the Court to take responsibility for this in the starkest terms by directly acknowledging decisions as racist or misogynist or homophobic—not just wrong, not just "incorrect," but racist or misogynist or homophobic. *Use those words.* As Kendi says, we can't truly challenge racism unless we acknowledge it.[44]

DISCUSSION QUESTIONS

1. What is your understanding of the meaning of intersectionality, and how does it differ from that of any of the participants in this chapter's dialogue?

2. What does Lua Yuille mean when she says that she worries that the term *intersectionality* may be functioning as "'legitimacy branding,' instead of the heuristic it was intended to be"? What does it mean to call intersectionality a heuristic, meaning stimulating interest or problem-solving?

3. Lua Yuille says that Black Lives Matter "centers the experience of Black men" and "#MeToo resonates in the key of 'white woman.'" Do you agree? Why or why not?

4. Aya Gruber called the joyful reaction to Harvey Weinstein's conviction for rape and criminal sexual offense "a sad simulacrum of success for a social justice movement." What does she mean? What, ideally, should success for a social justice movement look like? Can a criminal conviction be treated as a "success" in Gruber's view?

5. What role do you think race, age, social class, and celebrity status (of both the victims and the perpetrator) had in Harvey Weinstein's initial sentencing? Phrased differently, do you think his sentence would have been longer or shorter if he had been a Black man? What if most of his victims had been women of color instead of mostly white women? What if his victims had been, say, housekeepers or nannies, instead of accomplished or aspiring actors?

6. What do you think will be the impact on the #MeToo movement of the overturning of Harvey Weinstein's conviction in New York, given that he was also convicted and sentenced to jail in California for other sex crimes?

7. What does Lua Yuille mean in saying that "The Law" is different from "law"?

8. What does Ruthann Robson mean by using the law versus being used by it? In what way do the Black Lives Matter and #MeToo movements use the law, and in what way, if at all, does the law "use" the movements?

NOTES

1. See Black Lives Matter, "About," accessed April 23, 2024, https://blacklivesmatter.com/about/ [https://perma.cc/BX59-WAWK].

2. Global Fund for Women, "'Me Too.' Global Movement," accessed April 23, 2024, https://www.globalfundforwomen.org/movements/me-too / [https://perma.cc/NA8R-UTXN].

3. Combahee River Collective, *The Combahee River Collective Statement*, April 1977, https://www.blackpast.org/african-american-history/combahee -river-collective-statement-1977/ [https://perma.cc/92A5–3Y7Q].

4. Kimberlé Crenshaw, "Demarginalizing the Intersection of Race and Sex: A Black Feminist Critique of Antidiscrimination Doctrine, Feminist Theory, and Antiracist Politics," *University of Chicago Legal Forum* (1989): 149.

5. Black Lives Matter, "About."

6. Time's Up Legal Defense Fund and National Women's Law Center Fund LLC, *Coming Forward: Key Trends and Data from the Time's Up Legal Defense Fund*, p. 1, https://nwlc.org/wp-content/uploads/2020/10/NWLC -Intake-Report_FINAL_2020-10-13.pdf [https://perma.cc/3ScPN -NKZR].

7. See Flavia Dzodan, "My Feminism Will Be Intersectional or It Will Be Bullshit!" *Tiger Beatdown* (blog), October 10, 2011, https://tigerbeatdown .com/2011/10/10/my-feminism-will-be-intersectional-or-it-will-be-bulls-hit/ [https://perma.cc/C58B-MUMR]; Aja Romano, "This Feminist's Most Famous Quote Has Been Sold All over the Internet; She Hasn't Seen a Cent," *Vox*, August 12, 2016, https://www.vox.com/2016/8/12/12406648/flavia

-dzodan-my-feminism-will-be-intersectional-merchandise [https://perma.cc/XLT4–98W4].

8. *Berkeley Journal of Gender, Law, and Justice*, "Mandate," accessed April 23, 2024, https://genderlawjustice.org/mandate [https://perma.cc/9TY9-DYF8].

9. See Crenshaw, "Demarginalizing the Intersection of Race and Sex."

10. Reports on this have been mixed. See, for example, Ram Subramanian and Leily Arzy, "State Policing Reforms Since George Floyd's Murder," Brennan Center for Justice, May 21, 2020, https://www.brennancenter.org/our-work/research-reports/state-policing-reforms-george-floyds-murder [https://perma.cc/NLY3-UTCM]; Keenanga-Yamahtta Taylor, "Did Last Summer's Black Lives Matter Protests Change Anything?," *New Yorker*, August 6, 2021, https://www.newyorker.com/news/our-columnists/did-last-summers-protests-change-anything [https://perma.cc/X6UB-AP2H].

11. Andrea Johnson, Samone Ijoma, and Da Hae Kim, *#MeToo Five Years Later: Progress and Pitfalls in State Workplace Anti-Harassment Laws* (Washington, DC: National Women's Law Center, 2022), 3, https://nwlc.org/wp-content/uploads/2022/10/final_2022_nwlcMeToo_Report.pdf [https://perma.cc/FY7S-F4RM].

12. Marcia A. Gillespie, "We Speak in Tongues," *Ms.*, January/February 1992, 41–42.

13. Gillespie, "We Speak in Tongues."

14. See, for example, Julian Bond, "Self Defense against Rape: The Joanne Little Case," *The Black Scholar* 6, no. 6 (1975): 29–31; "The Case of Joanne Little," *Crime and Social Justice*, no. 3 (1975): 42–44.

15. See, for example, Enid Nemy, "Women Begin to Speak Out against Sexual Harassment at Work," *New York Times*, August 19, 1975, https://www.nytimes.com/1975/08/19/archives/women-begin-to-speak-out-against-sexual-harassment-at-work.html [https://perma.cc/H6DS-MR4S]. For a brief history of the sexual harassment movement from which this account is drawn, see Susan Brownmiller and Dolores Alexander, "How We Got Here: From Carmita Wood to Anita Hill," *Ms.*, January/February 1992, 70–71; Peter Weber, "The Depressingly Long History of Sexual Harassment Turning Points," *The Week*, November 27, 2017, https://theweek.com/articles/738873/depressingly-long-history-sexual-harassment-turning-points [https://perma.cc/WK88–3FVX]; Sarah Burke, "A Short History of the Long Fight against Workplace Sexual Harassment," *Vice*, December 12, 2017, https://www.vice.com/en/article/evaz8k/a-short-history-of-the-long-fight-against-workplace-sexual-harassment [https://perma.cc/62UW-KV4M]. One

description of the 1975 case of Carmita Wood, who was repeatedly harassed by Boyce McDaniel, her boss at the Cornell University Laboratory of Nuclear Sciences, includes the following details: "For years, Carmita Wood endured the sexual advances of her boss, Boyce McDaniel. He looked her up and down lasciviously, brushed up against her body, intimated that he was touching himself when she was nearby. He put his hand underneath her shirt and pinned her up against her desk. Once, after a Christmas party, he accosted her in an elevator, kissing her repeatedly on the mouth." Nina Renata Aron, "Groping in the Ivy League Led to the First Sexual Harassment Suit—And Nothing Happened to the Man," *Medium.com*, October 20, 2017, https://medium.com/timeline/carmita-wood-sexual-harrassment-f2c537a0e1e8 [https://perma.cc/7L3K-4EAE]. Wood applied for unemployment benefits from the employer but was denied because she left her job "voluntarily" and for "personal reasons" (Aron, "Groping in the Ivy League"). Wood, along with Eleanor Holmes Norton, who was then Commissioner of Human Rights of the City of New York, cofounded Working Women United, which aimed to illuminate the scope of a problem newly called "sexual harassment" (Aron, "Groping in the Ivy League"); see also Burke, "A Short History." Note, however, that there is some question about Wood's racial identity. See, for example, Nora Berenstain, "White Feminist Gaslighting," *Hypatia*, no. 35 (2020): 753n10.

16. Meritor Savings Bank v. Vinson, 477 U.S. 57 (1986); Meritor Savings Bank v. Vinson at 59.

17. On October 6, 1991, National Public Radio aired a report on Anita Hill's accusation of sexual harassment against her former boss, Clarence Thomas, a nominee to become the newest Supreme Court justice. Jewish Women's Archive, "Transcript of Nina Totenberg's *NPR* Report on Anita Hill's Charges of Sexual Harassment by Clarence Thomas," October 6, 1991, accessed February 11, 2023, https://jwa.org/media/transcript-of-nina-totenbergs-npr-report-on-anita-hills-charges-of-sexual-harassment-by-0 [https://perma.cc/GMZ7-4QZE]. The Hill-Thomas hearings followed, watched by people in more than 20 million homes. "Anita Hill vs. Clarence Thomas: The Backstory," *CBS News*, October 20, 2010, https://www.cbsnews.com/news/anita-hill-vs-clarence-thomas-the-backstory/ [https://perma.cc/JUJ4-3XAM]. Those hearings covered extensive territory. By the time the three days ended, the confirmation now encompassed issues of race and opportunity at the highest levels of government, white men judging Black men and Black women, lynching, judicial philosophy and natural law, reproductive choice, gender politics, and Thomas's subjection

to what he referred to as a "high-tech lynching." Ron Elving, "A Refresher on Anita Hill and Clarence Thomas," radio broadcast transcript, *NPR*, December 10, 2017, https://www.npr.org/2017/12/10/569716802/a-refresher-on-anita-hill-and-clarence-thomas [https://perma.cc/T7YP-XKFG]; see also *Nomination of Judge Clarence Thomas to Be Associate Justice of the Supreme Court of the United States: Hearings Before the S. Judiciary Comm.*, 102nd Cong. (1991), https://www.govinfo.gov/app/details/GPO-CHRG-THOMAS/ [https://perma.cc/ZT9B-XV4A]. In the final analysis, the confirmation would be decided by the vote of seven southern Democrats who voted yes, three of whom were up for reelection, 52–48. Associated Press, "The Thomas Confirmation; How the Senators Voted on Thomas," *New York Times*, October 16, 1991, https://www.nytimes.com/1991/10/16/us/the-thomas-confirmation-how-the-senators-voted-on-thomas.html [https://perma.cc/XY4C-3FPR]. It was a palpable power struggle over the role of Blacks and women in society. The next year, in what might count as a gender expiration, voters elected thirty women to Congress (twenty-four in the House and six in the Senate), including Carol Moseley Brown, whom Illinois elected as the first Black woman in the United States Senate in what became known as "The Year of the Woman." Carol Moseley Braun, History, Art and Archives, U.S. House of Representatives, accessed April 23, 2024, https://history.house.gov/People/Listing/M/MOSELEY-BRAUN,-Carol-(M001025)/ [https://perma.cc/FE2M-PJ33].

18. Anna J. Cooper, *A Voice from the South* (Xenia, OH: Aldine Printing House, 1892).

19. See, for example, Vivian May, *Pursuing Intersectionality, Unsettling Dominant Imaginaries* (New York: Routledge, Taylor & Francis, 2015); Ange-Marie Hancock, *Intersectionality: An Intellectual History* (New York: Oxford University Press, 2016).

20. Avtar Brah and Ann Phoenix, "Ain't I a Woman? Revisiting Intersectionality," *Journal of International Women's Studies* 5, no. 3 (2004): 75–86.

21. New York Times Editorial Board, "Black Lives Matter in France, Too," *New York Times*, July 29, 2016, https://www.nytimes.com/2016/07/29/opinion/black-lives-matter-in-france-too.html [https://perma.cc/KU4D-LNHZ]; Sewell Chan, "Black Lives Matter Activists Stage Protests across Britain," *New York Times*, August 5, 2016, https://www.nytimes.com/2016/08/06/world/europe/black-lives-matter-demonstrations-britain.html [https://perma.cc/X2MV-W4LZ]; Amien Essif, "How Black Lives Matter

Has Spread into a Global Movement to End Racist Policing," *In These Times*, June 29, 2015, https://inthesetimes.com/article/black-lives-matter-in-europe-too [https://perma.cc/KC83-PPU6] (documenting the impact of the movement in London, Paris, Berlin, and Amsterdam); Giovanni Torre, "Indigenous Australians Use Tech to Expose Police Abuse," *New York Times*, August 14, 2018, https://www.nytimes.com/2018/08/14/world/australia /aboriginal-police-abuse.html [https://perma.cc/3BGG-8N53] (noting that Black Lives Matter served as inspiration for Indigenous activists in Australia); Amy McQuire, "Without Video Evidence, Australians Find It Hard To Believe That Black Lives Matter," *Newmatilda.com*, July 13, 2016, https://newmatilda.com/2016/07/13/without-video-evidence-australians -find-it-hard-to-believe-that-black-lives-matter/ [https://perma.cc/4V5J -H2Z3]; Georgina Siklossy, "Racist Murder in Italy is a Wake-up Call for a European #BlackLivesMatter," European Network Against Racism, July 7, 2016, https://www.enar-eu.org/Racist-murder-in-Italy-is-a-wake-up-call-for-a-European-BlackLivesMatter-1138/ [https://perma.cc/4FG5-E2RJ]; Agence France Presse, "Thousands Protest in Rome over Italy's 'Anti-Migrant' Decree," *The National*, November 11, 2018, https://www.thena-tionalnews.com/world/europe/thousands-protest-in-rome-over-italy-s-anti-migrant-decree-1.790276 [https://perma.cc/FDX2-BN8D].

22. At the Oscars in 2018, presenter Ashley Judd proclaimed, "We work together to make sure that the next 90 years empower these limitless possibilities of equality, diversity, inclusion, intersectionality—that's what this year has promised us." See Kory Stamper, "A Brief, Convoluted History of the Word 'Intersectionality,'" *TheCut.com*, March 9, 2018, https://www.thecut.com/2018/03/a-brief-convoluted-history-of-the-word-intersectionality.html [https://perma.cc/V7MG-HC3T] (reporting Judd's remarks in the context of several accusations against movie producer Harvey Weinstein).

23. Jan Ransom, "Mr. Weinstein's Criminal Convictions in California Still Stand," *New York Times*, April 25, 2024, https://www.nytimes.com/live /2024/04/25/nyregion/harvey-weinstein-appeal [https://perma.cc /D3R2-K95V].

24. Jodi Kantor et al., "'Finally': Ashley Judd and Other Weinstein Accusers Respond to Verdict," *New York Times*, February 24, 2020, https:// www.nytimes.com/2020/02/24/nyregion/harvey-weinstein-accusers.html [https://perma.cc/R692-VTNB].

25. See "Harvey Weinstein Jailed for 23 Years in a Rape Trial," *BBC News*, March 12, 2020, https://www.bbc.com/news/world-us-canada-51840532

[https://perma.cc/9936-XNU3] (quoting statement from one of Weinstein accusers).

26. See Natasha Lennard, "What's Wrong with Cheering Harvey Weinstein's Reported Coronavirus Diagnosis," *Theintercept.com*, March 23, 2020, https://theintercept.com/2020/03/23/harvey-weinstein-coronavirus/.

27. Oppression is, of course, technological, both literally and metaphorically. Katherine M. Franke, "What's Wrong with Sexual Harassment?," *Stanford Law Review* 49, no. 4 (1997): 691–772.

28. Lua Kamál Yuille, "Liberating Sexual Harassment Law," *Michigan Journal of Gender and Law* 22, no. 2 (2015): 345–412.

29. Johnson v. M'Intosh, 21 U.S. (8 Wheat.) 543 (1823).

30. Audre Lorde, "The Master's Tools Will Never Dismantle the Master's House," in *Sister Outsider* (Berkeley, CA: Crossing Press, 1984), 110–13.

31. Lorde, "The Master's Tools."

32. See, for example, Ruthann Robson, "Lesbian Jurisprudence," *Law and Inequality: A Journal of Theory and Practice* 8, no. 3 (1990): 443–68; Ruthann Robson, *Sappho Goes to Law School: Fragments in Lesbian Legal Theory* (New York: Columbia University Press, 1998).

33. Mark Tushnet, "Critical Legal Studies: A Political History," *Yale Law Journal* 100, no. 5 (1991): 1523 (explaining that one of the characteristics of CLS "was the identification, in numerous substantive areas of the law, of paired oppositions to the standard arguments deploying sets of claims from one side of those oppositions against sets drawn from the other side" and explaining that adherents "continue to hold to the general perception that there is no interesting difference between legal discourse and ordinary, moral and political discourse").

34. Brown v. Board of Education, 347 U.S. 483 (1954).

35. See, for example, Herbert Lovelace, "King Making: *Brown v. Board* and the Rise of a Racial Savior," *American Journal of Legal History* 57, no. 4 (2017): 402–03.

36. Shelley v. Kramer, 334 U.S. 1 (1948).

37. I hesitate to lean in to such a white male–dominated body of knowledge, but the analogy to the controversial international law concept is instructive.

38. See Scott Jaschik, "Poll: Public Opposes Affirmative Action," *Inside Higher Ed*, July 8, 2016, https://www.insidehighered.com/news/2016/07/08/poll-finds-public-opposition-considering-race-and-ethnicity-college-admissions [https://perma.cc/3K8F-PHDE] (stating that in 2016, a Gallup poll found that 65 percent of those surveyed by Gallup disagreed

with the *Fisher v. University of Texas* decision that permitted race conscious admissions in higher education, 31 percent supported the decision, and 4 percent had no opinion). Also see Fisher v. University of Texas, 579 U.S. 365, 377 (2016) (holding that a race conscious admissions plan must be "narrowly tailored to achieve the university's permissible goals, [and that] the school bears the burden of demonstrating that "available" and "workable" "race-neutral alternatives" do not suffice).

39. Adarand Constructors, Inc. v. Peña, 515 U.S. 200, 223–4 (1995).

40. *Peña* at 247 (Stevens, J., dissenting).

41. *Peña* at 247 (Stevens, J., dissenting).

42. Fisher v. University of Texas [Fisher I], 570 U.S. 297, 328 (2013) (Thomas, J., concurring).

43. Ibram X. Kendi, *How to Be an Antiracist* (New York: One World, 2019), 9, 19–20.

44. Kendi, *How to Be an Antiracist*, 9 ("the only way to undo racism is to consistently identify and describe it").

BIBLIOGRAPHY

Adarand Constructors, Inc. v. Peña, 515 U.S. 200, 223–4 (1995).
Agence France Presse. "Thousands Protest in Rome over Italy's 'Anti
-Migrant' Decree." *The National*, November 11, 2018. https://www
.thenationalnews.com/world/europe/thousands-protest-in-rome-over
-italy-s-anti-migrant-decree-1.790276 [https://perma.cc/FDX2-BN8D].
"Anita Hill vs. Clarence Thomas: The Backstory." *CBS News*, October 20,
2010. https://www.cbsnews.com/news/anita-hill-vs-clarence-thomas-
the-backstory/ [https://perma.cc/JUJ4-3XAM].
Aron, Nina Renata. "Groping in the Ivy League Led to the First Sexual
Harassment Suit—And Nothing Happened to the Man." *Timeline*,
October 20, 2017. https://medium.com/timeline/carmita-wood-sexual
-harrassment-f2c537a0e1e8 [https://perma.cc/7L3K-4EAE].
Associated Press. "The Thomas Confirmation; How the Senators Voted on
Thomas." *New York Times*, October 16, 1991. https://www.nytimes
.com/1991/10/16/us/the-thomas-confirmation-how-the-senators-voted
-on-thomas.html [https://perma.cc/XY4C-3FPR].
Bell, Derrick A. "Who's Afraid of Critical Race Theory?" *University of
Illinois Law Review* 1995, no. 4 (1995): 893–910.

Berenstain, Nora. "White Feminist Gaslighting." *Hypatia*, no. 35 (2020): 733–58.

Berkeley Journal of Gender, Law, and Justice. "Mandate." Accessed April 23, 2024. https://genderlawjustice.org/mandate [https://perma.cc /9TY9-DYF8].

Black Lives Matter. "About." Accessed January 10, 2023. https://black-livesmatter.com/about/ [https://perma.cc/NRJ3-67Y7].

Bond, Julian. "Self-Defense against Rape: The Joanne Little Case." *The Black Scholar* 6, no. 6 (1975): 29–31.

Brah, Avtar, and Ann Phoenix. "Ain't I a Woman? Revisiting Intersection-ality." *Journal of International Women's Studies* 5, no. 3 (2004): 75–86.

Braun, Carol Moseley. History, Art and Archives. U.S. House of Representa-tives. Accessed April 23, 2024. https://history.house.gov/People/Listing /M/MOSELEY-BRAUN,-Carol-(M001025)/ [https://perma.cc /FE2M-PJ33].

Brownmiller, Susan, and Dolores Alexander. "How We Got Here: From Carmita Wood to Anita Hill." *Ms.*, January/February 1992.

Brown v. Board of Education, 347 U.S. 483 (1954).

Burke, Sarah. "A Short History of the Long Fight against Workplace Sexual Harassment." *Vice*, December 12, 2017. https://www.vice.com /en/article/evaz8k/a-short-history-of-the-long-fight-against-workplace -sexual-harassment [https://perma.cc/62UW-KV4M].

Carbado, Devon W., and Cheryl I. Harris. "Intersectionality at 30: Mapping the Margins of Anti-Essentialism, Intersectionality, and Dominance Theory." *Harvard Law Review* 132, no. 8 (2019): 2193–239.

"The Case of Joanne Little." *Crime and Social Justice*, no. 3 (1975): 42–44.

Chan, Sewell. "Black Lives Matter Activists Stage Protests across Britain." *New York Times*, August 5, 2016. https://www.nytimes.com/2016/08 /06/world/europe/black-lives-matter-demonstrations-britain.html [https://perma.cc/X2MV-W4LZ].

Combahee River Collective. *The Combahee River Collective Statement.* April 1977. https://www.blackpast.org/african-american-history/combahee -river-collective-statement-1977/ [https://perma.cc/92A5-3Y7Q].

Cooper, Anna J. *A Voice from the South.* Xenia, OH: Aldine Printing House, 1892.

Crenshaw, Kimberlé. "Demarginalizing the Intersection of Race and Sex: A Black Feminist Critique of Antidiscrimination Doctrine, Feminist Theory, and Antiracist Politics." *University of Chicago Legal Forum* (1989): 139–68.

————. "Mapping the Margins: Intersectionality, Identity Politics, and Violence against Women of Color." *Stanford Law Review* 43, no. 6 (1991): 1241–300.

Dzodan, Flavia. "My Feminism Will Be Intersectional or It Will Be Bullshit!" *Tiger Beatdown* (blog). October 10, 2011. https://tigerbeatdown .com/2011/10/10/my-feminism-will-be-intersectional-or-it-will-be -bullshit/ [https://perma.cc/C58B-MUMR].

Elving, Ron. "A Refresher on Anita Hill and Clarence Thomas." Radio broadcast transcript. *NPR*, December 10, 2017. https://www.npr .org/2017/12/10/569716802/a-refresher-on-anita-hill-and-clarence -thomas [https://perma.cc/T7YP-XKFG].

Essif, Amien. "How Black Lives Matter Has Spread into a Global Movement to End Racist Policing." *In These Times*, June 29, 2015. https:// inthesetimes.com/article/black-lives-matter-in-europe-too [https:// perma.cc/KC83-PPU6].

Fink, Jessica. "Disgorging Harvey Weinstein's Salary." *Berkeley Journal of Employment and Labor Law* 41, no. 2 (2020): 285–332.

Fisher v. University of Texas [Fisher I], 570 U.S. 297 (2013).

Fisher v. University of Texas, 579 U.S. 365 (2016).

Fortin, Jacey. "Critical Race Theory: A Brief History." *New York Times*, November 8, 2021. https://www.nytimes.com/article/what-is-critical -race-theory.html [https://perma.cc/W9J4-YY6P].

Franke, Katherine M. "What's Wrong with Sexual Harassment?" *Stanford Law Review* 49, no. 4 (1997): 691–772.

Gillespie, Marcia A. "We Speak in Tongues." *Ms.*, January/February 1992.

Global Fund for Women. "'Me Too.' Global Movement." Accessed April 23, 2024. https://www.globalfundforwomen.org/movements/me-too/ [https://perma.cc/NA8R-UTXN].

Hancock, Ange-Marie. *Intersectionality: An Intellectual History*. New York: Oxford University Press, 2016.

"Harvey Weinstein Jailed for 23 Years in a Rape Trial." *BBC News*, March 12, 2020. https://www.bbc.com/news/world-us-canada-51840532 [https://perma.cc/9936-XNU3].

Hayman, Robert L. *The Smart Culture: Society, Intelligence, and Law*. New York: New York University Press, 2000.

Hill, Anita. *Speaking Truth to Power*. New York: Doubleday, 1998.

hooks, bell. *Feminist Theory: From Margin to Center*. 2nd ed. Cambridge, MA: South End Press, 2000.

Jaschik, Scott. "Poll: Public Opposes Affirmative Action." *Inside Higher Ed*, July 8, 2016. https://www.insidehighered.com/news/2016/07/08/poll-finds-public-opposition-considering-race-and-ethnicity-college-admissions [https://perma.cc/3K8F-PHDE].

Jewish Women's Archive. "Transcript of Nina Totenberg's *NPR* Report on Anita Hill's Charges of Sexual Harassment by Clarence Thomas." October 6, 1991. Accessed February 11, 2023. https://jwa.org/media/transcript-of-nina-totenbergs-npr-report-on-anita-hills-charges-of-sexual-harassment-by-0 [https://perma.cc/GMZ7-4QZE].

Johnson, Andrea, Samone Ijoma, and Da Hae Kim. *#MeToo Five Years Later: Progress and Pitfalls in State Workplace Anti-Harassment Laws*. Washington, DC: National Women's Law Center, 2022. https://nwlc.org/wp-content/uploads/2022/10/final_2022_nwlcMeToo_Report.pdf [https://perma.cc/FY7S-F4RM].

Johnson v. M'Intosh, 21 U.S. (8 Wheat.) 543 (1823).

Kantor, Jodi, Megan Twohey, Grace Ashford, Catrin Einhorn, and Ellen Gabler. "'Finally': Ashley Judd and Other Weinstein Accusers Respond to Verdict." *New York Times*, February 24, 2020. https://www.nytimes.com/2020/02/24/nyregion/harvey-weinstein-accusers.html [https://perma.cc/R692-VTNB].

Kendi, Ibram X. *How to Be an Antiracist*. New York: One World, 2019.

Lennard, Natasha. "What's Wrong with Cheering Harvey Weinstein's Reported Coronavirus Diagnosis." *Theintercept.com*, March 23, 2020. https://theintercept.com/2020/03/23/harvey-weinstein-coronavirus/ [https://perma.cc/2J22-SM3X].

Levit, Nancy, and Robert R. M. Verchick. *Feminist Legal Theory: A Primer*. 2nd ed. New York: New York University Press, 2016.

Lorde, Audre. "The Master's Tools Will Never Dismantle the Master's House." In *Sister Outsider*. Berkeley, CA: Crossing Press, 1984, 110–13.

Lovelace, Herbert. "King Making: *Brown v. Board* and the Rise of a Racial Savior." *American Journal of Legal History* 57, no. 4 (2017): 393–446.

MacKinnon, Catharine A. *Feminism Unmodified: Discourses on Life and Law*. Cambridge, MA: Harvard University Press, 1987.

May, Vivian. *Pursuing Intersectionality, Unsettling Dominant Imaginaries*. New York: Routledge, 2015.

McQuire, Amy. "Without Video Evidence, Australians Find It Hard to Believe That Black Lives Matter." *Newmatilda.com*, July 13, 2016. https://newmatilda.com/2016/07/13/without-video-evidence-australians-find-it-hard-to-believe-that-black-lives-matter/ [https://perma.cc/4V5J-H2Z3].

Meritor Savings Bank v. Vinson, 477 U.S. 57 (1986).

Nemy, Enid. "Women Begin to Speak Out against Sexual Harassment at Work." *New York Times*, August 19, 1975. https://www.nytimes.com/1975/08/19/archives/women-begin-to-speak-out-against-sexual-harassment-at-work.html [https://perma.cc/H6DS-MR4S].

New York Times Editorial Board. "Black Lives Matter in France, Too." *New York Times*, July 29, 2016. https://www.nytimes.com/2016/07/29/opinion/black-lives-matter-in-france-too.html [https://perma.cc/KU4D-LNHZ].

Nomination of Judge Clarence Thomas to Be Associate Justice of the Supreme Court of the United States: Hearings before the S. Judiciary Comm. 102nd Cong. (1991). Accessed February 11, 2023. https://www.govinfo.gov/app/details/GPO-CHRG-THOMAS/ [https://perma.cc/ZT9B-XV4A].

Ransom, Jan. "Mr. Weinstein's Criminal Convictions in California Still Stand." *New York Times*, April 25, 2024. https://www.nytimes.com/live/2024/04/25/nyregion/harvey-weinstein-appeal [https://perma.cc/D3R2-K95V].

Robson, Ruthann. "Lesbian Jurisprudence." *Law and Inequality: A Journal of Theory and Practice* 8, no. 3 (1990): 443–68.

———. *Sappho Goes to Law School: Fragments in Lesbian Legal Theory.* New York: Columbia University Press, 1998.

Robson, Ruthann, and S. E. Valentine. "Lov(h)ers: Lesbians as Intimate Partners and Lesbian Legal Theory." *Temple Law Review* 63, no. 3 (1990): 511–42.

Romano, Aja. "This Feminist's Most Famous Quote Has Been So All over the Internet; She Hasn't Seen a Cent." *Vox*, August 12, 2016. https://www.vox.com/2016/8/12/12406648/flavia-dzodan-my-feminism-will-be-intersectional-merchandise [https://perma.cc/XLT4–98W4].

Scales, Ann. *Legal Feminism: Activism, Lawyering, and Legal Theory.* New York: New York University Press, 2006.

Shelley v. Kramer, 334 U.S. 1 (1948).

Siklossy, Georgina. "Racist Murder in Italy Is a Wake-up Call for a European #BlackLivesMatter." European Network against Racism, July 7, 2016. https://www.enar-eu.org/Racist-murder-in-Italy-is-a-wake-up-call-for-a-European-BlackLivesMatter-1138/ [https://perma.cc/4FG5-E2RJ].

Stamper, Kory. "A Brief, Convoluted History of the Word 'Intersectionality.'" *TheCut.com*, March 9, 2018. https://www.thecut.com/2018/03/a-brief-

convoluted-history-of-the-word-intersectionality.html [https://perma
.cc/V7MG-HC3T].

Stanchi, Kathryn. "The Rhetoric of Racism in the United States Supreme
Court." *Boston College Law Review* 62, no. 4 (2021): 1251–320.

Subramanian, Ram, and Leily Arzy. "State Policing Reforms Since George
Floyd's Murder." Brennan Center for Justice. May 21, 2020. https://
www.brennancenter.org/our-work/research-reports/state-policing-
reforms-george-floyds-murder [https://perma.cc/NLY3-UTCM].

Taylor, Keeanga-Yamahtta. "Did Last Summer's Black Lives Matter
Protests Change Anything?" *New Yorker*. August 6, 2021. https://www
.newyorker.com/news/our-columnists/did-last-summers-protests
-change-anything [https://perma.cc/X6UB-AP2H].

Time's Up Legal Defense Fund and National Women's Law Center Fund
LLC. *Coming Forward: Key Trends and Data from the Time's Up Legal
Defense Fund.* https://nwlc.org/wp-content/uploads/2020/10/NWLC
-Intake-Report_FINAL_2020-10-13.pdf [https://perma.cc
/3SPN-NKZR].

Torre, Giovanni. "Indigenous Australians Use Tech to Expose Police Abuse."
New York Times, August 14, 2018. https://www.nytimes.com/2018
/08/14/world/australia/aboriginal-police-abuse.html [https://perma
.cc/3BGG-8N53].

Tushnet, Mark. "Critical Legal Studies: A Political History." *Yale Law
Journal* 100, no. 5 (1991): 1515–544.

Weber, Peter. "The Depressingly Long History of Sexual Harassment
Turning Points." *The Week*, November 27, 2017. https://theweek.com
/articles/738873/depressingly-long-history-sexual-harassment
-turning-points [https://perma.cc/WK88-3FVX].

Yuille, Lua Kamál. "Liberating Sexual Harassment Law." *Michigan
Journal of Gender and Law* 22, no. 2 (2015): 345–412.

Missing Voices and the Quest for Historic Unity and Inclusivity

WITH CONTRIBUTIONS BY

Noa Ben-Asher   *Osamudia James*

I. Bennett Capers   *Keisha Lindsay*

Bridget J. Crawford   *Ruthann Robson*

Linda S. Greene   *Lua Kamál Yuille*

Lolita Buckner Inniss

BACKGROUND

Direct testimonies about events of the past, although often hailed as key evidentiary sources in legal matters, may lack perspective. A central reason for this is that even those recollections that purport to be accurate may include voluntary or involuntary omissions, thereby skewing retrospective accounts. Hence, the most complete considerations of the past will come through *discourses*—dialogues between and among as many voices as possible. As a way of understanding the past, discourse is more than a methodological or theoretical consideration; individual voices that are woven into strands of a collective articulation yield insights into history. Discourse is an actual practice that enriches and determines the fuller shape of an expression.

In the act of discussing the Black Lives Matter and #MeToo movements, as well as in discourse about the way the movements are discussed, a significant concern is the absence of a fully developed and inclusive historical context. To date, there has been virtually no exploration of the legal, social, political, and economic events relating to the movements from the perspectives of multiple people over specific periods in time. This void of broadly inclusive historical framing limits understandings of these movements.

In some ways, it is not surprising that historic and contemporary discussions around rights and demands for empowerment of Black people and women are marked by absences and silences. There may be a tendency by those at the front of movements to ignore difference, in order to present a more "unified" front to the general public. Or those with the most privilege among an otherwise unprivileged group may have the greatest access to any metaphoric megaphone extended to the group. For that reason, just as Black people of all gender identities and women of all races and ethnicities have lived, and often continue to live, in conditions of literal or metaphoric spatial limitations—*separation* dampens the impact their voices and other audible evidence of their existence—so, too, are diverse voices within both demographic groups often silenced. Within these incomplete histories, the socio-political significance, or indeed *competence,* of those who are excluded from the group narrative or voice has been contested and denied. Accordingly, when acknowledging histories and experiences of those outside the power center of disempowered groups, or where these "outsiders" inside the group are accorded recognition, agency, or competence, the overall histories remain incomplete. Too often there are intentional or unintentional silences and gaps about the lived experience of all group members.[1] Hence, the interests of all who are purportedly represented by group identities or movements may not be fully articulated, or those interests may be distilled in ways that erase many essential concerns.

Historical silences, especially legal historical silences, first about the lives of Black people and women of all races and ethnicities, and then about the full range of identities and experiences within those demographic groups, are not unusual. Even though both Black Lives Matter and #MeToo have been characterized as novel in many respects, there are ways that they represent "old wine in new bottles" (or maybe old wine in old bottles that have remained on lower shelves) in two ways. First, they represent a coming-to-voice for people who historically have not been treated as equally important socio-political actors. Second, in the process of making their voices heard, members of historically disempowered groups may themselves replicate patterns of domination and exclusion.

The discussion below explores silences and voids in the Black Lives Matter and/or #MeToo movements. We invited our contributors to consider this question:

> What voices or conversations, if any, are missing from
> the Black Lives Matter and/or #MeToo movements,
> and, if there are absences in these regards, how do we
> address them?

DIALOGUE

Bennett Capers: In terms of conversations, I'd love to hear about what we do with the past. Black Lives Matter has benefited from the widespread availability of cameras and video to document and "prove" blue-on-Black violence. To borrow from Lolita Buckner Inniss, these cameras now serve as a "white witness," proof to make real the claims of Black and brown folks.[2] On this level, Black Lives Matter, notwithstanding its broader agenda, as understood in the public imagination, is focused on present acts of violence. #MeToo, by contrast, can be as historical as it wants, alleging sexual abuses that took place last week as easily as twenty years ago—see, for example, Justice Kavanaugh. But really, Black Lives Matter has a much bigger agenda, and its concerns are historical too. There is a historical link

VIDEO CAMERAS AS THE CREDIBLE "WHITE WITNESS"?

Video surveillance sometimes provides much needed valorization for . . . less regarded private people [those possessing little power or authority]. This is because private people are far more often lied about, lied to and deemed liars. Hence private people often lose in battles of opposing narratives with public people about what has occurred. In such cases, video surveillance becomes a mostly neutral, unlikely to lie, legitimizing witness. For many of these private people, especially women, people of color or other relatively powerless people, video surveillance is the modern day white witness.

Excerpt from Lolita Buckner Inniss, "Video Surveillance as White Witnesses," *Ain't I a Feminist Legal Scholar Too?* (blog), September 30, 2012, http://innissfls.blogspot.com/2012/09/video-surveillance-as-white-witnesses.html [https://perma.cc/SF39-NMKD].

between slave patrols, the creation of police departments, and contemporary police brutality. That brings me to the conversation I want to hear.

What should we do with past behavior that seemed more acceptable at the time (at least to some people) than it does now? When we think of removing Confederate monuments, for example, or no longer playing Kate Smith's "God Bless America" at baseball games,[3] do we think of them the same way as removing serial sexual harassers? In other words, should we remove the names of historic sexual harassers from buildings? How are the situations the same, and how are they different?

The relatively recent fallout in Virginia politics, with the governor allegedly having a past of wearing blackface and the lieutenant governor allegedly having a past of sexual assault, brings this into sharp focus for me.[4] Does it matter that apparently every white person in Virginia donned blackface back then? (I'm exaggerating of course, but this is what it seems like.) Should it matter that probably lots of guys didn't take "no" as a final answer back then? (Again, maybe I'm exaggerating. Maybe not.)

Osamudia James: Bennett makes an important point—that we understand patriarchy and misogyny as having a historical legacy, but we don't understand racism and white supremacy as having the same. Our nation has never fully come to grips with how foundational white supremacy has been to the development of the United States—so foundational that eliminating slavery was a necessary, but by no means sufficient, step toward racial equality. And yet, the cataclysmic event of the Civil War has allowed us to run from that truth— "We fought a war, the 'right' side won, so it's over, right? Sure, we had some readjustments in the 1960s, but after that it was over, right?"

In addition, the passage of major civil rights laws in the mid-twentieth century provided a "break with the past" that allows Americans to double down on the meritocracy myth, which suggests that discrimination must not happen because *the law doesn't allow it.*[5] In contrast, the absence of wars or landmark civil rights legislation aimed at gender discrimination has enabled us to understand sexism and misogyny as ongoing. That long historical arc, ironically, renders us more comfortable with addressing not just current acts of sexual violence and abuse, but also the legacies created by individual perpetrators. Finally, when white women confront patriarchy, they serve as those "white witnesses" Lolita has written about, the ones who can legitimize grievance.

Accordingly, what is missing from the conversation about Black Lives Matter is that which is missing from all engagement with race and racial subordination: a shared understanding of the psychic and material legacy of slavery in the United States, such that all fields, and certainly law, are better informed about the doctrines, theories, ideologies, and policies that are anchored in white supremacy. Outside of an academic sphere, entertainment and media have told the story of slavery, and even Jim Crow, over and over again; but very little has been told about the enduring legacies of those periods.[6] When reading *Homegoing* a few years ago, I repeatedly thought, "This should be made into a movie."[7] I long to see more stories in popular culture that might help Americans understand how the traumas and thefts of slavery and Jim Crow are very much still with us today.

Noa Ben-Asher: I agree that facing the past is critical for both movements. In this context, I wonder about possible meanings of forgiveness. What does it mean to forgive someone or something? Are there unforgivable acts? How would a politics of forgiveness inform our social justice movements? What are the prices of unforgiveness? Is an apology necessary for forgiveness?

Shortly after the 2015 racist massacre in the Charleston church, the victims' relatives, one after the other, faced the murderer during the bond hearing and forgave him.[8] He had not apologized for his appalling deeds (one wonders if he had the emotional capacity to), yet they forgave him, nonetheless. To me, those gracious acts of forgiveness were ethical existence at its purest form.

Ruthann Robson: Movements are not perfect or all-inclusive. I think we too often fall into heightened and unrealistic expectations for a movement to be a "grand theory" that will address everyone and offer solutions for the myriad problems plaguing us. But we are always engaged in triage. We are always leaving something and someone out. At times, these omissions are problematic and hurtful. At other times, these omissions are necessary for focus. Just as no one can do everything, one movement cannot possibly encompass every single possible grievance. A movement can and should make demands, offer theories, and provide alternatives. But while we should expect our polity, our institutions, and our governments to be expansive and inclusive, I think we should recognize that a movement is not a government or even a blueprint for one.

THE LEGACY OF SLAVERY AND JIM CROW

Very visible signs of improvement mask deep inequities that relegate tens of millions of Black Americans to second-class status, with far fewer opportunities to achieve good health, political influence, prosperity and security than other Americans. Leading indicators of social and economic well-being [show] that, on average, Black Americans face much more difficult circumstances than their White counterparts.

- Historically, the unemployment rate for Black Americans has been approximately twice the rate for Whites. That is the case today—6.0% for Black workers and 3.1% for Whites.
- The typical Black household earns a fraction of White households—just 59 cents for every dollar. The gap between Black and White annual household incomes is about $29,000 per year.
- Black Americans are over twice as likely to live in poverty as White Americans.
- Much less than half (42%) of Black families own their homes, compared to almost three-quarters (73%) of White families.
- Persistent segregation leads to large disparities in the quality of secondary education, leading to worse economic outcomes.
- The incarceration rate for Black Americans is falling, but is still nearly six times the rate for White Americans.
- Non-Hispanic Black Americans have a life expectancy 3.6 years lower than non-Hispanic White Americans.

Excerpt from United States Congress Joint Economic Committee, *The Economic State of Black America in 2020*, https://perma.cc/AR4P-QQVZ.

THE WORK OF TIME'S UP

The [Time's Up] Legal Defense Fund has now paid attorneys across the country who take on sexual harassment cases for thousands of workers, most of them low-income. McDonald's cashiers and NFL cheerleaders alike used the fund's financial resources and Rolodex to advance their complaints against employers.

The movement's intangible effects are harder to quantify, though no less significant. In addition to good laws and funding to sue those who break them, two social mechanisms are necessary to combat workplace sexual harassment: Victims have to be willing to speak up, and people in power have to be willing to listen and take action.

Excerpt from Christina Cauterucci, "The Parts of #MeToo That Still Endure," *Slate*, October 9, 2022, https://slate.com/news-and-politics/2022/10/metoo-fifth-anniversary-what-lasts.html [https://perma.cc/G6SA-8MZ6].

For observers and "intellectuals" who are not deeply embedded in a particular movement as their primary work to "call out" a movement for its absences seems to me misguided. Instead of critiquing, we should use our voices to generate specific movements that "fill in the gaps" and which may be in alliance with other movements. That said, I admit I always "look for the lesbian" in any social justice movement. The Movement for Black Lives policy platform originally included a rigorous demand to "END THE WAR ON BLACK TRANS, QUEER, GENDER NONCONFORMING AND INTERSEX PEOPLE" with specific recognitions of the pervasiveness of LGBTQ+ inequities that must be addressed.[9] As for #MeToo and Time's Up, while certainly its representatives have mentioned LGBTQ+ concerns, the policy focus is eliminating sexual harassment in employment.

Figure 7. Alicia Garza, 2016.

Further, while #MeToo is not focused exclusively on employment and work, Time's Up does seem to be so. There is certainly a need to go beyond "work." This is true because our doctrinal definitions of "work" can be so limited, and our statutory frameworks such as Title VII even more limiting, even when the employment threshold is met.[10] Further the "space" of work and employment is not a central or stable one.

Linda Greene: Alicia Garza, a co-founder of Black Lives Matter and a queer Black woman, focuses her leadership on challenging "the misconception that only cisgender Black men encounter police and state violence."[11] That the media focuses on Black men who have fallen victim to police violence, including Trayvon Martin, Tamir

Rice, Walter Scott, Michael Brown, Laquan McDonald—as well as the frequency with which those images are rebroadcast—operates as a symbolic fetishization of these public executions. But Black women also face violence at the hands of police officers.

One such case involved a Black woman named Eula Love whom Los Angeles Police Department agents shot and killed in 1979.[12] The incident occurred after a gas company employee demanded that she pay an outstanding balance on her gas bill and threatened to turn her gas off if she did not. She physically stopped the employee from turning off the gas and proceeded to retrieve a check from the local social security office. When she returned, she was confronted with two police officers. The officers alleged that she was carrying a knife "and seething, with 'froth' coming from her mouth."[13] They drew their guns, demanded she drop the knife, and shot her eight times when she raised the knife and threw it. On April 17, 1979, the district attorney announced that there would be no criminal charges filed against the two police officers in the killing of Eula Love, ruling that they had acted in self-defense and were justified in using deadly force.[14]

Lolita Buckner Inniss: I remember that case. Maxine Waters was in the California State Assembly at the time. She played a huge role in bringing attention to the practices of the Los Angeles Police Department and its over-policing of Black people.[15] She later served for twenty-four years as member of U.S. House of Representatives and was a fierce critic of President Trump. Who can forget Representative Waters' assertion "I am reclaiming my time" when then-Treasury Secretary Steve Mnuchin was testifying before the committee in 2017 and not directly answering her questions?[16]

Linda Greene: Today we see the legacy of the Eula Love case and Maxine Waters' work, too, in the #SayHerName Movement.[17] That seeks to create a more inclusive narrative within the Black Lives Matter movement, including police violence and sexual assault (the second most reported form of police misconduct after use of excessive force) against Black women.[18]

Lolita Buckner Inniss: I am in deep accord with Bennett's query about what we do with the past. Much of my current scholarship takes a legal historical approach to questions of race and gender, often in the service of clarifying the present. In the context of analyzing how race and gender have been treated over the course of U.S. history, "past is prologue" is more than a trite Shakespearean quote. Exploring the past illuminates how we got to be where we are, and why, despite clear gains, there are frequent setbacks in access to social and legal rights.

Historically, Black men and all women have, for instance, often been said to have lesser faculties than white men.[19] Additionally, Black men and all women have often been said to possess physical and social characteristics that function to exclude them systematically and explicitly from opportunities to which members of other groups might aspire.[20] These historic claims about intellectual and physical deficits have been used to justify offering Black men and all women a lesser quantum of rights and of justice. These types of troubling claims are less often explicitly articulated as contemporary rationales for rights denials, but they nonetheless continue to exist as sub rosa rationales for rights denials. Explicit and implicit bias are the legacy of slavery.[21]

I also resonate with Linda Greene's observation that women at the head and the heart of the Black Lives Matter movement have frequently been overlooked in discussions of the movement. While it is true that many of the ills facing contemporary Black people affect men and women alike, Black women frequently face separate burdens. This has been well noted and is often described as the "Black woman question."[22] One of the burdens addressed in querying the Black woman question is how Black women have often been relegated to being silent partners to Black men in racial uplift projects, even where Black women have themselves crafted the projects.

Keisha Lindsay: I wholeheartedly agree that Black women's voices are increasingly absent from both movements. Let me put forward an additional explanation regarding why this is so. Plainly put, both movements are evidence that intersectionality is not always a progressive means of understanding the social world. Instead, it is a politically fluid heuristic that can be used to advance diverse political agendas. Or, put another way, while intersectional analysis highlights how racial, gendered, and other spheres of difference are co-constitutive, intersectionality's underlying logic does not dictate *which* spheres are mutually constructing, *who* experiences oppression in the process, or *how* to relieve their oppression. Instead, these are political decisions that are made by people who embrace intersectionality and not by intersectionality itself. As a result, Black men, white women, and other social groups who engage in intersectional analysis can and do use it to make diverse arguments about their own and others' socioeconomic status—including arguments that silence Black women's experiences of oppression.

The #MeToo movement and the Black Lives Matter movement exemplify this reality. First, some of the most prominent #MeToo voices are now those of white women who assert that they are oppressed not only because they are women who have experienced sexual harassment and assault, but also because they are *white* women whose experience of assault and/or harassment unjustly prevents them enjoying the same racist power as their white male peers. Consider comedian Bette Midler's recent assertion that Brett Kavanaugh's successful appointment to the Supreme Court is evidence that "women are the n-word of the world."[23] At first glance, Midler's claim is anything but intersectional given that she mistakenly presumes that "women" and "Blacks" are mutually exclusive social categories. A closer reading, however, reveals that Midler does, in fact, make an intersectional argument, albeit one that reinscribes rather than resists racism.[24] What I mean here is that Midler not only claims that white women who experience sexual assault are victims of gender-based oppression. She goes further and suggests that white women's status, as such, means that they are *racially* disempowered. Hence, her claim that "women are the n-word of the world."

There is also evidence that the Black Lives Matter movement is sometimes informed by a less than progressive intersectional framework.[25] A case in point are those Black male participants in the movement who conclude that they are oppressed not only because they are Black in a racist society, but also because they are Black *men* who have long been denied their "rightful" or "natural" status as leaders of the race. Paul McKinley, a self-defined "grassroots" activist, exemplified this sentiment when, during a 2015 march against police brutality in Chicago, he declared that queer Black women "want to get in front of the movement and all they want to do is promote the gay agenda! . . . You can't promote that. This is a Black man thing!"[26] In positing Black men as both the primary victims and primary challengers of racism, McKinley ultimately advances an anti-feminist ethos that obscures Black women's feminized experiences of racism and attempts to resist their racial oppression at the intersection of race and gender.

Lua Yuille: Linda and Keisha highlight what I think are the most glaring omissions from the conversations. One, whatever happened to Black women in the movements they started? And two, "All my skinfolk ain't kinfolk." Keisha's thoughts about regressive intersectionality also calls to my mind that there is insufficient reckoning with how women and Black people can be agents of their own oppression.

But I have noticed another omission. Black Lives Matter—to a great extent—wages its battles on the street. #MeToo does too. They shine their light on the things that happen when women and Black people go out into the world, on the public lives of Black people and women. However, the lives we call *private*—which includes the *institutions* we call private—are no less central to the objects of these movements.

The dominant strategy to deal with this reality has been to reframe the private as public. But that leaves unexamined how the private spaces, in which the issues against which Black Lives Matter and #MeToo position themselves arise, are actually the product and purview of very public exercises of power. This may be a complicated way to reject the public/private divide, or to re-spin "the personal is political," but I do want to see more of this conversation. Property law, for example, is the foundation of the segregation and exclusion that facilitates over-policing of Black people and Black space. These are important conversations if either Black Lives Matter or #MeToo are to pursue true liberation, rather than to merely set up the conditions in which Black people and women can emulate white men.

Bridget Crawford: I'm not sure that #MeToo wages its battles in the streets very much. I tend to think that the movement has forever changed how we talk about workplace sexual harassment; "#MeToo" is now shorthand for just that. That part is inclusive de facto.

But look at the original leadership of the external, political manifestation of the #MeToo movement: the street marches in January 2017. The leaders of that initiative were criticized as nonrepresentative of the nation as whole.[27] Three of them—a Palestinian American woman who wears hijab, a Black woman involved in gun control advocacy, and a white man—resigned over allegations of anti-Semitism.[28]

Inclusivity remains elusive. My sense is that movements such as these are created in response to a metaphoric door, and that, once they manage to crack that door open, there is a sense that "finally, there will be some attention to this issue that is important." This is followed by tremendous frustration from those who are within the group of rights claimants supposedly being heard. Not only do they not see themselves represented in the leadership that has most access to the press, to power, and to financial support, but they also believe that the movement's symbols or language aren't fully inclusive.

What would real inclusion look like? Despite the enormous number of people who have marched in favor of Black lives or women's rights, I don't think we yet know the answer to that question.

DISCUSSION QUESTIONS

1. The introduction to this chapter queries the imperfections of direct testimony and personal recollections and proposes as a solution to this problem the inclusion of multiple voices in crafting historic context. Might this create a challenge to what we mean by "testimony," and might it undermine any typical understandings of "history"?

2. What role have videos and photographs played in the success of the Black Lives Matter and #MeToo movements?

3. Osamudia James says, "The passage of major civil rights laws in the mid-twentieth century provided a 'break with the past' that allows Americans to double down on the meritocracy myth, which suggests that discrimination must not happen because *the law doesn't allow it.*" Do you agree that the passage of laws means that most people think discrimination is a thing of the past?

4. For those who believe that racial disparities of the past have been largely remedied, consider some of the facts laid out in the textbox labeled "The Legacy of Slavery and Jim Crow." Based on your own research, which of those facts have changed in recent years?

5. In light of statistics showing that, at least in New York City in 2013, racial disparities in police stops are roughly the same for both men and women, why do you think that most of the attention is on police profiling of Black men?

6. Lua Yuille uses the term *regressive intersectionality* in this chapter. What does she mean by that?

7. The contributors to this chapter are engaged in a debate about inclusivity in social movements. Ruthann Robson argues that "movements are not . . . all-inclusive. . . . We are always engaged in triage." But Lolita Buckner Inniss describes how Black women are frequently relegated to the role of silent partners to Black men in social movements and Keisha Lindsay notes the anti-feminism of Paul McKinley's insistence that the "gay agenda" has no place in Black Lives Matter. Do you feel that the tension between focusing on issues in order to achieve measurable progress and including the concerns of multiple groups can be resolved in social movement work?

8. In this chapter, Bennett Capers and Lolita Buckner Inniss discuss the question of "what to do with the past." What do they mean by this phrase? Why is this issue problematic for both #MeToo and Black Lives Matter?

9. Lua Yuille frames "true liberation" as something different from a world "in which Black people and women can emulate white men." What does she mean?

10. Can there ever be a truly inclusive movement for all Black lives or all women? What would that look like?

NOTES

1. Whether intentional or unintentional, this silence itself may offer a rich field for analysis, and indeed a number of scholars have applied critical discourse analysis to silence in discourse as well as to actual text or talk. See, for example, Shoko Okazaki Yohena, "Conversational Styles and Ellipsis in Japanese Couples' Conversations," in *Discourse and Silencing: Representation and the Language of Displacement*, ed. Lynn Thiesmeyer, 79–112 (Amsterdam: J. Benjamins, 2003).

2. See Lolita Buckner Inniss, "Video Surveillance as White Witness," *Ain't I a Feminist Legal Scholar Too?* (blog), September 30, 3012, http://innissfls.blogspot.com/2012/09/video-surveillance-as-white-witnesses.html [https://perma.cc/SF39-NMKD].

3. See, for example, "Confederate Monuments Are Coming Down across the United States. Here's a List," *New York Times*, updated August 28, 2017, https://www.nytimes.com/interactive/2017/08/16/us/confederate-monuments-removed.html [https://perma.cc/SF39-NMKD]; Des Bieler and Michael Errigo, "Yankees, Flyers Drop Kate Smith's 'God Bless America' amid Questions of Possible Racism," *Washington Post*, April 19, 2019, https://www.washingtonpost.com/sports/2019/04/19/yankees-drop-kate-smiths-god-bless-america-after-questions-possible-racism-arise/ [https://perma.cc/5APC-D74N]. See also Nancy Coleman, "The Rich and Complicated History of 'God Bless America,'" *New York Times*, July 3, 2019, https://www.nytimes.com/2019/07/03/arts/music/kate-smith-god-bless-america.html (explaining the post-9/11 history of playing "God Bless America").

4. The scandal did not result in resignations or even discipline. See Campbell Robertson, "'It Just Went Poof': The Strange Aftermath of Virginia's

Cascade of Political Scandals," *New York Times*, April 2, 2019, https://www.nytimes.com/2019/04/02/us/virginia-scandal-northam-fairfax.html [https://perma.cc/A8X5-MBCG]. For the background on the scandal, see also Alan Binder, "Was That Ralph Northam in Blackface? An Inquiry Ends without Answers," *New York Times* (May 22, 2019), https://www.nytimes.com/2019/05/22/us/ralph-northam-blackface-photo.html (explaining that in 2019, the governor "admitted that he was one of the people in a picture in his medical school yearbook from 35 years ago that contained two men: one in blackface and the other in a Ku Klux Klan robe," but that he later denied that one of the men in the picture was him and he went on to complete his full term in office).

5. See Kimberlé Williams Crenshaw, "Race, Reform, and Retrenchment: Transformation and Legitimation in Antidiscrimination Law," *Harvard Law Review* 101, no. 7 (1988): 1347.

6. See Maya C. Jackson, "Artificial Intelligence and Algorithmic Bias: The Issues with Technology Reflecting History and Humans," *Journal of Business and Technology Law* 16, no. 2 (2021): 306–07 (explaining that during Reconstruction, "white southern state legislatures created laws to prevent Black people from obtaining various rights including the right to vote, gain employment and receive an education. Like Black codes, any defiance could result in arrests, fines, and even violence or death.").

7. See Yaa Gyasi, *Homegoing* (New York: Alfred A. Knopf, 2017). *Homegoing* is a novel that follows the stories of two sisters who were born in Ghana in the eighteenth century. One is captured and sold into slavery. The other marries a white man and lives a life of comparative ease. Their descendants lead very different lives. Gyasi's novel won several awards, including a PEN/Hemingway Award (2017) and the American Book Award (2017).

8. See Mark Berman, "'I Forgive You.' Relatives of Charleston Church Shooting Victims Address Dylann Roof," *Washington Post*, June 19, 2015, https://www.washingtonpost.com/news/post-nation/wp/2015/06/19/i-forgive-you-relatives-of-charleston-church-victims-address-dylann-roof/ [https://perma.cc/U6B8-TYAZ]; see also Elahe Izadi, "The Powerful Words of Forgiveness Delivered to Dylann Roof by Victims' Relatives," *Washington Post*, June 19, 2015, https://www.washingtonpost.com/news/post-nation/wp/2015/06/19/hate-wont-win-the-powerful-words-delivered-to-dylann-roof-by-victims-relatives/ [https://perma.cc/HJ9X-EV4T] ("You hurt me. You hurt a lot of people. If God forgives you, I forgive you."; "Every fiber in my body hurts. . . . May God have mercy on you."; "I am very angry. . . . We have no room for hating, so we have to forgive.").

9. See Movement for Black Lives, *Policy Platform: End the War on Black People*, accessed February 13, 2023, https://m4bl.org/policy-platforms/end-the-war-trans/ [https://perma.cc/6G22-XK5S] ("Discrimination, harassment, and violence against Black trans, intersex, queer, and gender nonconforming (LGBTQ+) people pervade virtually every institution and setting, including schools, workplaces, systems of policing, prisons, parole and probation, immigration, health care, and family and juvenile courts. As a result, Black LGBTQ+ people experience high levels of poverty, criminalization, health disparities, and exclusion in the U.S. Black trans women and gender nonconforming people in particular experience some of the highest levels of killings, violence, poverty, policing, criminalization, and incarceration of any group in the U.S.").

10. Regarding whether employers are bound by Title VII, "simply put, Title VII does not apply to each and every employer. In fact, as a general rule, Title VII typically only covers private and public sector employers with 15 or more employees . . . [who] may include part-time employees, full-time employees, suspended employees, and employees on leave or vacation." One important exception to this rule? "Title VII typically does not cover independent contractors." "What You Need to Know about Title VII of the Civil Rights Act," *Thomson Reuters Legal*, May 10, 2022, https://legal.thomsonreuters.com/en/insights/articles/what-is-title-vii-civil-rights-act [https://perma.cc/FQT6-YEL7].

11. "Black Leaders You Should Know," *Seramount Research and Insights* (blog), February 11, 2021, https://seramount.com/articles/black-leaders-you-should-know/ [https://perma.cc/M44R-F5QH].

12. The description of the incident that appears in this paragraph is based on Los Angeles Board of Police Commissioners, "Concerning the Shooting of Eulia [*sic*] Love," *Crime and Social Justice*, no. 14 (1980): 2–9.

13. See Jamilah King, "Maxine Waters' Battle against Powerful White Men Began When Eula Love Was Killed in 1979," *MIC*, April 26, 2017, https://www.mic.com/articles/174565/maxine-waters-battle-against-powerful-white-men-began-when-eula-love-was-killed-in-1979 [https://perma.cc/WCZ7-TURK].

14. Los Angeles Board, "Love," 2.

15. See King, "Maxine Waters' Battle."

16. See, for example, Aja Romano, "Reclaiming My Time: Maxine Waters' Beleaguered Congressional Hearing Led to Mighty Meme," *Vox*, July 31, 2017, https://www.vox.com/culture/2017/7/31/16070822/reclaiming-my-time-maxine-waters-mnuchin-meme [https://perma.cc/83NP-QBDH].

17. "The #SayHerName campaign brings awareness to the often invisible names and stories of Black women and girls who have been victimized by racist police violence, and provides support to their families." African American Policy Forum, "#SayHerName: Black Women are Killed by Police Too," accessed February 14, 2023, https://www.aapf.org/sayhername [https://perma.cc/7JVW-BLS2].

18. See, for example, African American Policy Forum, "#SayHerName: Towards a Gendered Analysis of Racialized State Violence," March 30, 2015, https://www.aapf.org/hdd-2015 [https://perma.cc/MG9L-FDBD].

19. See, for example, Robert L. Hayman, *The Smart Culture: Society, Intelligence, and Law* (New York: New York University Press, 2000), 19.

20. See generally William Henry Chafe, *Women and Equality: Changing Patterns in American Culture* (Oxford: Oxford University Press, 1978), 77.

21. See B. Keith Payne, Heidi A. Vuletich, and Jazmin L. Brown-Iannuzzi, "Historical Roots of Implicit Bias in Slavery," *Proceedings of the National Academy of Sciences* 116, no. 24 (2019): 11693–98 (discussing the widespread incidence of implicit racial bias).

22. See Lolita Buckner Inniss, "Toward a Sui Generis View of Black Rights in Canada? Overcoming the Difference-Denial Model of Countering Anti-Black Racism," *Berkeley Journal of African-American Law and Policy* 9, no. 1 (2007): 68–69 (referring to the "Black woman question" as the multiplicity of oppressions faced by Black women).

23. See Timothy Bella, "Women 'Are the N-Word of the World,' Bette Midler Tweeted. She Apologized Hours Later," *Washington Post*, October 5, 2018, https://www.washingtonpost.com/news/morning-mix/wp/2018/10/05/women-are-the-n-word-of-the-world-bette-midler-tweeted-she-apologized-hours-later/[https://perma.cc/5TYY-V5TN].

24. Bella, "Women 'Are the N-Word of the World.'"

25. "West Siders Protest on the Magnificent Mile," *Austin Weekly News*, November 30, 2015, https://www.austinweeklynews.com/2015/11/30/west-siders-protest-on-the-magnificent-mile/ (describing march attended by over 2,500 to protest police killing of Laquan McDonald).

26. "West Siders Protest," *Austin Weekly News* (quoting Paul McKinley, a member of the Black Nationalists movement, criticizing the Black Youth Project 100).

27. See, for example, Anna North, "The Women's March Changed the American Left. Now Anti-Semitism Allegations Threaten the Group's Future," *Vox*, December 21, 2018, https://www.vox.com/identities/2018/12

/21/18145176/feminism-womens-march-2018–2019-farrakhan-intersec-
tionality [https://perma.cc/NXZ2-L5AU].

28. See, for example, Farah Stockman, "Three Leaders of Women's March
Group Step Down after Controversies," *New York Times*, September 16,
2019, https://www.nytimes.com/2019/09/16/us/womens-march-anti
-semitism.html [https://perma.cc/8VMC-SL6A].

BIBLIOGRAPHY

African American Policy Forum. "#SayHerName: Black Women Are
    Killed by Police Too." Accessed February 14, 2023. https://www.aapf
    .org/sayhername [https://perma.cc/7JVW-BLS2].
———. "#SayHerName: Towards a Gendered Analysis of Racialized State
    Violence." March 30, 2015. https://www.aapf.org/hdd-2015 [https://
    perma.cc/MG9L-FDBD].
African American Policy Forum and Center for Intersectionality and
    Social Policy Studies. *Say Her Name: Resisting Police Brutality
    against Black Women*. July 2015. https://www.aapf.org/_files/ugd/62e1
    26_9223ee35c2694ac3bd3f2171504ca3f7.pdf [https://perma.cc
    /JCS7-C3B3].
Armstrong, Megan. "From Lynching to Central Park Karen, How White
    Women Weaponize White Womanhood." *Hastings Women's Law
    Journal* 32, no. 1 (2021): 27–52.
Baradaran, Mehrsa. *The Color of Money: Black Banks and the Racial
    Wealth Gap*. Cambridge, MA: Harvard University Press, 2019.
Brathwaite, Les Fabian. "The New Black Vanguard: Alicia Garza on What
    Really Matters." *Out*, May 18, 2016. https://www.out.com/news-opinion
    /2016/5/18/new-black-vanguard-alicia-garza-matters [https://perma
    .cc/YSV2-QPNX].
Bella, Timothy. "Women 'Are the N-Word of the World,' Bette Midler
    Tweeted. She Apologized Hours Later." *Washington Post*, October 5,
    2018. https://www.washingtonpost.com/news/morning-mix
    /wp/2018/10/05/women-are-the-n-word-of-the-world-bette-midler-
    tweeted-she-apologized-hours-later/ [https://perma.cc/5TYY-V5TN].
Berman, Mark. "'I Forgive You.' Relatives of Charleston Church Shooting
    Victims Address Dylann Roof." *Washington Post*, June 19, 2015.
    https://www.washingtonpost.com/news/post-nation/wp/2015

/06/19/i-forgive-you-relatives-of-charleston-church-victims-address
-dylann-roof/ [https://perma.cc/U6B8-TYAZ].

Bieler, Des, and Michael Errigo. "Yankees, Flyers Drop Kate Smith's 'God
Bless America' amid Questions of Possible Racism." *Washington Post*,
April 19, 2019. https://www.washingtonpost.com/sports/2019/04/19
/yankees-drop-kate-smiths-god-bless-america-after-questions-
possible-racism-arise/ [https://perma.cc/5APC-D74N].

Binder, Alan. "Was That Ralph Northam in Blackface? An Inquiry Ends
without Answers." *New York Times*, May 22, 2019. https://www
.nytimes.com/2019/05/22/us/ralph-northam-blackface-photo
.html.

"Black Leaders You Should Know." *Seramount Research and Insights*
(blog). February 11, 2021. https://seramount.com/articles/black
-leaders-you-should-know/ [https://perma.cc/M44R-F5QH].

"Black Women and the Struggle for Equality." National Park Service. Last
modified January 27, 2021. https://www.nps.gov/subjects/womenshis-
tory/black-women-and-the-struggle-for-equality.htm [https://perma.cc
/7QTJ-ECYJ].

Brown, Dorothy A. *The Whiteness of Wealth: How the Tax System
Impoverishes Black Americans and How We Can Fix It*. New York:
Crown, 2021.

Cauterucci, Christina. "The Parts of #MeToo That Still Endure." *Slate*,
October 9, 2022. https://slate.com/news-and-politics/2022/10/metoo-
fifth-anniversary-what-lasts.html [https://perma.cc/G6SA
-8MZ6].

Chafe, William Henry. *Women and Equality: Changing Patterns in
American Culture*. Oxford: Oxford University Press, 1978.

Coleman, Nancy. "The Rich and Complicated History of 'God Bless
America.'" *New York Times*, July 3, 2019. https://www.nytimes.
com/2019/07/03/arts/music/kate-smith-god-bless-america.html.

"Confederate Monuments Are Coming Down across the United States.
Here's a List." *New York Times*, updated August 28, 2017. https://www
.nytimes.com/interactive/2017/08/16/us/confederate-monuments-
removed.html [https://perma.cc/SF39-NMKD].

Cott, Nancy F. *The Grounding of Modern Feminism*. New Haven, CT:
Yale University Press, 1987.

Crenshaw, Kimberlé Williams. "Race, Reform, and Retrenchment:
Transformation and Legitimation in Antidiscrimination Law."
Harvard Law Review 101, no. 7 (1988): 1331–87.

Franklin, John Hope, and Alfred A. Moss Jr. *From Slavery to Freedom: A History of African Americans.* 10th ed. New York: McGraw-Hill, 2021.

Gyasi, Yaa. *Homegoing.* New York: Alfred A. Knopf, 2016.

Hayman, Robert L. *The Smart Culture: Society, Intelligence, and Law.* New York: New York University Press, 2000.

Inniss, Lolita Buckner. "Toward a Sui Generis View of Black Rights in Canada? Overcoming the Difference-Denial Model of Countering Anti-Black Racism." *Berkeley Journal of African-American Law and Policy* 9, no. 1 (2007): 32–73.

———. "Video Surveillance as White Witnesses." *Ain't I a Feminist Legal Scholar Too?* (blog). September 30, 2012. http://innissfls.blogspot.com/2012/09/video-surveillance-as-white-witnesses.html [https://perma.cc/SF39-NMKD].

Izadi, Elahe. "The Powerful Words of Forgiveness Delivered to Dylann Roof by Victims' Relatives." *Washington Post,* June 19, 2015. https://www.washingtonpost.com/news/post-nation/wp/2015/06/19/hate-wont-win-the-powerful-words-delivered-to-dylann-roof-by-victims-relatives/ [https://perma.cc/HJ9X-EV4T].

Jackson, John P., Nadine M. Weidman, and Gretchen Rubin. "The Origins of Scientific Racism." *Journal of Blacks in Higher Education* 50, no. 50 (2005): 66–79.

Jackson, Maya C. "Artificial Intelligence and Algorithmic Bias: The Issues with Technology Reflecting History and Humans." *Journal of Business and Technology Law* 16, no. 2 (2021): 299–316.

King, Jamilah. "Maxine Waters' Battle against Powerful White Men Began When Eula Love Was Killed in 1979." *MIC,* April 26, 2017. https://www.mic.com/articles/174565/maxine-waters-battle-against-powerful-white-men-began-when-eula-love-was-killed-in-1979 [https://perma.cc/WCZ7-TURK].

Los Angeles Board of Police Commissioners. "Concerning the Shooting of Eulia [*sic*] Love." *Crime and Social Justice,* no. 14 (1980): 2–9.

Lott, Eric. *Love and Theft: Blackface Minstrelsy and the American Working Class.* New York: Oxford University Press, 2013.

McKinney Cait. *Information Activism: A Queer History of Media Technologies.* Durham, NC: Duke University Press, 2020.

Movement for Black Lives. *Policy Platform: End the War on Black People.* Accessed February 13, 2023. https://m4bl.org/policy-platforms/end-the-war-trans/ [https://perma.cc/6G22-XK5S].

Norris, Jesse J. "Why Dylann Roof Is a Terrorist under Federal Law, and Why It Matters." *Harvard Journal on Legislation* 54, no. 1 (2017): 259–300.

North, Anna. "The Women's March Changed the American Left. Now Anti-Semitism Allegations Threaten the Group's Future." *Vox*, December 21, 2018. https://www.vox.com/identi-ties/2018/12/21/18145176/feminism-womens-march-2018–2019-farra-khan-intersectionality [https://perma.cc/NXZ2-L5AU].

Payne, B. Keith, Heidi A. Vuletich, and Jazmin L. Brown-Iannuzzi. "Historical Roots of Implicit Bias in Slavery." *Proceedings of the National Academy of Sciences* 116, no. 24 (2019): 11693–98.

Robertson, Campbell. "'It Just Went Poof': The Strange Aftermath of Virginia's Cascade of Political Scandals." *New York Times*, April 2, 2019. https://www.nytimes.com/2019/04/02/us/virginia-scandal-northam-fairfax.html [https://perma.cc/A8X5-MBCG].

Romano, Aja. "Reclaiming My Time: Maxine Waters' Beleaguered Congressional Hearing Led to Mighty Meme." *Vox*, July 31, 2017. https://www.vox.com/culture/2017/7/31/16070822/reclaiming-my-time-maxine-waters-mnuchin-meme [https://perma.cc/83NP-QBDH].

Scott-Jones, Gwendolyn, and Mozella Richardson Kamara. "The Trau-matic Impact of Structural Racism on African Americans." *Delaware Journal of Public Health* 6, no. 5 (2020): 80–82.

Smithey, Lee A. "Social Movement Strategy, Tactics, and Collective Identity." *Sociology Compass* 3, no. 4 (2009): 658–71.

Solomon, Danyelle, Connor Maxwell, and Abril Castro. *Systematic Inequality and Economic Opportunity*. Washington, DC: Center for American Progress, 2019. https://www.americanprogress.org/article/systematic-inequality-economic-opportunity/ [https://perma.cc/8N2Y-YT4V].

Stockman, Farah. "Three Leaders of Women's March Group Step Down after Controversies." *New York Times*, September 18, 2019. https://www.nytimes.com/2019/09/16/us/womens-march-anti-semitism.html [https://perma.cc/8VMC-SL6A].

Strausbaugh, John. *Black Like You: Blackface, White Face, Insult and Imitation in American Popular Culture*. New York: Tarcher, 2007.

United States Congress Joint Economic Committee. *The Economic State of Black America in* 2020. https://www.jec.senate.gov/public/_cache

/files/ccf4dbe2-810a-44f8-b3e7-14f7e5143ba6/economic-state-of-black-america-2020.pdf [https://perma.cc/AR4P-QQVZ].

"West Siders Protest on the Magnificent Mile." *Austin Weekly News*, November 30, 2015. https://www.austinweeklynews.com/2015/11/30/west-siders-protest-on-the-magnificent-mile/.

"What You Need to Know about Title VII of the Civil Rights Act." *Thomson Reuters Legal*, May 10, 2022. https://legal.thomsonreuters.com/en/insights/articles/what-is-title-vii-civil-rights-act [https://perma.cc/FQT6-YEL7].

Yohena, Shoko Okazaki. "Conversational Styles and Ellipsis in Japanese Couples' Conversations." In *Discourse and Silencing: Representation and the Language of Displacement,* edited by Lynn Thiesmeyer, 79–112. Amsterdam: J. Benjamins, 2003.

Defining Success

WITH CONTRIBUTIONS BY

I. Bennett Capers   *Osamudia James*

Linda S. Greene   *Ruthann Robson*

Lolita Buckner Inniss

BACKGROUND

We often speak of success in the undertaking of any endeavor, large or small. But what is success? Success is the achievement of a desired outcome by a person, group of individuals, or an entity. The outcome may be in the realm of the personal, economic, legal, social, or political. That said, success is best understood as something other than an end in itself. Instead, success requires action—or many actions—taken with the objective of reaching a goal. Such goals are often centered on notions of satisfaction, which itself is premised on increasing self-measured or externally focused choice, happiness, or pleasure. In the sociolegal and political realms with which the Black Lives Matter and #MeToo movements engage, success of both the self-focused and the externally focused varieties are evident in the goal of alleviating persistent harms.

If a movement centers its own members, or an individual focuses on their own goals, that does not mean that the group or individual is not also externally focused. That said, notwithstanding the common saying that there is more pleasure in giving than in receiving, an important part of what will make the successful elimination of racist and sexist behaviors more likely is frequent, carefully executed, condoned self-regard.[1] Happiness is involved in all success, our own as well as that of others.

Observe, also, that success, while often measurable, must not meet a specific metric. There does not need to be degrees of success (e.g., "big" or "small" victories); success can be any victory. Furthermore, there is no specific technique or immediate prescription to achieve success. The movement toward success may be gradual, sometimes iterative, and often long, which may give rise to more frustration than satisfaction at times. This is certainly true for Black Lives Matter, #MeToo, and beyond. Indeed, many people embrace and promote ideals of immediate or instant success and recognition. However, it is important to sound a cautionary note: even where this sort of immediacy is possible, success that is too quick in coming may be ephemeral at best.

With this cautionary framing, we invited our participants' views on these questions:

> How do the two movements define success? How do
> you measure the success or failure of the movements?
> What has been the trajectory of success? Have the
> movements experienced setbacks? Has the public
> embraced or rejected these movements and how do
> you evaluate that embrace or rejection?

DIALOGUE

Bennett Capers: Others may not like my answer because of its simplicity, but this applies to almost everything I teach and care about. Success is when the movement becomes no longer necessary. I am thinking of Evan Wolfson's role as founder and president of Freedom to Marry, and his decades-long campaign to secure marriage equality for same-sex couples.[2] When *Obergefell v. Hodges* was decided in 2015, Wolfson decided the movement had achieved what it set out to do, and walked away.[3]

Of course, achieving an end to blue-on-Black violence and the excessive use of force by the police, as well as ending sexual harassment and assault, are much harder tasks, tied up as they are with the broader goals of true racial equality and true gender equality. But again, success will be when both those movements can pack their bags and move on to something else.

Osamudia James: "Success is when the movement no longer becomes necessary," Bennett said. I love that, and also want to add this: I want the upside of being Black, but not the (currently) attendant vulnerabilities. I want to delight in being a woman, without the psychic and material inequalities that I can't currently escape. It sometimes seems that we are envisioning a colorblind, gender-neutral world where neither race nor gender has any meaning for their identity holders, and I'm not sure that's what I want. To be sure, our society would be a better one if we weren't so fixated on the roles, rights, and obligations we've attached to gender. But that doesn't mean I want a world where being a woman has no meaning, or one where Black culture ceases to exist. And it feels to me, particularly when interrogating universal equality movements or the Supreme Court's refusal to properly engage race, that we're being told, "If you don't want the bad, then you can no longer have the good."

Bennett Capers: I'm totally down with Osamudia's friendly amendment!

Ruthann Robson: Success includes harm reduction. Every life spared or improved must count as a success, even if that success is not permanent. #SayHerName and #SayTheir Names are also marks of success: we must recognize the very real persons who are harmed. Individual lawsuits based on these harms that seek legal remedies, even while understanding that any remedies available will be inadequate to compensate for the injuries caused by the harms, are also marks of success. Yet success and its measures can falter on the opposing poles of over-individualization and under-individualization.

Individualization, perhaps better described as over-individualization, can lead to an analysis of the particular details of an incident, or even an ongoing relationship, so that each incident becomes unique and perhaps even explicable. This seems to me to occur in reactions to both Black Lives Matter and #MeToo incidents. Shouldn't the "victim" have acted differently? If only they had! They should not have been on that street corner, at that protest; they should not have gone to that hotel room; they should not have had those friends.

Yet we also under-individualize. There are so many incidents that they can blur together, erasing the individual humanity of those who have been affected. That is why I think "Say Her Name" and "Say Their Names" are so powerful.

I think it is also powerful to say the names of the perpetrators. Naming and shaming, derided as "cancel culture," and sometimes combatted with defamation lawsuits, is an important consequence of both Black Lives Matter and #MeToo. For example, Mark and Patricia McCloskey, the St. Louis lawyers who brandished an AK-47 and a handgun as Black Lives Matter protestors marched by their house, not only have been charged with felony weapon possession, but also have sued the UPI news photographer who captured the widely disseminated photograph. (Interestingly, "UPI said recently it was considering whether to send a 'cease and desist' order to the couple because of their use of the UPI photo as part of a personal greeting card.")[4]

I find it interesting that #MeToo has been much more viral and attractive than Time's Up. As Bridget described earlier, Time's Up may be less a movement in the way that we understand it. This may be because of its "corporate" structure, at least when it was rolled out. Now only the Time's Up Legal Defense Fund remains.[5] That said, the public embrace—if we can judge by traditional and social media—of #MeToo rather than Time's Up contrasts the claiming of individual harm (and trauma) versus a demand for responsibility by perpetrators.

I also think we would be remiss not to contextualize the success of these movements in the rise of Trumpian fascism. Of course, it is not that this era originated the issues; they are inveterate: one need only recall Mechelle Vinson (discussed later) or Rodney King.[6] Nevertheless, just having these movements occupy space in this time of authoritarianism has been vital. In that way, they are important successes.

Linda Greene: One way to measure the success of a movement is by assessing whether it is able to move the needle. Do its concerns eventually migrate to the mainstream political or legal policymaking agenda? Do suggested reforms eventually become actual policy?

In this respect, with regard to Black Lives Matter, we have achieved the following: legislation; criminal prosecutions that led to criminal convictions of officers in a few egregious circumstances; civil settlements; and federal court consent decrees, incorporating transitional justice truth and reconciliation principles and structures that have the potential to transform policing in Black communities in America.

The popularity of the slogan "All Lives Matter" is the latest iteration of the trope of colorblindness.[7] Its proponents erase the past and present of racialized policing in America, arguing normatively for a colorblind approach to prospective policy, despite the postulate "colorblind" theory.

Additionally, the Blue Lives Matter campaign seeks to reframe the issue as one of police discretion in times of high pressure[8]—this, of course, misses the point of the Black Lives Matter campaign. Blue Lives Matter has established a strong foothold in the highest levels of American politics, at least on the right. When he was running for president in 2015, Donald Trump said that, if he were elected, he would use an executive order to make the death penalty mandatory for anyone who killed a police officer.[9] At the 2016 Republican National Convention, Milwaukee Sheriff David Clarke opened his speech by saying that "blue lives matter" and blaming the Black Lives Matter movement for "the collapse of social order."[10]

The idea of a Black Lives Matter-inspired "war on cops" continues to play a powerful role in the Blue Lives Matter counternarrative, and it appears to be working, at least on some political levels. These concerns, for example, have gained the attention of state legislatures: thirty-two Blue Lives Matter bills were introduced in fourteen states in 2017, following fifteen bills in 2016.[11] They were meant to extend hate crime protections to members of law enforcement. Even though most bills failed, hate crime protections have been extended to police officers in Louisiana and Kentucky.[12]

One thing that this shows is that a measure of success is often imitation. Black Lives Matter's focus on policing issues has also driven mainstream civil rights and constitutional law organizations to seek to occupy the space.[13]

Some have pushed back on the idea that the Black Lives Matter movement is losing momentum. According to Frank Leon Roberts, a cultural and political critic who writes and performs about Black resistance, "the revolution is still happening—it is just not being televised."[14] Indeed, the idea that the Black Lives Matter movement is in a "decline" stage is false. Instead, what is true is that American mainstream media has been much less willing to actually cover the concerns of the Black Lives Matter movement, in part because it has been consumed by the daily catastrophes of other aspects of partisan politics. Nonetheless, it would be a mistake to assume that Black Lives Matter is "dwindling" away simply because the cameras are no longer present. All throughout the country, Black Lives Matter organizers are at work in their local communities, feverishly fighting for change and relentlessly speaking truth to power.[15] Black Lives Matter continues its work.[16]

The #MeToo movement led to the accusation of over 250 powerful people, including celebrities, politicians, and CEOs. The main goal of #MeToo is to use "healing and survivorship" to create a community of survivors who "move forward together" to create "the start of a larger conversation."[17] It is meant to give people a voice, and seeks cultural transformation by "encouraging millions to speak out about sexual violence and harassment."[18]

Success can be seen in the amount of money donated to women's causes. In 2018, 180 organizations that serve women saw a 13 percent increase in donations. Additionally, the Time's Up Legal Defense Fund, which funds cases involving workplace sexual harassment and related retaliation for fast food workers, retail workers, and police officers, raised $21 million, which made it the most successful initiative ever on the popular crowd-funding program GoFundMe.[19]

Such prevalence and success are not without setbacks. Unfortunately, men are feeling "attacked" by the movement, and some are afraid that they will be falsely accused: "I now think twice about spending one-on-one time with a young female colleague," one American finance executive said at the World Economic Forum.[20] This line of thought, of course, sets women back in the workplace, particularly where men hold higher positions of power and can help their mentees advance in their careers. As Pat Milligan, a researcher on female leadership wrote: "A number of men have told me that they will avoid going to dinner with a female mentee, or that they're concerned about deploying a woman solo onsite with a male."[21]

Sexual harassment is actionable under Title VII of the Civil Rights Act of 1964 and the Supreme Court's 1986 decision in the case of *Meritor Savings Bank v. Vinson.*[22] *Meritor Savings Bank* requires severe and pervasive treatment, and the plaintiff in *Meritor* met that test after she showed that she had been raped multiple times by her boss, including in the bank vault at work. The Supreme Court has since clarified that *Meritor* set a ceiling, rather than a floor. While this standard does not require a significant effect on the plaintiff's "psychological well-being" or cause her to "suffer injury," it does require something more than a "mere utterance of an ... epithet which engenders offensive feelings in an employee."[23] Ultimately, severity is judged from the "perspective of a reasonable person in the plaintiff's position, considering 'all the circumstances.'"[24]

ABOUT *MERITOR SAVINGS BANK, FSB V. VINSON*

Erasure of the activism and experiences of poor women and women of color is not merely part of the social discourse in the United States; it is also reflected in the ways in which U.S. law is taught and created. In other words, this erasure is embedded in our governing structures. To illustrate this point, consider *Meritor Savings Bank, FSB v. Vinson,* the first case in which the U.S. Supreme Court recognized sexual harassment as a form of prohibited sex discrimination under Title VII of the Civil Rights Act of 1964.

In 1974, Mechelle Vinson began working for Meritor Savings Bank as a teller-trainee. Over the next four years, the bank promoted Vinson to teller, head teller, and assistant branch manager. Shortly after her probationary period ended, Vinson alleged that Sidney Taylor, who was an assistant vice-president of the bank and the manager of one of its branches, began to harass her. She testified that Taylor repeatedly demanded sexual favors, fondled her in front of other employees, exposed himself to her, and forcibly raped her on several occasions. Vinson initially refused Taylor's sexual demands but eventually complied because she feared losing her job. Vinson testified that she had sex with Taylor forty to fifty times over the course of her employment. Because Vinson was afraid of Taylor, she never reported his harassment to any of his supervisors and never attempted to use the bank's complaint procedures.

Taylor denied all of Vinson's allegations, contending that they were in response to a business-related dispute. The Bank also denied Vinson's allegations, asserting that "any sexual harassment by Taylor was unknown to the bank and engaged in without its consent or approval."

In its groundbreaking opinion, the U.S. Supreme Court recognized sexual harassment as a form of sex discrimination under Title VII, noting "[w]ithout question, when a supervisor sexually harasses a subordinate because of the subordinate's sex, that supervisor 'discriminates' on the basis of sex." Although the case reached the Court on a hostile environment theory, by adopting the EEOC's definition of harassment the Court endorsed both quid pro quo and hostile environment claims. Quid pro quo claims involve unwelcome employer demands for sexual favors in return for an employment benefit or to avoid an employment detriment. Hostile environment claims involve unwelcome conduct that is sufficiently severe or pervasive as to alter the terms or conditions of employment and create an abusive working environment.

In reaching these conclusions, the Court significantly advanced the ability of complainants to seek redress for workplace sexual harassment. Unfortunately, however, the Supreme Court omitted any reference in its analysis to Vinson's age, race, or economic class. Indeed, students often assume that Mechelle Vinson was an older, middle-class, White woman. She, however, was not. Both Vinson and Taylor were Black. Vinson was 19 when she met Taylor. She grew up poor and was a high school dropout with a general education diploma ("GED")— and subsequently earned equivalent to a high school diploma. Prior to her employment at the bank, Vinson had worked in lower level, female-dominated jobs in the service industry. In contrast, Taylor was old enough to be Vinson's father. He had worked his way up the bank's hierarchy from janitor to assistant vice-president. He was a father of seven children, the deacon of his church, and was revered by the local community.

We suggest that inclusion of these facts would have more clearly exposed the power dynamics at play between Vinson

(continued)

and Taylor and in sexual harassment cases more generally. Their inclusion would have demonstrated the ways in which race, class, and age intersect to heighten the vulnerability of certain women, particularly young, poor, women of color.

Excerpt from Trina Jones and Emma E. Wade, "Me Too? Race, Gender and Ending Workplace Sexual Harassment," *Duke Journal of Gender Law and Policy* 27, no. 1 (2020): 210–12.

#MeToo may help further redefine the standards under which these claims are evaluated—specifically, what a "reasonable person" in these circumstances may consider "severe." While some scholars argue that the standard should be a "reasonable woman," that standard has not been adopted by the federal courts.[25] But by continuing to keep these issues in the public eye, the movement may be able to shift men's perspectives on the topic. Additionally, while many sexual harassment lawsuits in the past have targeted individual employers for the environment in specific workplaces, some #MeToo litigation has targeted an expanded group of defendants, including entire companies, senior management, and corporate boards.[26]

#MeToo has potential to effect change in workplace culture, getting to the root of the cause of sexual assault so that lawsuits are not the only vehicle for redress.

Lolita Buckner Inniss: Both Black Lives Matter and #MeToo have as implicit goals the ending of harms that engendered the movements. So, in the case of Black Lives Matter, a core goal is reducing and ultimately eliminating state-based and vigilante violence against Black people. For #MeToo, a key objective is to reduce and ultimately eliminate sexual harassment and sexual abuse of women.

However, I think that, in both cases, the articulation of these more immediate goals obscures the fact that harms against Black people and women are only symptoms of broader situations of legal, social, political, and economic oppression. If somehow sexual harassment and sexualized violence against women were ended overnight, or if state-sanctioned and vigilante violence against Black people ceased immediately, we would still be left with other aspects of gender, racial, and other forms of oppression.

Of course, as others note, the Black Lives Matter and #MeToo movements have, in point of fact, multiple planks to their platforms that seek the eradication of harms across identity categories. However, while allyship and collaborative undertakings are often key to overcoming entrenched, structural harms, the narrow framing of goals—here, eliminating anti-Black racism and sexism—is an important way of meaningfully reaching the public.

However, even choosing only these two goals offers pitfalls. If, for instance, we treat anti-Black racism comprehensively, there is the risk of ignoring the gender dimension in certain harms. And if the focus is on sexism against women-identifying people, other aspects of identity, such as race, may be disregarded.

DISCUSSION QUESTIONS

1. Must movements such as Black Lives Matter and #MeToo explicitly define success, and mechanisms for measuring it, in order to offer coherence and meaning to their actions? Does it matter if such definitions shift along the way?

2. This chapter presents multiple perspectives about the #MeToo movement's capacity to bring about social change. Survey evidence suggests that a large proportion of U.S. men are reevaluating their behavior to ensure that it is not sexual harassment. In some people's minds, the movement won a "victory" in court with the Weinstein verdicts in New York and California (covered in chapter 2). The New York conviction was subsequently overturned. How does this impact your assessment of the success of the #MeToo movement? Consider also that some analyses of the movement's experience in courtrooms argue that it is more difficult for low-income women

workers to avail themselves of the court system to address sexual harassment and assault in the workplace. Given the various definitions of success the contributors have offered in this chapter, what is your view of what success would look like for #MeToo?

3. In 2019, when many of the contributors in this book first offered their views on the relationship between Black Lives Matter and #MeToo, there was some concern that Black Lives Matter was losing momentum. Then, in 2020, the movement was reignited in the wake of the murder of George Floyd. Nationwide protests challenged police authority and the police responded with extreme violence. These protests were catalyzed by the 2020 start of the COVID-19 crisis, as it became clear that the pandemic disproportionately harmed people in Black communities and other communities of color. After the protests ended, Republican states introduced legislation to protect police from being charged with hate crimes and "Blue Lives Matter" became a counter-slogan. As we write this book, the United States is still in the process of responding to the Black Lives Matter movement. Given the stated goals of the movement, what national policies would fulfill the vision of the movement? In your opinion, does the movement have the momentum it needs to move the needle on policy?

4. What point are people trying to make when they use the slogan "Blue Lives Matter" or "All Lives Matter"? Legal scholar India Thusi says that "Blue Lives Matter is evidence of the permanence of racism." Do you agree? Why or why not?

5. Similarly, what point are people trying to make when they use the slogan "Not All Men"? Is this evidence of the permanence of sexism? Why or why not?

NOTES

1. "Condoned self-regard" is an attitude of positive self-focus that includes, for example, the right to refuse demands of state and non-state actors that inappropriately inhibit personal autonomy. See Lolita Buckner Inniss, "(Un)Common Law and the Female Body," *Boston College Law Review* 61, E. Supp. (2020): I-100, citing Anita Bernstein, *The Common Law Inside the Female Body* (Cambridge: Cambridge University Press, 2019).

2. Freedom to Marry, "About Us," accessed April 24, 2024, http://www
.freedomtomarry.org/pages/about-us   [https://perma.cc/P2EM-EZ9S]
("Freedom to Marry was the campaign that won marriage in the United
States and ignited a global movement." The campaign deployed a "national
strategy focused from the beginning on setting the stage for a national
victory at the Supreme Court by winning a critical mass of states, building
a critical mass of public support, and ending federal marriage
discrimination.").

3. Obergefell v. Hodges, 135 S. Ct. 2017 (2015); Karen Heller, "Freedom to
Marry Is Going Out of Business. And Everybody's Thrilled," *Washington Post*,
July 20, 2015, https://www.washingtonpost.com/lifestyle/style/freedom-to-
marry-is-going-out-of-business-and-everybodys-thrilled/2015/07
/30/5ca89b5c-322b-11e5-8f36-18d1d501920d_story.html   [https://perma.
cc/8XSM-QPYL]; Evan Wolfson, "Opinion: What's Next in the Fight for Gay
Equality," *New York Times*, June 26, 2015, https://www.nytimes.com/2015/06
/27/opinion/evan-wolfson-whats-next-in-the-fight-for-gay-equality.html
[https://perma.cc/4FY2-P2AR].

4. "Gun-Waving St. Louis Couple Sues News Photographer," *Associated
Press*, updated November 7, 2020, https://apnews.com/article/st-louis
-lawsuits-us-news-07f1a5b2d119f527dcdbba0911998e14   [https://perma
.cc/7C9W-TTXH].

5. See Jocelyn Noveck, "Time's Up to Halt Operations, Shift Resources
to Legal Fund," *AP News*, January 22, 2023, https://apnews.com/article
/times-up-metoo-1ac800e48a96357d7fb29c18848c50d2   [https://perma
.cc/DRN3-7JWR].

6. Abraham L. Davis, "The Rodney King Incident: Isolated Occurrence
or a Continuation of a Brutal Past?," *Harvard Blackletter Journal* 10 (1993):
67–68 (providing a description of the 1991 beating of Mr. King and the five
days in Los Angeles following a jury verdict that four police officers were not
guilty of assault with a deadly weapon or excessive use of force).

7. See, for example, John Tawa, Ruiqian Ma, and Katsumoto Shinji, "'All
Lives Matter': The Cost of Colorblind Racial Attitudes in Diverse Social
Networks," *Race and Social Problems* 8 (2016): 196–208.

8. India Thusi, "Blue Lives and the Permanence of Racism," *Cornell Law
Review Online* 105 (2020), https://www.cornelllawreview.org/2020/03/03
/blue-lives-the-permanence-of-racism   [https://perma.cc/L7HA-ZERX]
(explaining that this phrase "has become the rallying call for those offended
by the suggestion that we should hold police officers accountable for killing
unarmed Black people").

9. See Ben Kamisar, "Trump: I Will Mandate Death Penalty for Killing Police Officers," *The Hill*, December 10, 2015, https://thehill.com/homenews /campaign/262897-trump-i-will-mandate-death-penalty-for-killing -police-officers/ [https://perma.cc/7NUK-CPWV].

10. See Nick Gass, "Milwaukee Sheriff at RNC: 'Blue Lives Matter,'" *Politico*, July 18, 2016, https://www.politico.com/story/2016/07/rnc-2016 -sheriff-dave-clarke-225768 [https://perma.cc/J55S-VPJM].

11. See Julia Craven, "32 Blue Lives Matter Bills Have Been Introduced across 14 States This Year," *HuffPost Politics*, updated December 11, 2017, https://www.huffpost.com/entry/blue-black-lives-matter-police-bills -states_n_58b61488e4b0780bac2e31b8 [https://perma.cc/M8H4-ZPVJ].

12. For Louisiana, see La. Rev. Stat. § 14:107.2(E) (2022). For Kentucky, see Ky. Rev. Stat. § 532.031(A) (2022).

13. These organizations include the American Civil Liberties Union and the NAACP Legal Defense Fund. American Civil Liberties Union, "Police Practices," accessed February 18, 2023, https://www.aclu.org/feature /police-practices [https://perma.cc/P6P2-DL8L]; NAACP Legal Defense Fund, "Policing Reform Campaign," accessed March 13, 2024, https:// perma.cc/7SBU-8AXW.

14. See, for example, Frank Leon Roberts, Cynthia Erivo, and Ledisi, "5 Ways of Understanding Black Lives Matter," Broadway for Black Lives Matter, Columbia University, New York, August 1, 2016, YouTube video, 16:59, https://www.youtube.com/watch?v=D7ERPOddqZw [https:// perma.cc/GJ2T-9NTF]. The quote is a paraphrase of the song "The Revolution Will Not Be Televised" by Gill Scott-Heron from his debut album *Small Talk at 125th and Lenox*. Scott-Heron, "The Revolution Will Not Be Televised," Songfacts, accessed February 18, 2023, https://www.songfacts. com/facts/gil-scott-heron/the-revolution-will-not-be-televised [https:// perma.cc/L6QG-T5CG]. See also Darren Sands, "What Happened to Black Lives Matter?," *BuzzFeed News*, June 28, 2017, https://www.buzzfeednews. com/article/darrensands/what-happened-to-black-lives-matter [https:// perma.cc/VUN2-NBHS].

15. Roberts, Erivo, and Ledisi, "5 Ways of Understanding."

16. See, for example, Ann M. Simmons and Jaweed Kaleem, "Q&A: A Founder of Black Lives Matter Answers a Question on Many Minds: Where Did It Go?," *Los Angeles Times*, August 25, 2017, https://www.latimes.com /nation/la-na-patrisse-cullors-black-lives-matter-2017-htmlstory.html [https://perma.cc/QDE5-NBMM]; Jamiles Lartey, "'We've Ignited a New Generation': Patrisse Khan-Cullors on the Resurgence of Black Activism,"

The Guardian, January 28, 2018, https://www.theguardian.com/us -news/2018/jan/28/patrisse-khan-cullors-black-lives-matter-interview [https://perma.cc/JH8W-KNHV].

17. Alix Langone, "#MeToo and Time's Up Founders Explain the Difference between the 2 Movements—And How They're Alike," *Time,* March 8, 2018, https://time.com/5189945/whats-the-difference-between-the-metoo-and-times-up-movements/ [https://perma.cc/57H5-NLV3].

18. Langone, "#MeToo and Time's Up Founders" (quoting the website metoomvmt.org [https://perma.cc/5HGZ-ZTCJ]).

19. Alix Langone, "These Are the Biggest Donors to Hollywood's Record-Breaking #TimesUp Campaign," *Money,* January 18, 2018, https://money .com/times-up-go-fund-me-donations/ [https://perma.cc/4VJY-RW3Z].

20. Maya Salam, "What Happens When Men Are Too Afraid to Mentor Women?," *New York Times,* January 29, 2019, https://www.nytimes .com/2019/01/29/us/metoo-men-women-mentors.html [https://perma.cc /N2F8-H36B].

21. Salam, "What Happens When Men Are Too Afraid."

22. Meritor Savings Bank v. Vinson, 477 U.S. 57 (1986).

23. Harris v. Forklift Systems, 510 U.S. 17, 21 (1993).

24. Oncale v. Sundowner Offshore Services, 523 U.S. 75 (1998).

25. Kathleen A. Kenealy, "Sexual Harassment and the Reasonable Woman Standard," *Labor Lawyer* 8, no. 2 (1992): 203–10.

26. Susan L. Saltzstein and Jocelyn E. Strauber, "#MeToo Litigation: The Changing Landscape," *New York Law Journal* 261, no. 40 (2019), https:// www.skadden.com/-/media/files/publications/2019/03/metoo_litigation _the_changing_landscape.pdf [https://perma.cc/EUR7-T24V].

BIBLIOGRAPHY

American Civil Liberties Union. "Police Practices." Accessed February 18, 2023. https://www.aclu.org/feature/police-practices [https://perma .cc/P6P2-DL8L].

Bernstein, Anita. *The Common Law Inside the Female Body.* Cambridge: Cambridge University Press, 2019.

Bernstein, Danielle. "#MeToo Has Changed the World—Except in Court." *The Atlantic,* August 13, 2021. https://www.theatlantic.com/ideas /archive/2021/08/metoo-courts/619732/ [https://perma.cc/Y5K5–7MD3].

Brown, Anna. *More Than Twice as Many Americans Support Than Oppose the #MeToo Movement.* Washington, DC: Pew Research Center, 2022. https://www.pewresearch.org/social-trends/wp-content/uploads/sites/3/2022/09/ST_2022.09.29_Me-Too_FINAL.pdf [https://perma.cc/4CFR-985T].

Chen, Teresa. *Black Lives Matter: Power, Perception, and Press.* Cambridge, MA: Harvard Kennedy School Carr Center for Human Rights Policy, 2021. https://carrcenter.hks.harvard.edu/files/cchr/files/21_chen_topol_paper.pdf [https://perma.cc/BQ58-4TBU].

Coglianese, Cary. "Social Movements, Law, and Society: The Institutionalization of the Environmental Movement." *University of Pennsylvania Law Review* 150, no. 1 (2001): 85–118.

Craven, Julia. "32 Blue Lives Matter Bills Have Been Introduced across 14 States This Year." *HuffPost Politics*, updated December 11, 2017. https://www.huffpost.com/entry/blue-black-lives-matter-police-bills-states_n_58b61488e4b0780obac2e31b8 [https://perma.cc/M8H4-ZPVJ].

Crenshaw, Kimberlé Williams. "Twenty Years of Critical Race Theory: Looking Back to Move Forward." *Connecticut Law Review* 43, no. 5 (2011): 1253–354.

Davis, Abraham L. "The Rodney King Incident: Isolated Occurrence or a Continuation of a Brutal Past?" *Harvard Blackletter Journal* 10 (1993): 67–78.

Della Porta, Donatella, and Mario Diani. *Social Movements: An Introduction.* Malden, MA: Blackwell, 1999.

Dobbs v. Jackson Women's Health Organization, 142 S. Ct. 2228 (2022).

Dwyer, Colin. "The Harvey Weinstein Trial: A Brief Timeline of How We Got Here." *NPR*, January 22, 2020. https://www.npr.org/2020/01/22/798222176/the-harvey-weinstein-trial-a-brief-timeline-of-how-we-got-here [https://perma.cc/WJT8-UZVE].

Eskridge, William N., Jr. "Channeling: Identity-Based Social Movements and Public Law." *University of Pennsylvania Law Review* 150, no. 1 (2001): 419–526.

Freedom to Marry. "About Us." Accessed April 24, 2024. https://perma.cc/P2EM-EZ9S.

Gass, Nick. "Milwaukee Sheriff at RNC: 'Blue Lives Matter.'" *Politico*, July 18, 2016. https://www.politico.com/story/2016/07/rnc-2016-sheriff-dave-clarke-225768 [https://perma.cc/J55S-VPJM].

Gruber, Aya. *The Feminist War on Crime: The Unexpected Role of Women's Liberation in Mass Incarceration*. Berkeley: University of California Press, 2020.

———. "#MeToo and Mass Incarceration." *Ohio State Journal of Criminal Law* 17, no. 2 (2020): 275–92.

"Gun-Waving St. Louis Couple Sues News Photographer." *Associated Press*, updated November 7, 2020. https://apnews.com/article/st-louis-lawsuits-us-news-07f1a5b2d119f527dcdbba0911998e14 [https://perma.cc/7C9W-TTXH].

Harris v. Forklift Systems, 510 U.S. 17 (1993).

"Harvey Weinstein Jailed for 23 Years in a Rape Trial." *BBC News*, March 12, 2020. https://www.bbc.com/news/world-us-canada-51840532 [https://perma.cc/9936-XNU3].

Heller, Karen. "Freedom to Marry Is Going Out of Business. And Everybody's Thrilled." *Washington Post*, July 20, 2015. https://www.washingtonpost.com/lifestyle/style/freedom-to-marry-is-going-out-of-business-and-everybodys-thrilled/2015/07/30/5ca89b5c-322b-11e5-8f36-18d1d501920d_story.html [https://perma.cc/8XSM-QPYL].

Inniss, Lolita Buckner. "(Un)Common Law and the Female Body," *Boston College Law Review* 61, E. Supp. (2020): I-95-I-104.

Jones, Trina, and Emma E. Wade. "Me Too? Race, Gender and Ending Workplace Sexual Harassment." *Duke Journal of Gender Law and Policy* 27, no. 1 (2020): 203–26.

Kamisar, Ben. "Trump: I Will Mandate Death Penalty for Killing Police Officers." *The Hill*, December 10, 2015. https://thehill.com/homenews/campaign/262897-trump-i-will-mandate-death-penalty-for-killing-police-officers/ [https://perma.cc/7NUK-CPWV].

Kantor, Jodi, Megan Twohey, Grace Ashford, Catrin Einhorn, and Ellen Gabler. "'Finally': Ashley Judd and Other Weinstein Accusers Respond to Verdict." *New York Times*, February 24, 2020. https://www.nytimes.com/2020/02/24/nyregion/harvey-weinstein-accusers.html [https://perma.cc/R692-VTNB].

Kenealy, Kathleen A. "Sexual Harassment and the Reasonable Woman Standard." *Labor Lawyer* 8, no. 2 (1992): 203–10.

Kinsey, Jennifer M. "Black Speech Matters." *University of Louisville Law Review* 59, no. 1 (2020): 1–22.

KY. REV. STAT. § 532.031(A) (2022).

Langone, Alix. "#MeToo and Time's Up Founders Explain the Difference between the 2 Movements—And How They're Alike." *Time*, updated

March 8, 2018. https://time.com/5189945/whats-the-difference
-between-the-metoo-and-times-up-movements/ [https://perma
.cc/57H5-NLV3].

———. "These Are the Biggest Donors to Hollywood's Record-Breaking
#TimesUp Campaign." *Money*, January 18, 2018. https://money.com
/times-up-go-fund-me-donations/ [https://perma.cc/4VJY-RW3Z].

La. Rev. Stat. § 14:107.2(E) (2022).

Lartey, Jamiles. "'We've Ignited a New Generation': Patrisse Khan-
Cullors on the Resurgence of Black Activism." *The Guardian*, January
28, 2018. https://www.theguardian.com/us-news/2018/jan/28
/patrisse-khan-cullors-black-lives-matter-interview [https://perma
.cc/JH8W-KNHV].

Lee, Cynthia. "Firearms and Initial Aggressors." *North Carolina Law
Review* 101, no. 1 (2022): 1–80.

Lennart, Natasha. "What's Wrong with Cheering Harvey Weinstein's
Reported Coronavirus Diagnosis." *Theintercept.com*, March 23, 2020.
https://theintercept.com/2020/03/23/harvey-weinstein-coronavirus
/ [https://perma.cc/2J22-SM3X].

Levenson, Eric, Lauren del Valle, and Sonia Moghe. "Harvey Weinstein
Sentenced to 23 Years in Prison after Addressing His Accusers in
Court." *CNN*, March 11, 2020. https://www.cnn.com/2020/03/11/us
/harvey-weinstein-sentence/index.html [https://perma.cc/ZLV7
-27VK].

Malik, Nesrine. "'I Have a Lot of Resentment': Patrisse Cullors on Co-
founding Black Lives Matter, the Backlash—and Why the Police Must
Go." *The Guardian*, February 28, 2022. https://www.theguardian.com
/world/2022/feb/28/i-have-a-lot-of-resentment-patrisse-cullors-on-co-
founding-black-lives-matter-the-backlash-and-why-the-police-must-go
[https://perma.cc/S6MJ-DZZ5].

Medina, Eduardo, and Chris Cameron. "Missouri Governor Pardons St.
Louis Couple Who Aimed Guns at Protestors." *New York Times*, August
3, 2021. https://www.nytimes.com/2021/08/03/us/politics/mark
-patricia-mccloskey-pardon.html [https://perma.cc/NG68-UF9R].

Meritor Savings Bank v. Vinson, 477 U.S. 57 (1986).

"The #MeToo Backlash." *Harvard Business Review*, September/October
2019. https://hbr.org/2019/09/the-metoo-backlash [https://perma.cc
/BA69-TV54].

Mulvaney, Erin, and Lydia Beyoud. "Cuomo Harassment Scandal
Underscores Limits of #MeToo Movement." *Bloomberg Law*, August 9,

2021. https://news.bloomberglaw.com/daily-labor-report/cuomo
-harassment-scandal-underscores-limits-of-metoo-movement
[https://perma.cc/HR9P-3AY7].

NAACP Legal Defense Fund. "Policing Reform Campaign." Accessed
March 13, 2024. https://perma.cc/7SBU-8AXW.

Nardini, Gia, Tracy Rank-Christman, Melissa G. Bublitz, Samantha N. N.
Cross, and Laura A. Peracchio. "Together We Rise: How Social
Movements Succeed." *Journal of Consumer Psychology* 31, no. 1 (2021):
112–45.

Noveck, Jocelyn. "Time's Up to Halt Operations, Shift Resources to Legal
Fund." *AP News*, January 22, 2023. https://apnews.com/article/times-
up-metoo-1ac800e48a96357d7fb29c18848c50d2 [https://perma.cc
/DRN3-7JWR].

Obergefell v. Hodges, 576 U.S. 644 (2015).

Oncale v. Sundowner Offshore Services, 523 U.S. 75 (1998).

Quinton, Sophie. "Republicans Respond to Black Lives Matter with
Anti-Protest Bills." *Pew Charitable Trust: Stateline*, February 4, 2021.
https://stateline.org/2021/02/04/republicans-respond-to-black-lives-
matter-with-anti-protest-bills/ [https://perma.cc/AFM4-EUEM].

Roberts, Frank Leon, Cynthia Erivo, and Ledisi. "5 Ways of Understanding Black Lives Matter." Broadway for Black Lives Matter, Columbia
University, New York, August 1, 2016. YouTube video, 16:59. https://
www.youtube.com/watch?v=D7ERPOddqZw [https://perma.cc/GJ2T-
9NTF].

Rubin, Edward. L. "Passing through the Door: Social Movement Literature and Legal Scholarship." *University of Pennsylvania Law Review*
150 no. 1 (2001): 1–84.

Salam, Maya. "What Happens When Men Are Too Afraid to Mentor
Women?" *New York Times*, January 29, 2019. https://www.nytimes
.com/2019/01/29/us/metoo-men-women-mentors.html [https://perma
.cc/N2F8-H36B].

Saltzstein, Susan L., and Jocelyn E. Strauber. "#MeToo Litigation: The
Changing Landscape." *New York Law Journal* 261, no. 40 (2019).
https://www.skadden.com/-/media/files/publications/2019/03
/metoo_litigation_the_changing_landscape.pdf [https://perma.cc
/EUR7-T24V].

Sands, Darren. "What Happened to Black Lives Matter?" *BuzzFeed News*,
June 28, 2017. https://www.buzzfeednews.com/article/darrensands
/what-happened-to-black-lives-matter [https://perma.cc/VUN2-NBHS].

Scott-Heron, Gil. "The Revolution Will Not Be Televised." Songfacts. Accessed February 18, 2023. https://www.songfacts.com/facts /gil-scott-heron/the-revolution-will-not-be-televised [https://perma .cc/L6QG-T5CG].

Simmons, Ann M., and Jaweed Kaleem. "Q&A: A Founder of Black Lives Matter Answers a Question on Many Minds: Where Did It Go?" *Los Angeles Times*, August 25, 2017. https://www.latimes.com/nation /la-na-patrisse-cullors-black-lives-matter-2017-htmlstory.html [https://perma.cc/QDE5-NBMM].

Tawa, John, Ruqian Ma, and Shinji Katsumoto. "'All Lives Matter': The Cost of Colorblind Racial Attitudes in Diverse Social Networks." *Race and Social Problems* 8 (2016): 196–208.

Teebagy, Elizabeth. "White Privilege and Racial Narratives: The Role of Race in Media Storytelling of Sexual Assaults by College Athletes." *Journal of Gender, Race, and Justice* 21, No. 2 (2018): 479–99.

Terwiel, Anna. "What Is Carceral Feminism?" *Political Theory* 48, no. 4 (2020): 421–42.

Thusi, India. "Blue Lives and the Permanence of Racism." *Cornell Law Review Online* 105 (2020). https://www.cornelllawreview.org/2020/03 /03/blue-lives-the-permanence-of-racism/ [https://perma.cc /B6WH-64ZV].

United States Sentencing Commission. *Demographic Differences in Sentencing: An Update to the* 2011 *Booker Report.* 2017. https://www .ussc.gov/sites/default/files/pdf/research-and-publications/research -publications/2017/20171114_Demographics.pdf [https://perma.cc /TBW2-QMT9].

———. *Quick Facts on Sexual Abuse Offenders.* 2018. https://www.ussc .gov/sites/default/files/pdf/research-and-publications/quick-facts /Sexual_Abuse_FY18.pdf [https://perma.cc/QL64-EJ8D].

Wolfson, Evan. "Opinion: What's Next in the Fight for Gay Equality." *New York Times*, June 26, 2015. https://www.nytimes.com/2015/06 /27/opinion/evan-wolfson-whats-next-in-the-fight-for-gay-equality .html [https://perma.cc/4FY2-P2AR].

6 *Dialogue*

Black Lives Matter and #MeToo

LAW, CULTURE, AND POSSIBILITIES
FOR CHANGE

WITH CONTRIBUTIONS BY

Noa Ben-Asher	*Lolita Buckner Inniss*
I. Bennett Capers	*Osamudia James*
Bridget J. Crawford	*Ruthann Robson*
Linda S. Greene	*Kathryn M. Stanchi*
Aya Gruber	*Lua Kamál Yuille*

BACKGROUND

In the previous chapter we discussed how the Black Lives Matter and #MeToo movements define success. Even in their short existences, both movements have seen advances. These include wide recognition of the movements' concerns as well as actual, concrete changes. However, it is clear from that discussion that what success looks like is different for each movement. Success is not only differently assessed; it is also subject to alternate possibilities and limits. The prospect of expanding ideas of formal legal rights, as well as of social views about what a fully inclusive society looks like, has implications for the roles of both law and culture in creating success.

Hence, this chapter queries how the Black Lives Matter and #MeToo movements have or have not affected law and culture.

In engaging in this conversation here, we recognize that *law* has myriad meanings. The most typical understandings have to do with formal renderings of law by state actors and institutions that occur in a systemic fashion, primarily involving the creation of rules and regulations that govern behavior in a society. Formal law offers enforcement mechanisms and explicit, even if not consistent, penalties for those who violate it. Typically, the stated goal of law is to ensure order and stability in society. Yet justice is, and must be, a goal of law too. It is important to note that while law frequently makes judgments (i.e., the legal system requires adjudicators to reach conclusions that are ostensibly premised on truth and fairness), law is not always just.[1]

Broadly speaking, *culture* refers to the beliefs, values, customs, practices, and social behaviors that are learned and shared among members of a group or society. It encompasses a wide range of aspects, including language, religion, cuisine, art, music, and more. Culture influences the way people think, behave, and interact with each other; it is often passed down from generation to generation. Notions of culture also include morals, belief systems, and values—all the way to the finer details of how people live and engage with the world. Undergirding this traditional notion of culture are multiple sublegal regulatory regimes that also shape, guide, and control our behavior. There are both official and unofficial frameworks that transmit rules.[2]

Acknowledging these plural understandings of culture, the dialogue that follows explores the interactions of law, culture, and the Black Lives Matter and #MeToo movements. What emerges is a picture of how, as one scholar has described, law is constitutive of culture and culture is constitutive of law.[3]

To start this discussion, we asked the following questions:

> What is law, and does it have the potential to produce
> meaningful and transformative solutions for either or
> both the Black Lives Matter and/or #MeToo

movements? How does culture, broadly defined, shape the movements? How have the movements shaped culture?

DIALOGUE

Lua Yuille: The first thing that comes to mind for me is that there is an invisible regulatory regime that shapes the terrain and reproduces the conditions that erase and legitimize racial and gender harassment and violence. This regime is "civility." Calls to civility delegitimize "call out" or "cancel" culture—which is really just the restorative act of publicly "naming, claiming, and blaming."

Transgressions of civility—or more accurately, servility—are used to justify, time and again, the use of fatal force to demand compliance. Sandra Bland was uncivil.[4] Michael Brown was uncivil.[5] Jordan Davis was uncivil.[6] Black Lives Matter protests are "riots," #MeToo complaints are "nasty," and it is all juxtaposed against proper civil discourse.

Lolita Buckner Inniss: I hear you, Lua. I might ask whether the discussion of civility is a move to dangerous ground. I recall that, as a child, my family gave me to understand that civility—defined as politeness, respect, and courtesy in all interactions—would protect us all from most negative interactions with other people. In the context of law, civility is important as it helps to maintain order and promote peaceful resolution of disputes. It is also a fundamental principle in legal systems, where parties are expected to conduct themselves with decorum and respect during legal proceedings. This helps to ensure that the proceedings are fair and impartial, and that the rights of all parties involved are protected.

Civility, however, assumes shared values. That is a big assumption.

Kathy Stanchi: I was recently reading Bryan Stevenson's book chapter on the policing of Black men.[7] He notes that America has never had a truth and reconciliation process like the ones in South Africa or Rwanda. We ended slavery, but we never grappled with the underlying social structures that made it acceptable to treat Black people like chattel. Law can be part of that truth and reparation process by owning and recognizing racism and the law's complicity in it.

Calls for civility are not enough, and as Lua and Lolita point out, can be counterproductive because it is always the oppressed who are called upon to be "civil."

Aya Gruber: One of the legacies of slavery and Jim Crow is segregation. These movements contribute to a critical cultural understanding of space and geography. For example, the Black Lives Matter movement spotlights how the police literally and figuratively discipline Black people's space and place. Through patrolling and profiling, the police, together with their private neighborhood-watch cousins, ensure that white spaces, or more accurately spaces that people like to imagine to be white, remain free from "outsiders."[8]

Having confined Black people to certain spaces, through policing, residential discrimination, redlining, and gentrification, the police then seek to exercise authoritarian control within those spaces, and do so through the use of aggressive stop and frisks, intense surveillance, jump-outs, and military-style home raids, among other tactics.

Black Lives Matter protesters have expressed their objection to the police's confinement and management of Black space by physically occupying certain spaces themselves—even, or especially, against the dictates of the police and state authorities. By occupying highly controlled, exclusionary, and racialized zones like commercial, governmental, and residential areas, protesters sought to challenge the state's geographic monopoly and use of violence to maintain it. This tactic, predictably, provoked a strong, even warlike, response from the police. To the protesters being out of place, officers reacted with weapons of war, disappearances, and unabashed brutality, and the true nature of the police as agents of violence and soldiers of racialized control was laid bare.[9]

The #MeToo movement is also concerned with the disciplining of geography, and in particular, how law and society enable men to dominate spaces like workplaces (or exclusive spaces within workplaces) and city streets. There are of course, many laws, policies, and cultural mores that maintain women's status of political and economic inferiority, but #MeToo concentrates specifically on the role *sexual* conduct plays in patriarchal spatial dominance. Regarding sexual harassment, the argument is that sexual words and acts, whether intended to denigrate, compliment, or achieve something else, create an environment that is inhospitable to women. This, in turn, constructively divests power spaces of a critical mass of women, and, at the same time, keeps women in their place as sexual objects. A similar argument is made about street hassling, asserting that catcalls and the like accrue to men geographic domination over urban streets and effectuate men's goal of relegating women to the domestic cage.

One big difference between #MeToo and Black Lives Matter lies in their responses to this unjust spatial disciplining, which reveal their fundamentally different relationships to the state. Black Lives Matter's counteractions involve organizing, uniting, and physically occupying off-limits spaces. By contrast, #MeToo has generally called on authorities, both state and institutional, to discipline individual sexual (and sexist) malefactors. Anti-street-harassment messages encourage women to report public hassling from men to the police or other authorities.

In #MeToo tweets and other narratives, street hassling incidents appear to often involve women receiving unwanted attention from certain types of men, including young men of color hanging out, the homeless, and men with mental health issues.[10] But these are also the types of men who regularly experience violence from state authorities intent on strictly curtailing the spaces they may occupy. The anti-street-hassling rhetoric elevates women's right to police protection from fear, confrontation, and discomfort in public spaces. But this ethic steps close to the motivations behind the many infamous "Karen"-calling-the-cops incidents of recent years. Indeed, Amy Cooper, who was filmed calling the cops on Christian Cooper (no relation), a Black birder in Central Park, eventually issued a public apology to him, stating that she regretted treating the police as her "protection agency" when "so many don't have that luxury."[11]

Bridget Crawford: That is helpful, Aya. The concept of spaces is an important one. Law is a "space" too. We keep coming back to this question of the movements' influence on law (noting that law is a part of culture).

Bennett Capers: Professor Deb Tuerkheimer at Northwestern has argued that #MeToo has not had much influence on the law.[12] To be sure, there have been modest changes at the margins, but nothing earth shattering.[13] Nothing that, in fact, has reduced unwanted sex and unwanted sexual advances.

By contrast, if nothing else, Black Lives Matter must be credited with the widespread adoption of police body-worn cameras. I have argued elsewhere that these cameras likely deter some excessive force; when they don't deter it, they at least record it, again serving as a "white witness."[14] But I have also borrowed from my colleague Jocelyn Simonson to argue that the impact of video evidence will likely go well beyond deterring and documenting.[15] Ultimately, when used in court, such evidence has the power to change not only how courts normally think about the police, which is often with uncritical deference and assumptions about police expertise,[16] but also how courts think about victims and everyday citizens. Eventually, this may have implications for how we think about anti-discrimination claims.

Ruthann Robson: Speaking of anti-discrimination claims, Bennett, I think often of the lawsuit filed in federal court by Alva John-

IS LAW MISSING IN ACTION FROM #METOO?

As the #MeToo movement has gathered force, the law has remained largely missing in action, with the perceived futility of invoking formal accountability measures taken as given. But the near absence of law is too damning to ignore. Rather than remain a dominant feature of our societal approach to sexual assault and harassment, the proliferation of informal complaint underscores the need to invigorate our systems of formalized redress. Unless we are willing to consign the laws that regulate sexual misconduct to a state of perpetual dormancy, the channels that activate legal consequences must be reimagined. By creating a next generation of official reporting channels, we can breathe new life into the law of sexual misconduct, along with the protections it offers victims and accused alike.

Excerpt from Deborah Tuerkheimer, "Beyond #MeToo," *New York University Law Review* 94, no. 5 (2019): 1150–51.

son, a Black woman who worked on the 2016 Trump campaign. According to court filings, she alleged that "Trump grabbed [her] by the hand, held her hand, and then kissed her without her consent. Plaintiff further alleges that she turned her head to avoid the kiss, and Defendant kissed her on the side of her mouth. She felt humiliated by this contact and, shortly thereafter, she was disappointed because her co-workers were aware of the incident and were joking about it."[17]

In evaluating Johnson's complaint on a motion to dismiss, the district court judge stated that, although "this simple battery appears to have lasted perhaps 10–15 seconds, Plaintiff has spent 29 pages and 115 paragraphs in the Complaint setting it forth," including "19 unrelated incidents involving women upon whom Defendant Trump allegedly committed nonconsensual acts, over the past four decades with differing circumstances."[18] The district court judge, who was appointed to the bench by President Trump, struck all the allegations pertaining to other incidents, citing the court's "broad discretion" to strike from a pleading "any redundant, immaterial, impertinent, or scandalous matter." He then reasoned that, even if the allegations do not constitute a "scandalous matter," they are nonetheless "immaterial and impertinent" to Johnson's simple battery claim, concluding that evidence of the other incidents would not be admissible at trial.

On the admissibility issue, the judge distinguished inadmissible character evidence from admissible habit evidence, noting that, under the Federal Rules of Evidence, although they are "close akin," a "habit is a behavior repeated so often as to become a reflex." The judge reasoned that this evidence did not show sufficient habit on the part of the perpetrator, not only because "only one of the 19 prior incidents happened during the presidential campaign," but also because some had occurred years before.[19]

In making this determination, the judge did not consider Federal Rule of Evidence 415, which allows admission of similar acts in civil cases involving sexual assaults.[20] Indeed, the change of Rule 415 was hard fought by feminists, and part of a package of rules originally proposed as part of the Women's Equal Opportunity Act in 1991, and which was eventually passed by Congress in 1994 as part of the Violent Crime Control and Law Enforcement Act.[21] Rule 415 applies to civil cases involving "sexual assault" and provides that the "court may admit evidence that the party committed any other sexual assault or child molestation." In her assessment and critique of Rule 415, feminist legal scholar Jane Aiken argued not only that the definition of sexual assault should be broadened to include sexual misconduct and harassment, but also that the definition of prior acts should be narrowed so that the acts should be similar.[22]

The Alva Johnson example, it seems to me, illustrates our perennial interactions with law. The evidentiary standards applicable to perpetrators of sexual violence need questioning, as do the standards applying to racialized violence, especially police brutality and misconduct, in which even access to police records can be impossible.[23]

We seek to reform the law and do enact reforms, even as conservatives do the same. And these reforms can produce progress for individual cases and instances, and even produce wider societal changes. Yet they are not transformative. I believe every progressive recognizes that they are not truly transformative. But reform is not nothing. And so I believe we should continue to reform rules of evidence, employment discrimination laws, and standards of judicial recusal, in addition to diversifying the bench. These are too late to assist Alva Johnson, whose lawsuit did not proceed,[24] but reformative struggles are important, even as we recognize our efforts are not transformative.

Osamudia James: I'm interested in Ruthann's reference to the specific feminist victory concerning evidentiary rules. Particularly when understood as a broad conceptual umbrella for the work of Black liberation groups, Black Lives Matter has produced a string of accomplishments that, while not necessarily resulting in new law, have impacted our understanding of our legal system and how it functions.

Consider Black Lives Matter protestors who were arrested while protesting the death of Alton Sterling in Baton Rouge, Louisiana. They sued the city for unconstitutional tactics intended to infringe on their First Amendment rights, and settled for $100,000.[25] Black Lives Matter-affiliated labor groups, like BYP100 and Assata's Daughters, successfully led the charge to unseat Cook County Prosecutor Anita Alvarez, who failed to charge police officers who were involved in at least sixty-eight killings.[26] The Dream Defenders and others led a successful campaign against the reelection bid of Angela Corey, the Florida state attorney who failed to convict Travyon Martin's killer, but prosecuted Melissa Alexander.[27]

Black Lives Matter's victories have not only been in the courts. For example, they successfully pushed the 2016 Democratic presidential candidates to address structural racism during their campaigns, and compelled the Democratic party to restructure its national platform to include criminal justice reform.[28] Additionally, in conjunction with allied organizations, the Black Lives Matter movement released a multiagenda policy platform addressing reparations, economic justice, community control, and political power.[29]

I'll also double down on Bennett's assertion that Black Lives Matter has impacted policing. I am not as optimistic as my colleagues about the potential of body-worn cameras. As long as police officers and the public continue to unjustifiably perceive Black people as criminal, dangerous, aggressive, and super- and sub-human, the cameras will only reflect and affirm that narrative. After all, what could justify the acquittal of Eric Garner's killers, despite video evidence of clear overreach?

I do think, however, that Black Lives Matter has succeeded in prompting conversations about the command and control culture of policing in the United States, opening up spaces for discussion about what policing could look like if the goal was not to routinely and immediately subdue and overpower civilians.

Linda Greene: Although Black Lives Matter aims for a "fundamental reordering of society wherein Black lives are free from systematic dehumanization,"[30] it began to seek legal reform shortly after Darrin Wilson, a white police officer in Ferguson, Missouri, shot and killed Michael Brown, a Black teenager, on August 9, 2014.[31] The Associated Press reported that by August 2015, a year after Michael Brown's death, twenty-four states had passed at least forty new measures addressing officer-worn cameras, racial bias training, independent investigations when police use force, and new limits on the flow of surplus military equipment to local law enforcement agencies.[32]

It is clear that Black Lives Matter seeks a "seat at the table." This was evident in an agreement that Black Lives Matter would play a role in the development of the federal court consent decree that now forms the framework for policing in Chicago.[33] Black Lives Matter joined a coalition of community and civil rights groups that criticized the Illinois attorney general's original draft of this consent decree as inadequate to address the history of police misconduct in Chicago.[34] That coalition had filed its own lawsuit to seek reform of policing in Chicago,[35] had developed its own proposed consent decree for the reform of policing in Chicago, and had reached an agreement with the city of Chicago and the Illinois attorney general that required both the city and the state not only to "consider the Coalition's consent decree terms," but also to empower the coalition "with the authority to enforce the decree in federal court."[36]

Lolita Buckner Inniss: While I do think that both Black Lives Matter and #MeToo have had a significant effect on some formal legal articulations and procedures, which I call law with a capital "L," perhaps more impact has been seen in sublegal, informal regulatory regimes, which I call law with a small "l." Small "l" law consists of the informal norms that govern how we shape social rule formulations, and how we interact with one another. An interesting change in small "l" regimes has been the way that many facets of society have examined their own behaviors and explored how they are sometimes complicit in promoting or valorizing women's sexual objectification, or in silencing Black people's articulation of the harms they suffer.

Consider, for example, how a distinct subcultural space in U.S. social media, Black Twitter, has moved toward the center of the culture. Black Twitter is a virtual space on X (formerly known as Twitter), a social media application, where a large, informally connected network of Black people offer opinions and social commentary on the news of the day. Black X/Twitter users decry injustice and assail white hegemony, typically using wry humor. In the advent of the Black Lives Matter movement, more people from the mainstream have followed and noted Black X/Twitter postings and have come to value them as the voice of a community that is not often heard.[37]

Another example of a small "l" response is seen in the fact that the Disney Company recently quietly deleted a joke about the casting couch from the end of the 1999 film version of *Toy Story* 2. The casting couch is as old as the film business; it refers to how powerful men sometimes use promises of film roles to entice or coerce women into sexual relationships.[38]

Bridget Crawford: The power of social media as a tool for organizing and spreading awareness brings us full circle to the discussion in chapter 2 of the methods of each movement. It will be interesting to see whether changes in ownership or content rules on social media platforms, like those associated with Elon Musk's purchase of Twitter, will change whether and how those platforms are used for progressive organizing. I think we just don't know yet what the future holds.

Linda Greene: At least for now, though, Black Lives Matter has become an important social media case study. And, as we have frequently seen, social media crosses into "mainstream" media. Police abuse issues have also been the subject in popular television shows and other forms of entertainment. For example, in the *Black-ish* episode "Hope," which aired on February 26, 2016, the Johnson family focused on a case involving an unarmed Black man whom the police tasered thirty-seven times for selling DVDs illegally, and wondered whether the grand jury would indict the police officers involved.[39] *Scandal*, which starred Kerry Washington, aired an episode with facts similar to those in the killing of Michael Brown in Ferguson.[40] In several episodes of the *Daily Show*, then-host Trevor Noah took up police killing of Black men, a subject which has been an ongoing theme for many years in the work of comedian David Chappelle.[41]

On the music front, which, from Beyoncé to Blood Orange, has long been a site of protest over racial injustice generally, and in the context of policing specifically, racialized policing is a frequent topic.[42] The song "I Can't Breathe," released in 2016, is a tribute to Eric Garner.[43] Five years later, in 2021, another song with that same title by the R&B artist H.E.R., which was "written in memory of

George Floyd and the many Black Americans who died at the hands of the police," won a Grammy for the song of the year.[44] Beyoncé's *Lemonade* track "Forward" features Black mothers holding pictures of their sons who have been killed by the police: Trayvon Martin, Eric Garner, and Michael Brown.[45] Jay-Z's "spiritual" protests, "I am not poison/Just a boy from the hood that got my hands in the air/In despair don't shoot/I just wanna do good."[46] QuestLove may have summed it up: "It ain't fair when your protector is your predator."[47]

Sexual assault and harassment have increased in TV representation as well. An episode of CBS's *Murphy Brown* featured staff members of "Murphy in the Morning" sitting through a sexual harassment seminar and the main character remembering a traumatic experience involving a professor who attacked her when she was nineteen years old. When the character confronted the harasser, he dismissed the account and criticized the #MeToo movement, saying it's just "women dredging up the past, pointing fingers, ruining reputations."[48] Episodes of *The Handmaid's Tale, Law & Order: SVU*, and *13 Reasons Why* also addressed rape and sexual assault victims calling out their accusers.[49]

The #MeToo movement's effect continues to be palpable in popular culture as well: books published around sociology, feminism, and feminist theory spiked by 70 percent; Merriam-Webster's 2017 Word of the Year was *feminism*; and *Time*'s Person of the Year in 2017 was "The Silence Breakers," those who came forward with their stories of sexual assault.[50] In the music world, Kesha's song "Praying" discussed her sexual assault by her producer, though some have noted that #MeToo has not infiltrated the music world in the same way it has politics, television, and movies.[51]

Noa Ben-Asher: Linda mentioned the *Handmaid's Tale*. To my eye, *Handmaid's Tale* and the TV show *Big Little Lies* communicate some of the strongest messages of #MeToo. Though different in style and genre, the messages of white male dominance, female solidarity, trauma, and reproductive and sexual freedom loom large in both shows. I think they both call for close and critical analysis, as they very much represent, in my mind, a certain predominant feminist mindset. Unsurprisingly, and this fits with the critiques made by many of you, the treatment of race on these shows is simplistic or absent.

Bridget Crawford: The *Handmaid's Tale* also anticipates a regime in which women are primarily valued for their ability to bear children. Given the Supreme Court's 2022 rollback of federal protections for abortion rights in the *Dobbs* decision,[52] I wonder if we will not see reproductive rights overtaking sexual harassment as a subject in popular culture.

Osamudia James: Before adding about pop culture, I want to note the impact of social media on Black Lives Matter. I noted earlier that Black Lives Matter was the first movement for Black liberation unanchored in the Black church. I would further suggest that social media replaced the church as the meeting place for activists. Indeed, the ability to quickly galvanize protestors through viral social media posts made the movement agile in ways it might not have otherwise been. It also provided a platform to anyone with a social media account to promote the movement's goals and ideals, although this decentralized leadership network also made the movement vulnerable to critique when independent chapters took action that others considered excessive (such as the refusal of protestors to allow Bernie Sanders to speak at a Seattle rally in 2015).[53]

I'm not sure about the impact of the Black Lives Matter movement on pop culture. In one sense, yes—the slogan caught like wildfire, and became a convenient, all-encompassing heuristic for racism and white supremacy, not just in the United States, but around the world. And as Linda has pointed out, reference to the movement, in particular, and the dehumanizing treatment of Black people more generally, has certainly been reflected in popular music.

And yet, the use of art as a medium for exposing brutality is not new, even if the slogan #BlackLivesMatter is. Rather, Black people in the United States have been creating Black culture and Black art as witness to, and explanation and critique of, racial subordination since the first slave ships departed from African shores. Moreover, despite the potency of that art, I nevertheless read Black Lives Matter as part of a larger societal trend where Black racial identity is celebrated in pop and cultural spaces (such as the success of Beyoncé's *Lemonade*), but still marginalized in social, legal, and substantively material spaces.

DISCUSSION QUESTIONS

1. The beginning of this chapter offers a brief discussion of the difference between law and culture. What difference does this distinction have in terms of how we think about Black Lives Matter and #MeToo?

2. In any discussion of U.S. law and culture, the implicit understanding is that we mean Anglo-American law and Euro-descendant cultural ideas, often from a masculine point of view. Do the Black Lives Matter and #MeToo movements move us to broader understandings of law and culture?

3. Bennett Capers addresses the role of video evidence in how we understand the harms that occur and the need for reform. Do you agree that video evidence plays a crucial role in obtaining legal change? Why or why not?

4. What are some manifestations of the influence of Black Lives Matter and #MeToo in books, television, movies, music, and other forms of popular culture, other than the ones mentioned in this chapter?

NOTES

1. Lolita Buckner Inniss, "A Message from Dean Inniss on MLK Jr. Day," Colorado Law: University of Colorado Boulder, January 16, 2023, https://www.colorado.edu/law/2023/01/16/message-dean-inniss-mlk-jr-day [https://perma.cc/9DAK-9CS4].

2. See Lolita Buckner Inniss, "Abortion Law as Protection Narrative," *Oregon Law Review* 101, no. 2 (2023): 213–55.

3. Menachem Mautner, "Three Approaches to Law and Culture," *Cornell Law Review* 96, no. 4 (2011): 841–42.

4. David Montgomery, "The Death of Sandra Bland: Is There Anything Left to Investigate?," *New York Times*, May 9, 2019, https://www.nytimes.com/2019/05/08/us/sandra-bland-texas-death.html [https://perma.cc/ZMJ8-KT9N].

5. #TeamEbony, "A Look Back on the Death of Mike Brown in Ferguson," *Ebony*,August9,2019,https://www.ebony.com/a-look-back-on-the-death-of-mike-brown-in-ferguson/ [https://perma.cc/6T6B-R3WC].

6. Jordan Davis was a Black teenager who was shot and killed by a white man in a dispute over the volume at which Davis was playing music in his car at a Florida gas station. Richard Luscombe, "Florida Man Found Guilty of First-Degree Murder in 'Loud Music' Retrial," *The Guardian*, October 1, 2014, https://www.theguardian.com/world/2014/oct/01/florida-man-guilty-first-degree-loud-music-retrial [https://perma.cc/8TQH-8UCJ].

7. Bryan Stevenson, "A Presumption of Guilt: The Legacy of America's History of Racial Injustice," in *Policing the Black Man*, ed. Angela J. Davis (New York: Vintage Books, 2018), 3.

8. See Angela Onwuachi-Willig, "Policing the Boundaries of Whiteness: The Tragedy of Being 'Out of Place' from Emmett Till to Trayvon Martin," *Iowa Law Review* 102, no. 3 (2017): 1113–86; Aya Gruber, "Race to Incarcerate: Punitive Impulse and the Bid to Repeal Stand Your Ground," *University of Miami Law Review* 68, no. 4 (2014): 983–94.

9. See Francine Prose, "Watching Trump's Paramilitary Squads Descend on Portland, It's Hard Not to Feel Doomed," *The Guardian*, July 20, 2020, https://www.theguardian.com/commentisfree/2020/jul/20/trump-shock-troops-portland-doomed [https://perma.cc/A7G2-Y2JK].

10. Elizabeth Apondi, "'Unprintable Comments from the Young Men,'" Stop Street Harassment, April 24, 2020, http://www.stopstreetharassment.org/author/contributor/ [https://perma.cc/ZAE8-E795].

11. Aya Gruber, "Why Amy Cooper Felt the Police Were Her Personal 'Protection Agency,'" *Slate*, May 27, 2020, https://slate.com/news-and-politics/2020/05/amy-cooper-white-women-policing.html [https://perma.cc/NQ9H-8BQ3].

12. See Deborah Tuerkheimer, "Beyond #MeToo," *New York University Law Review* 94, no. 5 (2019): 1146–208.

13. See Cara Kelly and Aaron Hegarty, "#MeToo Was a Culture Shock. But Changing Laws Will Take More Than a Year," *USAToday.com*, October 4, 2018, https://www.usatoday.com/story/news/investigations/2018/10/04 /metoo-me-too-sexual-assault-survivors-rights-bill/1074976002/ [https:// perma.cc/TRS8-DNRT]. See also Catharine MacKinnon, "What #MeToo Has Changed," *The Atlantic*, March 24, 2019, https://www.theatlantic.com /ideas/archive/2019/03/catharine-mackinnon-what-metoo-has-changed /585313/ [https://perma.cc/G2HD-P965] (acknowledging that #MeToo has primarily moved "the culture beneath the law of sexual abuse" rather than moving the law itself).

14. Bennett Capers, "Race, Policing, and Technology," *North Carolina Law Review* 95, no. 4 (2017): 1268–83.

15. See Jocelyn Simonson, "Copwatching," *California Law Review* 104, no. 2 (2016): 442–43.

16. See Anna Lvovsky, "The Judicial Presumption of Police Expertise," *Harvard Law Review* 130, no. 8 (2017): 1999.

17. Johnson v. Trump for President, Inc., No. 819CV00475T02SPF, 2019 WL 2492122, at *1 (M.D. Fla. June 14, 2019). I discuss this lawsuit and its resolution further in my 2020 article published in the *Michigan Journal of Gender and Law*. Ruthann Robson, "The Sexual Misconduct of Donald J. Trump: Toward A Misogyny Report," *Michigan Journal of Gender and Law* 27, no. 1 (2020): 114–116.

18. *Johnson*, 2019 WL 2492122, at *1.

19. *Johnson*, 2019 WL 2492122, at *1.

20. Federal Rule of Evidence 415, entitled "Similar Acts in Civil Cases Involving Sexual Assault or Child Molestation," provides: "Permitted Uses. In a civil case involving a claim for relief based on a party's alleged sexual assault or child molestation, the court may admit evidence that the party committed any other sexual assault or child molestation." FED. R. EVID. 415.

21. For discussions of adoption of Federal Rule of Evidence 415, see Jane Harris Aiken, "Sexual Character Evidence in Civil Actions: Refining the Propensity Rule," *Wisconsin Law Review* 1997, no. 6 (1997): 1221–74; Daniel L. Overbey, "Federal Rule of Evidence 415 and *Paula Corbin Jones v. William Jefferson Clinton*: The Use of Propensity Evidence in Sexual Harassment Suits," *Notre Dame Journal of Law, Ethics, and Public Policy* 12, no. 1 (1998): 343–68; Michael Teter, "Acts of Emotion: Analyzing Congressional Involvement in the Federal Rules of Evidence," *Catholic University Law Review* 58, no. 1 (2008): 153–98.

22. Aiken, "Sexual Character Evidence."

23. The literature describes how police officer misconduct records are protected from being viewed by the public as follows:

> Police officer misconduct records are protected from public disclosure in the vast majority of states. Many states also make these records very difficult for criminal defendants to obtain, even when the officers who are the subject of these records are key witnesses in a prosecution against those defendants. Misconduct records may contain information ranging from claims of excessive force to planting evidence to arriving late or intoxicated to work. The common justification for denying access to these records is that police officers have a privacy interest in the content of the records. When in 2018 the New York Police Department—which has for the past several years refused to disclose even anonymized police misconduct records—floated a proposal to release redacted information about its disciplinary process, the city's largest police union immediately sued to halt the release on grounds that disclosure of these records would constitute a breach of the officers' privacy.

Rachel Moran, "Police Privacy," *UC Irvine Law Review* 10, no. 1 (2019): 154–55.

24. Although she was given leave to file an amended complaint, Alva Johnson declined to pursue the case, given the odds of success: "I'm fighting against a person with unlimited resources, and repeatedly the judicial system has failed to find fault in his behavior." Olivia Messer, "Alva Johnson Drops Lawsuit against President Trump: 'I'm Fighting against a Person with Unlimited Resources,'" *Daily Beast*, September 5, 2019, https://www.thedailybeast.com/alva-johnson-drops-lawsuit-against-president-trump-im-fighting-against-a-person-with-unlimited-resources-6.

25. Chris Sommerfeldt, "Baton Rouge Dishes out $100,000 to Settle Lawsuit Brought By Arrested Alton Sterling Protestors," *New York Daily News*, November 23, 2016, https://www.nydailynews.com/news/national/baton-rouge-settles-lawsuit-brought-alton-sterling-protesters-article-1.2884260 [https://perma.cc/3UES-6R57].

26. Miles Kampf-Lassin, "How Black Youth Helped Unseat Anita Alvarez and Transform the Face of Criminal Justice in Chicago," *In These Times*, March 16, 2016, https://inthesetimes.com/article/chicago-black-youth-anita-alvarez-kim-foxx-cook-county [https://perma.cc/8TTT-KX8H].

27. Serafina Wright, "State's Attorney in Trayvon Martin Case Ousted," *Washington Informer*, September 7, 2016, https://www.washingtoninformer.com/states-attorney-in-trayvon-martin-case-ousted/ [https://perma.cc/UJR2-ZBF4]; Christine Hauser, "Florida Woman Whose 'Stand Your Ground' Defense Was Rejected Is Released," *New York Times*, February 7, 2017, https://www.nytimes.com/2017/02/07/us/marissa-alexander-released-stand-your-ground.html [https://perma.cc/F97S-8NBE].

28. Brandon E. Patterson, "Black Lives Matter Just Officially Became Part of the Democratic Primary," *Mother Jones*, October 21, 2015, https://www.motherjones.com/crime-justice/2015/10/democratic-national-committee-asks-black-lives-matter-activists-organize-racial-jusitce/ [https://perma.cc/7XQU-MMNQ]; Jeff Stein, "Bernie Sanders Moved Democrats to the Left. The Platform Is Proof," *Vox*, July 25, 2016, https://www.vox.com/2016/7/25/12281022/the-democratic-party-platform [https://perma.cc/VB38-ZJQB]; James Downie, "Opinion: The Democratic Platform Is Far More Liberal Than Four Years Ago. Here's Why That Matters," *Washington Post*, July 7, 2016, https://perma.cc/GH5B-P2ZF.

29. Movement for Black Lives, *Vision for Black Lives: Policy Platforms*, accessed February 26, 2023, https://m4bl.org/policy-platforms/ [https://perma.cc/T3QC-8VCJ].

30. Frank Leon Roberts, "How Black Lives Matter Changed the Way Americans Fight for Freedom," *ACLU*, July 13, 2018, https://www.aclu.org/news/racial-justice/how-black-lives-matter-changed-way-americans-fight [https://perma.cc/4XK7-CQL9].

31. The Department of Justice's report on its investigation of the Ferguson Police Department after Michael Brown's death describes the events of that day as follows:

> On August 9, 2014, in Ferguson, Missouri, Officer Wilson suspected Brown and another, walking on the sidewalk, to have stolen cigarillos from a local convenience store. He parked in front of the men to stop them from walking any further. At that point, Officer Wilson attempted to open his door, but Brown's body stopped the door from opening. Officer Wilson then claimed that Brown reached in squad car, and a struggle ensued. Eventually, Officer Wilson shot Brown in the hand. Brown turned and ran away and when he was 180 feet away from Officer Wilson, Officer Wilson fatally shot him.

United States Department of Justice Civil Rights Division, *Investigation of the Ferguson Police Department*, March 4, 2015, https://www.justice.gov/sites/default/files/opa/press-releases/attachments/2015/03/04/ferguson_police_department_report.pdf.

32. David A. Lieb, "Ferguson Spurs 40 New State Measures; Activists Want More," *AP News*, August 3, 2015, https://apnews.com/article/2cd834a26ad146ceb04ba6f265566ec5 [https://perma.cc/H3AX-M6TF].

33. Final Consent Decree, State of Illinois v. City of Chicago, No. 17-cv-6260 (N.D. Ill., January 31, 2019), https://perma.cc/7N6U-98GX.

34. Dan Hinkel, "ACLU, Black Lives Matter Say Plans to Reform the Chicago Police Don't Go Far Enough," *Chicago Tribune*, August 14, 2018, https://www.chicagotribune.com/news/breaking/ct-met-consent-decree

-criticisms-20180813-story.html [https://perma.cc/E94E-UWJH];
"Coalition of Community and Civil Rights Groups Call on City of Chicago
and Illinois Attorney General to Improve the Draft Chicago Police Consent
Decree," ACLU Illinois, August 14, 2018, https://www.aclu-il.org/en/press
-releases/coalition-community-and-civil-rights-groups-call-city-chicago
-and-illinois-attorney [https://perma.cc/96EP-759P]. See Consent Decree
Draft for Public Review, State of Illinois v. City of Chicago, No. 17-cv-6260
(N.D. Ill., July 27, 2018), https://perma.cc/K32Z-UEQX.

35. Amended Class Action Complaint, Campbell v. City of Chicago, No.
1:17-cv-04467 (N.D. Ill., September 9, 2017).

36. See *Memorandum of Agreement between the Office of the Illinois
Attorney General and the City of Chicago and* Campbell v. City of Chicago
Plaintiffs and Communities United v. City of Chicago *Plaintiffs*, March
2018, https://perma.cc/3LCY-HTC2.

37. Jenna Wortham, "Black Tweets Matter," *Smithsonian Magazine*,
September 2016, https://www.smithsonianmag.com/arts-culture/black
-tweets-matter-180960117/ [https://perma.cc/X5JY-U73J]. See also Bryan
Adamson, "'Thugs,' 'Crooks,' and 'Rebellious Negroes': Racist and Racialized
Media Coverage of Michael Brown and the Ferguson Demonstrations,"
Harvard Journal on Racial and Ethnic Justice 32 (2016): 272–73 (describing Black Twitter).

38. See Jason Silverstein, "Disney Deletes 'Toy Story 2' Scene That Jokes
about Casting Couch Sex," *CBS News*, July 3, 2019, https://www.cbsnews
.com/news/disney-deletes-toy-story-2-scene-that-jokes-about-casting
-couch-sex/ [https://perma.cc/8U7Y-LPCL]. Note that the casting couch is
but one industry's metaphor for coerced sex in the workplace. Several years
ago, a Michigan attorney was sanctioned for allowing some clients to discharge their legal fees by having sex with him on his "couch of restitution."
Lolita Buckner Inniss, "'The Couch of Restitution' (Or, The Devil and the
Deep Blue Sea vs. The Devil in Miss Jones)," *Ain't I a Feminist Legal Scholar
Too?* (blog), December 4, 2009, http://innissfls.blogspot.com/2009/12/
couch-of-restitution-or-devil-and-deep.html [https://perma.cc/JMB2-NHVY].

39. *Black-ish*, season 2, episode 16, "Hope," aired February 24, 2016, on
ABC, https://www.imdb.com/title/tt4831844/; see also Michael Rothman
and Vanessa Wilkins, "'Black-ish' Lauded for Police Brutality Episode 'Hope,'"
ABCNews, February 25, 2016, https://abcnews.go.com/Entertainment/black
-ish-lauded-police-brutality-episode-hope/story?id=37188031 [https://
perma.cc/CDZ3-TEL9].

40. *Scandal*, season 4, episode 14, "The Lawn Chair," aired March 5, 2015, on ABC, https://www.imdb.com/title/tt4430626/ [https://perma.cc /VQ2D-WLBL]. After the police shot his son, the father planted himself in a lawn chair in front of his dead son's body while awaiting answers as to what happened. NewsOne Now, "#BlackLivesMatter on ABC's 'Scandal': Actor Courtney B. Vance Talks Racism, Police Brutality," *NewsOne.com*, March 10, 2015, https://newsone.com/3097311/blacklivesmatter-on-abcs -scandal-actor-courtney-b-vance-talks-racism-police-brutality/ [https:// perma.cc/SN4A-ZQUE].

41. See, for example, *The Daily Show with Trevor Noah*, "The Truth about the Philando Castile Verdict," June 21, 2017, YouTube video, 5:26, https://www. youtube.com/watch?v=wqgz7kRGVxg [https://perma.cc/9RU9-P32H]; *The Daily Show with Trevor Noah*, "Breaking the Cycle of Police Violence," July 22, 2016, YouTube video, 7:56, https://www.youtube.com/watch?v=cJ4fHIfkB_k [https://perma.cc/N2GN-35NW]; *The Daily Show with Trevor Noah*, "The Fatal Shootings of Alton Sterling and Philando Castile," July 7, 2016, YouTube video, 7:56, https://www.youtube.com/watch?v=tP0awqth0XI [https:// perma.cc/GZH8-LGKN]; Dave Chappelle, "Police Brutality (Killin' Them Softly)," July 6, 2009, YouTube video, 9:44, https://www.youtube.com /watch?v=VFHpvPwq2i8 [https://perma.cc/YMX4-YYR2].

42. See, for example, Britany Spanos and Sarah Grant, "Songs of Black Lives Matter: 22 New Protest Anthems," *Rolling Stone*, July 13, 2016, https://www.rollingstone.com/music/music-lists/songs-of-black-lives-mat ter-22-new-protest-anthems-15256/ [https://perma.cc/BSM4–3VGL]; Billie Holiday, "Strange Fruit," January 14, 2022, YouTube video, 3:02, https://www.youtube.com/watch?v=649wWWkW_1o; Bruce Springsteen and the E Street Band, "American Skin (41 Shots)," track 1 on *Live in New York City*, Columbia Records, 2001, https://brucespringsteen.net/track /american-skin-41-shots/ [https://perma.cc/PVA2-F4M9] (memorializing Amadou Diallo); "Top 10 Hip Hop Songs against Police Brutality," HipHop Golden Age, May 27, 2020, https://hiphopgoldenage.com/list/top-10-hip-hop-songs-police-brutality/ [https://perma.cc/X764-QQCX].

43. Daniel Kreps, "Eric Garner's Family Drop Moving New Song 'I Can't Breathe,'" *Rolling Stone*, July 11, 2016, https://www.rollingstone.com /music/music-news/eric-garners-family-drops-moving-new-song-i-cant -breathe-192574/ [https://perma.cc/Z2EX-3HR2].

44. Suzy Exposito, "In Surprise Win, H.E.R.'s 'I Can't Breathe' Takes Grammy for Song of the Year," *Los Angeles Times*, March 14, 2021, https:// perma.cc/L32P-7YC3.

45. Spanos and Grant, "Songs of Black Lives Matter."

46. Spanos and Grant, "Songs of Black Lives Matter"; see also Daniel Kreps, "Hear Jay Z Tackle Police Brutality on Raw New Song 'spiritual,'" *Rolling Stone*, July 8, 2016, https://www.rollingstone.com/music/music-news/hear-jay-z-tackle-police-brutality-on-raw-new-song-spiritual-165528/ [https://perma.cc/6NZ2-WMXA].

47. The Roots, Featuring Bilal, "It Ain't Fair," track 7 on *Detroit: Original Motion Picture Soundtrack*, Motown Records, 2017, https://perma.cc/YBZ5-WVMC.

48. Don Scardino, dir., *Murphy Brown*, season 11, episode 3, "#MurphyToo," aired October 11, 2018, on CBS, https://www.imdb.com/title/tt9090130/ [https://perma.cc/U2V9-2BXV].

49. Jeremy Podeswa, dir., *The Handmaid's Tale*, season 2, episode 10, "The Last Ceremony," aired June 28, 2018, on Hulu, https://www.imdb.com/title/tt7435256/ [https://perma.cc/N4KY-JYZW]; Alex Chapple, dir., *Law & Order: SVU*, season 19, episode 24, "Remember Me Too," aired May 23, 2018, on NBC, https://www.imdb.com/title/tt7846634/ [https://perma.cc/YDQ4-ASUS]; Kyle Patrick Alvarez, dir., *13 Reasons Why*, season 2, episode 13, "Bye," aired May 18, 2018, on Netflix, https://www.imdb.com/title/tt7414990/ [https://perma.cc/V782-NCA9]. This episode of *13 Reasons Why* deals with a woman of color testifying against her white male harasser, saying that she was afraid that she wasn't the "right victim" to stand up to him in what would come down to a "he-said, she-said" trial. Her account was followed by the accounts of multiple women accusing the same man. The white, male judge in the show lets the young man off with a stern warning and three months of probation.

50. Kristine Phillips, "'Feminism' Is Merriam-Webster's Word of the Year, Thanks in Part to Kellyanne Conway," *Washington Post*, December 12, 2016, https://www.washingtonpost.com/news/arts-and-entertainment/wp/2017/12/12/feminism-is-merriam-websters-word-of-the-year-thanks-in-part-to-kellyanne-conway/ [https://perma.cc/YTC6-Q7VV].

51. Hanif Abdurraqib, "Year In Music: The Slow Road to Music's #MeToo Moment," *Billboard*, December 13, 2018, https://perma.cc/5A3K-A9FT.

52. Dobbs v. Jackson Women's Health Organization, 142 S. Ct. 2228 (2022).

53. Dara Lind, "Black Lives Matter v. Bernie Sanders, Explained," *Vox*, August 11, 2015, https://www.vox.com/2015/8/11/9127653/bernie-sanders-black-lives-matter [https://perma.cc/6JSH-QWEC] (documenting the refusal of protestors to allow Bernie Sanders to speak at a Seattle rally in 2015, and the ensuing critique).

BIBLIOGRAPHY

Abdurraqib, Hanif. "Year in Music: The Slow Road to Music's #MeToo Moment." *Billboard*, December 13, 2018. https://perma.cc/5A3K -A9FT.

Adamson, Bryan. "'Thugs,' 'Crooks,' and 'Rebellious Negroes': Racist and Racialized Media Coverage of Michael Brown and the Ferguson Demonstrations." *Harvard Journal on Racial and Ethnic Justice* 32 (2016): 189–278.

Aiken, Jane Harris. "Sexual Character Evidence in Civil Actions: Refining the Propensity Rule." *Wisconsin Law Review* 1997, no. 6 (1997): 1221–74.

Alvarez, Kyle Patrick, dir. *13 Reasons Why*. Season 2, episode 13, "Bye." Aired May 18, 2018, on Netflix. https://www.imdb.com/title/tt7414990/ [https://perma.cc/V782-NCA9].

Amended Class Action Complaint, Campbell v. City of Chicago, No. 1:17-cv-04467 (N.D. Ill., September 9, 2017).

Apondi, Elizabeth. "Unprintable Comments from the Young Men." Stop Street Harassment, April 24, 2020. http://www.stopstreetharassment. org/author/contributor/ [https://perma.cc/ZAE8-E795].

Bonnett-Bailey, Lakeyta, and Adolphus Belk, eds. *For the Culture: Hip-Hop and the Fight for Social Justice*. Ann Arbor: University of Michigan Press, 2022.

Brandt, Jenn, and Sam Kizer. "From Street to Tweet." In *Feminist Theory and Pop Culture*, edited by Adrienne Trier-Bieniek, 2nd ed., 139–54. Boston: Brill, 2019.

Capers, Bennett. "Race, Policing, and Technology." *North Carolina Law Review* 95, no. 4 (2017): 1241–92.

Chappelle, Dave. "Police Brutality (Killin' Them Softly)." July 6, 2009. YouTube video, 9:44. https://www.youtube.com/ watch?v=VFHpvPwq2i8 [https://perma.cc/YMX4-YYR2].

Chapple, Alex, dir. *Law & Order: SVU*. Season 19, episode 24, "Remember Me Too." Aired May 23, 2018, on NBC. https://www.imdb.com/title /tt7846634/ [https://perma.cc/YDQ4-ASUS].

"Coalition of Community and Civil Rights Groups Call on City of Chicago and Illinois Attorney General to Improve the Draft Chicago Police Consent Decree." ACLU Illinois, August 14, 2018. https://www.aclu-il .org/en/press-releases/coalition-community-and-civil-rights-groups -call-city-chicago-and-illinois-attorney [https://perma.cc/96EP -759P].

Consent Decree Draft for Public Review. State of Illinois v. City of Chicago, No. 17-cv-6260 (N.D. Ill., July 27, 2018). https://perma.cc/K32Z-UEQX.

The Daily Show with Trevor Noah. "Breaking the Cycle of Police Violence." July 22, 2016. YouTube video, 7:56. https://www.youtube.com/watch?v= cJ4fHIfkB_k [https://perma.cc/N2GN-35NW].

———. "The Fatal Shootings of Alton Sterling and Philando Castile." July 7, 2016. YouTube video, 7:56. https://www.youtube.com/watch?v= tPoawqthoXI [https://perma.cc/GZH8-LGKN].

———. "The Truth about the Philando Castile Verdict." June 21, 2017. YouTube video, 5:26. https://www.youtube.com/ watch?v=wqgz7kRGVxg [https://perma.cc/9RU9-P32H].

Dniven, Zackary Okun, Harry Yaojun Yane, Jelani Ince, and Fabio Rojas. "Black Lives Matter Protests Shift Public Discourse." *Proceedings of the National Academy of Sciences* 119, no. 10 (2022): e2117320119. https://doi.org/10.1073/pnas.2117320119.

Dobbs v. Jackson Women's Health Organization, 142 S. Ct. 2228 (2022).

Downie, James. "Opinion: The Democratic Platform Is Far More Liberal Than Four Years Ago. Here's Why That Matters." *Washington Post,* July 7, 2016. https://perma.cc/GH5B-P2ZF.

Exposito, Suzy. "In Surprise Win, H.E.R.'s 'I Can't Breathe' Takes Grammy for Song of the Year." *Los Angeles Times,* March 14, 2021. https://perma .cc/L32P-7YC3.

Fed. R. Evid. 415.

Final Consent Decree. State of Illinois v. City of Chicago, No. 17-cv-6260 (N.D. Ill., Jan. 31, 2019). https://perma.cc/7N6U-98GX.

Gruber, Aya. "Race to Incarcerate: Punitive Impulse and the Bid to Repeal Stand Your Ground." *University of Miami Law Review* 68, no. 4 (2014): 961–1024.

———. "Why Amy Cooper Felt the Police Were Her Personal 'Protection Agency.'" *Slate,* May 27, 2020. https://slate.com/news-and-politics /2020/05/amy-cooper-white-women-policing.html [https://perma .cc/NQ9H-8BQ3].

Hauser, Christine. "Florida Woman Whose 'Stand Your Ground' Defense Was Rejected Is Released." *New York Times,* February 7, 2017. https:// www.nytimes.com/2017/02/07/us/marissa-alexander-released-stand -your-ground.html [https://perma.cc/F97S-8NBE].

Hinkel, Dan. "ACLU, Black Lives Matter Say Plans to Reform the Chicago Police Don't Go Far Enough." *Chicago Tribune,* August 14, 2018. https://

www.chicagotribune.com/news/breaking/ct-met-consent-decree
-criticisms-20180813-story.html [https://perma.cc/E94E-UWJH].

Holiday, Billy. "Strange Fruit." January 14, 2022. YouTube video, 3:02.
https://www.youtube.com/watch?v=649wWWkW_10.

Inniss, Lolita Buckner. "Abortion Law as Protection Narrative." *Oregon
Law Review* 101, no. 2 (2023): 213–55.

———. "'The Couch of Restitution' (Or, The Devil and the Deep Blue Sea vs.
The Devil in Miss Jones)." *Ain't I a Feminist Legal Scholar Too?* (blog).
December 4, 2009. http://innissfls.blogspot.com/2009/12/couch-of-
restitution-or-devil-and-deep.html [https://perma.cc/JMB2
-NHVY].

———. "A Message from Dean Inniss on MLK Jr. Day." Colorado Law:
University of Colorado Boulder. January 16, 2023. https://www
.colorado.edu/law/2023/01/16/message-dean-inniss-mlk-jr-day
[https://perma.cc/9DAK-9CS4].

Johnson v. Trump for President, Inc., No. 819CV00475T02SPF, 2019 WL
2492122 (M.D. Fla. June 14, 2019).

Kampf-Lassin, Miles. "How Black Youth Helped Unseat Anita Alvarez
and Transform the Face of Criminal Justice in Chicago." *In These
Times*, March 16, 2016. https://inthesetimes.com/article/chicago-black-
youth-anita-alvarez-kim-foxx-cook-county [https://perma.cc
/8TTT-KX8H].

Kelly, Cara, and Aaron Hegarty. "#MeToo Was a Culture Shock. But
Changing Laws Will Take More than a Year." *USAToday.com*, October 4,
2018. https://www.usatoday.com/story/news/investigations/2018/10/04
/metoo-me-too-sexual-assault-survivors-rights-bill/1074976002/
[https://perma.cc/TRS8-DNRT].

Kreps, Daniel. "Eric Garner's Family Drops Moving New Song 'I Can't
Breathe.'" *Rolling Stone*, July 11, 2016. https://www.rollingstone.com
/music/music-news/eric-garners-family-drops-moving-new-song-i-
cant-breathe-192574/ [https://perma.cc/Z2EX-3HR2].

———. "Hear Jay Z Tackle Police Brutality on Raw New Song 'spiritual.'"
Rolling Stone, July 8, 2016. https://www.rollingstone.com/music
/music-news/hear-jay-z-tackle-police-brutality-on-raw-new-song
-spiritual-165528/ [https://perma.cc/6NZ2-WMXA].

Lieb, David A. "Ferguson Spurs 40 New State Measures; Activists
Want More." *AP News*, August 3, 2015. https://apnews.com/article
/2cd834a26ad146cebo4ba6f265566ec5 [https://perma.cc/H3AX
-M6TF].

Lind, Dara. "Black Lives Matter v. Bernie Sanders, Explained." *Vox*, August 11, 2015. https://www.vox.com/2015/8/11/9127653/bernie-sanders-black-lives-matter [https://perma.cc/6JSH-QWEC].

Luscombe, Richard. "Florida Man Found Guilty of First-Degree Murder in 'Loud Music' Retrial." *The Guardia*n, October 1, 2014. https://www.theguardian.com/world/2014/oct/01/florida-man-guilty-first-degree-loud-music-retrial [https://perma.cc/8TQH-8UCJ].

Lvovsky, Anna. "The Judicial Presumption of Police Expertise." *Harvard Law Review* 130, no. 8 (2017): 1995–2081.

MacKinnon, Catharine. "What #MeToo Has Changed." *The Atlantic*, March 24, 2019. https://www.theatlantic.com/ideas/archive/2019/03/catharine-mackinnon-what-metoo-has-changed/585313/ [https://perma.cc/G2HD-P965].

Mautner, Menachem. "Three Approaches to Law and Culture." *Cornell Law Review* 96, no. 4 (2011): 839–68.

McKinnon-Crowley, Saralyn. "After #MeToo: How Visual Media Can Provide an Alternative to Cultural Scripts: A Quarterly of Women's Studies Resources." *Feminist Collections* 41, no. 1 (2020): 7–8.

Memorandum of Agreement between the Office of the Illinois Attorney General and the City of Chicago and Campbell v. City of Chicago *Plaintiffs and* Communities United v. City of Chicago *Plaintiffs*. March 2018. https://perma.cc/3LCY-HTC2.

Messer, Olivia. "Alva Johnson Drops Lawsuit against President Trump: 'I'm Fighting against a Person with Unlimited Resources.'" *Daily Beast*, September 5, 2019. https://www.thedailybeast.com/alva-johnson-drops-lawsuit-against-president-trump-im-fighting-against-a-person-with-unlimited-resources-6 [https://perma.cc/EZB8-4HPG].

Montgomery, David. "The Death of Sandra Bland: Is There Anything Left to Investigate?" *New York Times*, May 9, 2019. https://www.nytimes.com/2019/05/08/us/sandra-bland-texas-death.html [https://perma.cc/ZMJ8-KT9N].

Moran, Rachel. "Police Privacy." *UC Irvine Law Review* 10, no. 1 (2019): 153–98.

Movement for Black Lives. *Vision for Black Lives: Policy Platforms*. https://m4bl.org/policy-platforms/ [https://perma.cc/T3QC-8VCJ].

NewsOne Now. "#BlackLivesMatter on ABC's '*Scandal*': Actor Courtney B. Vance Talks Racism, Police Brutality." *NewsOne.com*, March 10, 2015. https://newsone.com/3097311/blacklivesmatter-on-abcs-scandal-

actor-courtney-b-vance-talks-racism-police-brutality/ [https://perma
.cc/SN4A-ZQUE].

Onwuachi-Willig, Angela. "Policing the Boundaries of Whiteness: The
Tragedy of Being 'Out of Place' from Emmett Till to Trayvon Martin."
Iowa Law Review 102, no. 3 (2017): 1113–86.

Overbey, Daniel L. "Federal Rule of Evidence 415 and *Paula Corbin Jones
v. William Jefferson Clinton*: The Use of Propensity Evidence in Sexual
Harassment Suits." *Notre Dame Journal of Law, Ethics, and Public
Policy* 12, no. 1 (1998): 343–68.

Patterson, Brandon E. "Black Lives Matter Just Officially Became Part of
the Democratic Primary." *Mother Jones*, October 21, 2015. https://
www.motherjones.com/crime-justice/2015/10/democratic-national-
committee-asks-black-lives-matter-activists-organize-racial-jusitce/
[https://perma.cc/7XQU-MMNQ].

Phillips, Kristine. "'Feminism' Is Merriam-Webster's Word of the Year,
Thanks in Part to Kellyanne Conway." *Washington Post*, December 12,
2017. https://www.washingtonpost.com/news/arts-and-entertainment
/wp/2017/12/12/feminism-is-merriam-websters-word-of-the-year
-thanks-in-part-to-kellyanne-conway/ [https://perma.cc/YTC6-
Q7VV].

Podeswa, Jeremy, dir. *The Handmaid's Tale*. Season 2, episode 10, "The
Last Ceremony." Aired June 28, 2018, on Hulu. https://www.imdb
.com/title/tt7435256/ [https://perma.cc/N4KY-JYZW].

Prose, Francine. "Watching Trump's Paramilitary Squads Descend on
Portland, It's Hard Not to Feel Doomed." *The Guardian*, July 20, 2020.
https://www.theguardian.com/commentisfree/2020/jul/20/trump
-shock-troops-portland-doomed [https://perma.cc/A7G2-Y2JK].

Roberts, Frank Leon. "How Black Lives Matter Changed the Way
Americans Fight for Freedom." *ACLU*, July 13, 2018. https://www.aclu
.org/news/racial-justice/how-black-lives-matter-changed-way
-americans-fight [https://perma.cc/4XK7-CQL9].

Robson, Ruthann. "The Sexual Misconduct of Donald J. Trump: Toward
A Misogyny Report." *Michigan Journal of Gender and Law* 27, no. 1
(2020): 81–148.

The Roots, Featuring Bilal. "It Ain't Fair." Track 7 on *Detroit: Original
Motion Picture Soundtrack*, Motown Records, 2017. https://perma.cc
/YBZ5-WVMC.

Rothman, Michael, and Vanessa Wilkins. "*Black-ish* Lauded for Police
Brutality Episode 'Hope.'" *ABCNews*, February 25, 2016. https://

abcnews.go.com/Entertainment/black-ish-lauded-police-brutality-episode-hope/story?id=37188031 [https://perma.cc/CDZ3-TEL9].

Scardino, Don, dir. *Murphy Brown*. Season 11, episode 3, "#MurphyToo." Aired October 11, 2018, on CBS. https://www.imdb.com/title/tt9090130/ [https://perma.cc/U2V9-2BXV].

Silverstein, Jason. "Disney Deletes 'Toy Story 2' Scene That Jokes about Casting Couch Sex." *CBS News*, July 3, 2019. https://www.cbsnews.com/news/disney-deletes-toy-story-2-scene-that-jokes-about-casting-couch-sex/ [https://perma.cc/8U7Y-LPCL].

Simonson, Jocelyn. "Copwatching." *California Law Review* 104, no. 2 (2016): 391–446.

Sommerfeldt, Chris. "Baton Rouge Dishes out $100,000 to Settle Lawsuit Brought By Arrested Alton Sterling Protestors." *New York Daily News*, November 23, 2016. https://www.nydailynews.com/news/national/baton-rouge-settles-lawsuit-brought-alton-sterling-protesters-article-1.2884260 [https://perma.cc/3UES-6R57].

Spanos, Brittany, and Sarah Grant. "Songs of Black Lives Matter: 22 New Protest Anthems." *Rolling Stone*, July 13, 2016. https://www.rollingstone.com/music/music-lists/songs-of-black-lives-matter-22-new-protest-anthems-15256/ [https://perma.cc/BSM4-3VGL].

Springsteen, Bruce, and the E Street Band. "American Skin (41 Shots)." Track 1 on *Live in New York City*, Columbia Records, 2001. https://brucespringsteen.net/track/american-skin-41-shots/ [https://perma.cc/PVA2-F4M9].

Stein, Jeff. "Bernie Sanders Moved Democrats to the Left. The Platform Is Proof." *Vox*, July 25, 2016. https://www.vox.com/2016/7/25/12281022/the-democratic-party-platform [https://perma.cc/VB38-ZJQB].

Stevenson, Bryan. "A Presumption of Guilt: The Legacy of America's History of Racial Injustice. In *Policing the Black Man*, edited by Angela J. Davis, 3–30. New York: Vintage Books, 2018.

#TeamEbony. "A Look Back on the Death of Mike Brown in Ferguson." *Ebony*, August 9, 2019. https://www.ebony.com/a-look-back-on-the-death-of-mike-brown-in-ferguson/ [https://perma.cc/6T6B-R3WC].

Teter, Michael. "Acts of Emotion: Analyzing Congressional Involvement in the Federal Rules of Evidence." *Catholic University Law Review* 58, no. 1 (2008): 153–98.

"Top 10 Hip Hop Songs against Police Brutality." HipHop Golden Age, May 27, 2020. https://hiphopgoldenage.com/list/top-10-hip-hop-songs-police-brutality/ [https://perma.cc/X764-QQCX].

Tuerkheimer, Deborah. "Beyond #MeToo." *New York University Law Review* 94, no. 5 (2019): 1146–208.

United States Department of Justice Civil Rights Division. *Investigation of the Ferguson Police Department.* March 4, 2015. https://www.justice.gov/sites/default/files/opa/press-releases/attachments/2015/03/04/ferguson_police_department_report.pdf.

van Haperen, Sander, Justus Uitermark, and Walter Nicholls. "The Swarm versus the Grassroots: Places and Networks of Supporters and Opponents of Black Lives Matter on Twitter." *Social Movement Studies* 22, no. 2 (2022): 171–89.

Verica, Tom, dir. *Scandal.* Season 4, episode 14, "The Lawn Chair." Aired March 5, 2015, on ABC. https://www.imdb.com/title/tt4430626/ [https://perma.cc/VQ2D-WLBL].

Wellman, Mariah L. "Black Squares for Black Lives? Performative Allyship As Credibility Maintenance for Social Media Influencers on Instagram." *Social Media + Society* 8, no. 1 (2022).

Wilz, Kelly. *Resisting Rape Culture through Popular Culture: Sex after #MeToo.* Lanham, MD: Lexington Books, 2020.

Wortham, Jenna. "Black Tweets Matter." *Smithsonian Magazine,* September 2016. https://www.smithsonianmag.com/arts-culture/black-tweets-matter-180960117/ [https://perma.cc/X5JY-U73J].

Wright, Serafina. "State's Attorney in Trayvon Martin Case Ousted." *Washington Informer,* September 7, 2016. https://www.washingtoninformer.com/states-attorney-in-trayvon-martin-case-ousted/ [https://perma.cc/UJR2-ZBF4].

Conclusion   # Continuing Conversations about Law, Social Movements, Black Lives Matter, and #MeToo

Lolita Buckner Inniss
Bridget J. Crawford

In choosing the subtitle of this book, we sought to capture the existence of dialogue between and among participants on the topics of Black Lives Matter and #MeToo. Although in some respects the dialogue presented here reads as an ordinary conversation (even if a well-cited one) we are mindful of the ways that *conversation itself* is a primary method by which we hope to increase the reach of this scholarly endeavor. We who "speak" in this book do so as scholars of varied disciplines, racial backgrounds, and social backgrounds; yet we have a common goal. We embrace the hope that the conversations here will stimulate further conversations, especially outside of academia, about Black Lives Matter and #MeToo, and positively influence thinking about the law and sublegal renderings, and their many manifestations in all aspects of life.

This book's discussion of the past, present, and future of the Black Lives Matter and #MeToo movements does not relate exclusively to sociolegal possibilities. There is a decidedly political bent here; ideas of justice are inseparable from the functions and the authority of the state. This conversation takes place in the larger sociolegal and socio-political contexts that exist in our world today, where news and images can be shared more rapidly and widely than ever before and at a time when public opinion is sharply divided, even polarized, on many issues. Indeed, during the presidency of Donald J. Trump from 2017 to 2021, the United States experienced nine of the ten fiscal quarters having the lowest level of political unity in the preceding forty years, according to the Vanderbilt Project on Unity and American Democracy, which tracks presidential approval ratings, polarization in Congress, frequency of public opinion polls that ask about political protest or unrest, and self-reports of political ideology and levels of trust.[1] The lack of unity can be explained, at least in part, by the proliferation of highly partisan television news outlets, such as Fox News and MSNBC; the echo chamber effect of social media algorithms; "nationalized" elections for state-wide and national office, where voters are more swayed by the candidate's party affiliation than particular viewpoints; hyperpartisan judicial nominations, especially at the Supreme Court level; ongoing culture wars over issues such as gay marriage, transgender rights, and abortion; and the rise of populist leaders on both the left and the right.[2] At the time of this writing, college campuses across the United States were exploding with protests over the Israel-Hamas war and the Israeli military's actions in Gaza.[3] Campus protests in this context may themselves constitute a new social movement, embodying solidarity, activism, and advocacy for human rights along with, in many cases, bitterly divided sentiments on who stands on the side of "right."

OPINION DIVIDED

In this context, it is hardly surprising that support for Black Lives Matter and #MeToo is divided along partisan and other lines. According to research conducted by the Pew Research Center in March 2022, 56 percent of American adults overall said that they "somewhat support" or "strongly support" the Black Lives Matter movement, which is largely consistent with figures from September

2020 and September 2021 for the same population. As of 2023, the level of support had dropped to 51 percent overall. Support for the Black Lives Matter movement is generally weaker among adults who are self-identified Republican and those who lean Republican (22 percent support the movement at least in part) compared to self-identified Democrats or those who lean Democratic (85 percent). Stark divisions are visible along generational lines, especially on the right. Among those ages 13–17, 70 percent of all teenagers "somewhat support" or "strongly support" the Black Lives Matter movement, including 42 percent of self-identified Republican or Republican-leaning teenagers and 94 percent of Democratic or Democratic-leaning teenagers. These generational divides carry over to racial or ethnic groups too. The percentage who "somewhat support" or "strongly support" the movement reflects this: of whites, 50 percent of adults are supporters, compared to 70 percent of teens; among Blacks, 80 percent of adults are supporters, compared to 92 percent of teens; and among Hispanics, 66 percent of adults are supporters, compared to 82 percent of teens.[4]

Support for the Black Lives Matter Movement is somewhat higher than that for the #MeToo movement. According to Pew Research Center surveys, as of July 2022, of American adults who had heard of the #MeToo movement, 49 percent "somewhat support" or "strongly support" it. Adults who self-identify as Republican and who lean Republican support the #MeToo movement at the same level (22 percent) as they support the Black Lives Matter movement, compared to self-identified Democrats and those who lean Democratic (70 percent) who support the #MeToo movement dramatically more than those on the right, but at a lower rate overall than the 85 percent rate at which they support the Black Lives Matter movement. Of those who had heard of the #MeToo movement in 2022, women were more likely (54 percent) to be supporters than men are (32 percent). Within partisan ranks, support for #MeToo is divided along gender lines. Support among Republican and Republican-leaning men (15 percent) is lower than among

51%   49%

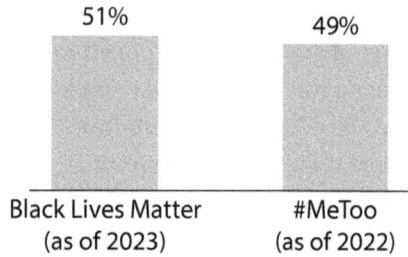

Figure 8. Percentage of American
  adjults who support or strongly
  support Black Lives Matter and   **Black Lives Matter**   **#MeToo**
  #MeToo (Pew Research Center).   (as of 2023)   (as of 2022)

Republican and Republican-leaning women (28 percent), and lower among Democratic and Democrat-leaning men (65 percent) than among Democratic and Democratic-leaning women (76 percent).[5]

These differences exist and persist along partisan and other lines, despite the widespread attention that both Black Lives Matter and #MeToo have brought to the need for reform. Although millions of people have taken to the streets in favor of either or both movements, the dehumanization that Black people in this country continues, seemingly unabated. In fact, more Black people were killed by police in the year *after* George Floyd's death (and subsequent years) than any other year since the tracking of statistics began in 2015.[6] Black people are twice as likely as white people to be killed by police officers.[7] Indeed, most Black people live with the daily fear that they, their family members, or their loved ones could be the victims of violence because of their race.[8] Combined with disproportionately high rates of COVID-19 infection and death during the pandemic, people of color understandably may feel pessimistic about the possibility of meaningful reform.[9]

It is vitally important that the Black Lives Matter and #MeToo movements be understood as engaging in the *actual* reform of law and society, and not just the *discourse* of the reform—that is, talking about improving or changing things. There is, no doubt, a significant relationship between outcomes and words, between reform and how we talk about and compare tools of reform. All talk about the Black Lives Matter and #MeToo movements, including the conversations in this book, have numerous aims: to explain the possibilities of reform, to justify the need for it, and to explore the limits of the movements.

In terms of progress made by #MeToo, the movement seems to have increased confidence that those who engage in sexual harassment or sexual assault will be held accountable for their actions, but a significant number of people (46 percent) say that it is somewhat or extremely common that workplace sexual harassment or assault continue to be unreported, with more women (55 percent) than men (36 percent) believing this to be the case. Another consequence of the #MeToo movement is a sense among all adults (46 percent) that its advocacy has made it "harder" for men to know how to interact with women at work, with many more men (53 percent) than women (39 percent) and many more who are Republican or who lean Republican (59 percent) than those who are Democratic or who lean Democratic (36 percent) believing this to be true.[10]

In France, a group of prominent French women, including film star Catherine Deneuve, denounced the #MeToo movement as a misguided form of "expedited justice" that makes men victims when they are "prevented from practicing their profession as punishment, forced to resign, etc., when the only thing they did wrong was touching a knee, trying to steal a kiss, a speaking about 'intimate' things at dinner, or sending messages with sexual connotations to a woman whose feelings were not mutual."[11] Concerns about the well-being and livelihood of accused men, more than their (usually) female accusers, cast the #MeToo movement as a collective threat to men's inability to earn a living, as opposed to increasing our understanding about unwanted sexual advances as obstacles to women's success at work.

FATIGUE IS REAL

In considering the present state of Black Lives Matter and #MeToo, as well as the possible future directions the movements may take, there is another important factor to consider: *exhaustion*. We are mindful that, too often, current academic and social trends mediate for a reemergence of concern about socioeconomic disadvantage in lieu of discussions about racial or gender oppression. It is as if there is an "identity politics fatigue" or "racial fatigue" regarding gender and race.[12]

However, turning the focus away from race and gender to class alone would ignore the very real, myriad, and pernicious ways in which race and gender impact not only people, both collectively and individually, without regard to their class status, but also the spaces they inhabit within society.[13] Referring to the spatial metaphors laid out in the book's introductory chapter and running throughout, the exhaustion can be understood from three perspectives: (1) internal, meaning the viewpoint of those who are active in either or both movements; (2) external-supportive, meaning those who stand outside one or both of the movements, but are generally supportive of the cause they represent; and (3) external-oppositional, meaning those who stand outside the movements and are either unsupportive or actively critical of their goals and/or methods. For each group, the exhaustion is real.

Movement insiders face the perpetual question, How does one continue the work without experiencing what Professor Cher Weixia has called the "chronic phenomenon of activist burnout"?[14] For a series it was creating, *Being Black in America*, National Public Radio issued a call in June 2020, asking Black Americans to describe their personal experiences. Approximately five hundred people responded with comments, with several talking about how to maintain engagement with antiracist work without burning out. Respondents cited the "cumulative impact of experiencing racism day to day," and the particular emotional toll of the constant influx of videos of violent police attacks against Black people.[15] Some talked about the need to take breaks from social media to focus on family or connect with nature. As one activist explained, "It's really prioritizing yourself, which many people are uncomfortable with, especially people who are activists, who really are selfless and give everything that they have to others, to their movement, to what they believe in. But you really also have to protect and preserve yourself, because if you don't, you'll have nothing left to give."[16]

For those who are generally sympathetic to the Black Lives Matter movement, the attempt to show support can unwittingly operate as another demand on the time and emotional well-being of activists. As one Black Lives Matter participant explained, "I do appreciate that many white or non-BIPOC people are stepping in to say, 'I'm an ally. Can you teach me?' or 'I didn't realize this.' [However, t]hat's an additional burden for Black activists."[17] When white people—often with good intentions—look to Black people or other people of color to be experts about all things race related, or to do the hard work of calling out racist language and practices, that is an exercise of white privilege. It is privilege that takes the form of the absence of white people's investment in self-education about race, and their abdication of a responsibility to develop their own voice in calling on others, especially other white people, to account for racism.[18] Likewise, white allies who may be supportive, but who are concerned about saying the wrong thing, may be anxious or withdraw, choosing to say nothing at all.[19]

For those who are external-oppositional to the Black Lives Matter movement, in that they stand outside it and may even critique its goals or methods, it is hard to imagine that any newly discovered facts will convince them that there is ongoing and systemic racism in the United States. For people in this external-oppositional group, many of whom are conservative, Black Lives Matter stands for rioting, "the indoctrination of children," "struggle sessions at work," and "an attempt to change the American way of life" in a negative manner.[20] These conservatives believe that race consciousness and discussion of race are racist; no evidence to the contrary will change their views.[21]

Turning to the #MeToo movement, fatigue is again evident in three domains: internally; among the external-supporters; and among the external-oppositional. For participants in the #MeToo movement, the public act of telling one's story or using the hashtag #MeToo on social media can bring positive feelings of relief, liberation, or solidarity.[22] Doing so without details, however, may bring unwanted attention. Supporters as well as detractors often want to know more. Follow-up demands and questions, such as "Tell me what happened," "How did you respond?" and "Where were you?" can feel invasive, judgmental, or traumatizing. This is especially true if the narrative does not follow a triumphal arc, or the survivor's behavior did not comport with some people's view of a "perfect" victim who reports the incident right away or fights back in some way.[23]

For supporters who are consuming the stories of assault and abuse, the cumulative effect may be a level of rage that is so overwhelming that it becomes a kind of numbness.[24] For other supporters, reading about others' experiences of sexual assault and sexual harassment can be triggering of their own past traumas. Given that an estimated 25 percent of all women and 10 percent of all men have experienced sexual assault or harassment, it is indeed a large population that might be upset or disturbed by #MeToo stories because of their own personal experiences.[25] Among supporters, some movement fatigue arguably has set in, at least insofar as conventional protests in the form of organized women's marches appear to have disappeared. At the same time, in the wake of the Supreme Court's 2022 decision in *Dobbs*, which eliminated *Roe v. Wade*' s longstanding federal protections for abortion rights,[26] there is surge of future activism around women's rights. In the first national elections after *Dobbs*, the 2022 mid-term elections, pro-choice voters contributed to important victories in several states.[27]

Those located outside the #MeToo movement, who are external-oppositional in that they do not support its goals or methods, are like those who are external-oppositional to the Black Lives Matter movement: no amount of persuasion or newly discovered evidence likely will change their position. For critics of the #MeToo movement, their opposition has nothing to do with the absence of data. When asked for the reasons for their opposition, detractors cite factors such lack of due process for the accused (22 percent); the possibility of false accusations (18 percent); and a perception that claimants are seeking attention, publicity, or money (14 percent).[28] For those external-oppositional, many of whom are conservative, the #MeToo movement is founded on a shared *victimhood*, and victimhood is to be avoided. As one writer who attended a conservative political conference explained, "the best way to address misogyny is to ignore it. To sneer at male animalism, to reject self-pity, and above all else, to resist hysteria. Victimhood, according to this logic, is a liberal complex, and rising above it means rejecting such nonsense."[29] In other words, it is not that conservatives, especially conservative women, do not believe that sexual assault and harassment occur. They simply believe that women should put men in their place, never think of themselves as weak, and handle their own "business" with zero expectation of assistance from anyone else, let alone the support of an entire movement.

THE ROLE OF LAW IN SOCIAL MOVEMENTS

In both the Black Lives Matter and the #MeToo movements, law occupies both practical and aspirational spaces. Protests—both online and in the streets—are ways of bringing attention that are understood to have some solutions that contemplate a clear role for law. Victories in court cases, such as the successful prosecution of the police officers who killed George Floyd, as well as the conviction, leading to a lengthy prison sentence, of Harvey Weinstein for rape and sexual assault (a conviction since overturned in New York), the latter of which is discussed at length in chapter 3, are just two of the most prominent examples where the law has been invoked to bring justice in specific cases. The law has also brought about larger-scale reform. Examples of this include the passage of legislation reforming police practices and extending protections for workers against sexual harassment, as discussed in chapters 4, 5 and 6.

The embrace of the law that one sees in the Black Lives Matter and #MeToo movements goes well beyond what law can do in one case or to solve one problem. Both movements embrace the foundational American value of *equality*, the self-evident truth that all people are created equal. Law is a constituent part of that, to be sure: equal justice under the law is the promise carved above the entrance of U.S. Supreme Court. The movements embrace a vision of embodied self-evident equality, where all people can fully flourish in private and public life, regardless of their race or gender. Black Lives Matter and #MeToo have illuminated the path toward that embodied existence, just as an approach lighting system illuminates a runway. Whether all of us, collectively, can fly in that direction remains to be seen.

In summary, the conversation about Black Lives Matter and #MeToo may wane at times, but it is ongoing. And that conversation has long existed, albeit by other terms, in word and in deed, long before we arrived at the topic. Thus we offer this work as a reminder that there is nothing new under the sun—we are all participants in the unending conversation around these movements, much like that described by Kenneth Burke, wherein we enter a parlor where a conversation goes on that has long preceded us, and yet, while we are in that parlor, we are willing and able to join and contribute meaningfully, and a conversation will still continue even after our departure.[30] We have our eyes trained on the future and on that continuing conversation.

NOTES

1. Vanderbilt Project on Unity and American Democracy, *Vanderbilt Unity Index White Paper* (Nashville, TN: Vanderbilt University, 2022), 7, https://www.vanderbilt.edu/unity/wp-content/uploads/sites/380/2022/06/Vanderbilt-Unity-Index-White-Paper.pdf [https://perma.cc/R8RC-7CCQ] ("Of the 10 quarters scoring lowest on the VUI, nine of them were during the Trump administration.").

2. See, for example, John Geer and Mary Catherine Sullivan, "How Politically Divided is the U.S.? It's Complicated But Quantifiable," *Washington*

Post, June 7, 2022, https://www.washingtonpost.com/politics/2022/06/07/ public-opinion-polarization-partisan-republicans-democrats   [https:// perma.cc/665G-WDU4]; Matteo Cinelli, Gianmarco De Francisci Morales, Alessandro Galeazzi, and Michele Starnini, "The Echo Chamber Effect on Social Media," *Proceedings of the National Academy of Sciences* 118, no. 9 (2021): e2023301118, https://doi.org/10.1073/pnas.2023301118; Joel Sievert and Seth C. McKee, "Nationalization in U.S. Senate and Gubernatorial Elections," *American Politics Research* 47, no. 5 (2019): 1055–80; Simon Lazarus, "How to Rein In Partisan Supreme Court Justices," Brookings Institute, March 23, 2002, https://www.brookings.edu/articles/how-to-rein -in-partisan-supreme-court-justices/ [https://perma.cc/DX6N-XA4Z].

3. See, for example, Anna Betts, Matthew Eadie, and Nicholas Boel-Burroughs, "Crackdowns at 4 College Protests Lead to More Than 200 Arrests," *New York Times*, April 27, 2024, https://www.nytimes.com/2024/04/27/us /northeastern-arizona-state-university-protests-arrests.html [https://perma .cc/ZK4X-K5UF].

4. See Kiley Hurst, "U.S. Teens Are More Likely Than Adults to Support the Black Lives Matter Movement," Pew Research Center, June 15, 2022, https://www.pewresearch.org/fact-tank/2022/06/15/u-s-teens-are-more-likely-than-adults-to-support-the-black-lives-matter-movement/ [https:// perma.cc/QX84-FRC8].

5. See Anna Brown, *More Than Twice as Many Americans Support Than Oppose the #MeToo Movement*, Pew Research Center, September 29, 2022, https://www.pewresearch.org/social-trends/wp-content/uploads/sites /3/2022/09/ST_2022.09.29_Me-Too_FINAL.pdf [https://perma.cc/4CFR-985T]; Juliana Menasce Horowitz, Kiley Hurst, and Dana Braga, *Support for the Black Lives Matter Movement Has Dropped Considerably from Its Peak in 2020* Pew Research Center, June 14, 2023, https://www.pewresearch.org /social-trends/2023/06/14/support-for-the-black-lives-matter-movement-has-dropped-considerably-from-its-peak-in-2020 [https://perma.cc/R4EG-TZVM]; Silvia Foster-Frau, Arelis R. Hernandez, Scott Clement, and Emily Guskin, "Poll: Black Americans Fear More Racist Attacks after Buffalo Shooting," *Washington Post*, May 21, 2022, https://www.washingtonpost.com /nation/2022/05/21/post-poll-black-americans/ [https://perma.cc/VP3U-U6AM] (reporting results of *Washington Post*-Ipsos poll).

6. See Curtis Bunn, "Report: Black People Are Still Killed by Police at a Higher Rate Than Other Groups," *NBC News*, March 3, 2022, https://www .nbcnews.com/news/nbcblk/report-black-people-are-still-killed-police-higher-rate-groups-rcna17169 [https://perma.cc/2CA4-JG29].

7. Bunn, "Report: Black People Are Still Killed by Police."

8. See Foster-Frau et al., "Poll: Black Americans Fear More Racists Attacks."

9. See Latoya Hill and Samantha Artiga, "COVID-19 Cases and Deaths by Race/Ethnicity: Current Data and Changes Over Time," Kaiser Family Foundation, August 22, 2022, https://www.kff.org/coronavirus-covid-19 /issue-brief/covid-19-cases-and-deaths-by-race-ethnicity-current-data-and-changes-over-time/ [https://perma.cc/R7FR-G45F].

10. See Brown, *More Than Twice as Many Americans.*

11. See Valeriya Safronova, "Catherine Deneuve and Others Denounce #MeToo Movement," *New York Times*, January 9, 2018, https://www .nytimes.com/2018/01/09/movies/catherine-deneuve-and-others-denounce-the-metoo-movement.html [https://perma.cc/5K2T-KBYM].

12. The idea of fatigue around these issues suggests that racial or identity awareness has gone too far—that we are all now "tired" of hearing about the oppression of others. See Dana Y. Takagi, *The Retreat from Race: Asian-American Admissions and Racial Politics* (New Brunswick, NJ: Rutgers University Press, 1993), 207.

13. See Lolita Buckner Inniss, "Toward a Sui Generis View of Black Rights in Canada? Overcoming the Difference-Denial Model of Countering Anti-Black Racism," *Berkeley Journal of African-American Law and Policy* 9, no. 1 (2007): 32–73.

14. See Christianna Silva, "Black Activist Burnout: 'You Can't Do This Work If You're Running on Empty,'" *NPR*, August 10, 2020, https://www.npr .org/2020/08/10/896695759/black-activist-burnout-you-can-t-do-this -work-if-you-re-running-on-empty [https://perma.cc/SWN7-LAW8] (quoting Cher Weixia).

15. Silva, "Black Activist Burnout," quoting Paul Gorski, a researcher who focuses on "activism burnout."

16. Silva, "Black Activist Burnout," quoting Danielle Hairston.

17. Silva, "Black Activist Burnout," quoting Hairston.

18. See, for example, Melanie S. Morrison, "Becoming Trustworthy White Allies," Yale Divinity School, *Reflections*, Spring 2013, https://reflections .yale.edu/article/future-race/becoming-trustworthy-white-allies [https:// perma.cc/JL2Y-QEDL] (explaining, as a white woman, her reaction to a Black friend's challenge to speak about race: "I had to acknowledge that I and many of my well intentioned white friends did not have vocabulary to talk about racism in an everyday kind of way. We were frequently mired in feelings of guilt. When we encountered racism, we could not be counted on

to speak up and confront it. Too often, we fell mute, became confused, reacted with defensiveness, or simply wanted to disappear. I could see that I was not trustworthy, especially when things got hot.").

19. See, for example, Will Greenberg, "'You Say the Wrong Thing Then Suddenly You are a Racist': Voices on MTV's 'White People,'" *Washington Post*, July 9, 2015, https://www.washingtonpost.com/news/morning-mix/wp/2015/07/09/you-say-the-wrong-thing-then-suddenly-you-are-a-racist-voices-on-mtvs-white-people/ [https://perma.cc/2K64-MHHQ]; "How Do We Overcome Our Fear of Talking about Racism?," Vice President Finance and Operations Portfolio, University of British Columbia, March 15, 2021, https://vpfo.ubc.ca/2021/03/how-do-we-overcome-our-fear-of-talking-about-racism/ [https://perma.cc/PLT3-Q3XX].

20. Heritage Foundation, "Heritage Explains: BLM Is in Trouble, but Still Making Our Lives Worse," February 13, 2022, https://www.heritage.org/progressivism/heritage-explains/blm-trouble-still-making-our-lives-worse [https://perma.cc/724C-WMAU] (quoting author Mike Gonzalez).

21. But see T. Alexander Aleinikoff, "A Case for Race-Based Consciousness," *Columbia Law Review* 91, no. 5 (1991): 1060–125 (critiquing the "colorblind" strain of Supreme Court jurisprudence).

22. See Susan Kelleher, "Telling a #MeToo Story Can Help Survivors' Health," *Seattle Times*, March 23, 2018, https://www.seattletimes.com/seattle-news/telling-the-metoo-story-can-lighten-a-victims-burden/ [https://perma.cc/DZG3-L9MD].

23. See Brianna C. Delker, Rowan Salton, Kate C. McLean, and Moin Syed, "Who Has To Tell Their Trauma Story and How Hard Will It Be? Influence of Cultural Stigma and Narrative Redemption on the Storying of Sexual Violence," *PLoS One* 15, no. 6 (2020): e0234201, https://doi.org/10.1371/journal.pone.0234201; Rajvi Desai, "Stop Looking for the Perfect #MeToo Victim," *The Swaddle*, November 28, 2019, https://theswaddle.com/stop-looking-for-the-perfect-metoo-victim/ [https://perma.cc/WBH5-LA3A].

24. See Amanda Petrusich, "One Year of #MeToo: A Younger Generation's Remedy for Rage," *New Yorker*, October 10, 2018, https://www.newyorker.com/culture/culture-desk/one-year-of-metoo-a-younger-generations-remedy-for-rage [https://perma.cc/7KFL-TW32] ("To see women's pain reiterated so endlessly and broadly was depleting in ways I simply didn't expect. Here was progress, an extraordinary breakthrough, a large and welcome dialogue, but I did not feel good or liberated. I just felt incapacitated by my own fury.").

25. See Sandee LaMotte, "For Some, #MeToo Sexual Assault Stories Trigger Trauma Not Empowerment," *CNN*, October 19, 2017, https://www.cnn.com/2017/10/19/health/me-too-sexual-assault-stories-trigger-trauma/index.html [https://perma.cc/WST3-9PYR].

26. Dobbs v. Jackson Women's Health Organization, 142 S. Ct. 2228 (2022).

27. See Charlotte Alter, "How Abortion Helped Blunt a Red Wave in the Midterms," *Time*, November 9, 2022, https://time.com/6231550/how-abortion-helped-blunt-a-red-wave-in-the-midterms/ [https://perma.cc/Y4R6-UDA7].

28. See Brown, *More Than Twice as Many Americans*.

29. Tina Nguyen, "'Conservative Women Don't Feel Victimized': How the Kavanaugh Nomination Underscored the Right's Complex Inability to Cope with the #MeToo Reckoning," *Vanity Fair*, October 10, 2018, https://www.vanityfair.com/news/2018/10/kavanaugh-nomination-conservative-women-metoo-reckoning [https://perma.cc/8DFQ-QJZF].

30. See Kenneth Burke, *The Philosophy of Literary Form: Studies in Symbolic Action* (Baton Rouge: Louisiana State University Press, 1941), 110–11.

BIBLIOGRAPHY

Aleinikoff, T. Alexander. "A Case for Race-Based Consciousness." *Columbia Law Review* 91, no. 5 (1991): 1060–125.

Alter, Charlotte. "How Abortion Helped Blunt a Red Wave in the Midterms." *Time*, November 9, 2022. https://time.com/6231550/how-abortion-helped-blunt-a-red-wave-in-the-midterms/ [https://perma.cc/Y4R6-UDA7].

Betts, Anna, Matthew Eadie, and Nicholas Boel-Burroughs. "Crackdowns at 4 College Protests Lead to More Than 200 Arrests." *New York Times*, April 27, 2024. https://www.nytimes.com/2024/04/27/us/northeastern-arizona-state-university-protests-arrests.html [https://perma.cc/ZK4X-K5UF].

Brown, Anna. *More Than Twice as Many Americans Support Than Oppose the #MeToo Movement*. Pew Research Center, September 29, 2022. https://www.pewresearch.org/social-trends/wp-content/uploads/sites/3/2022/09/ST_2022.09.29_Me-Too_FINAL.pdf [https://perma.cc/4CFR-985T].

Bunn, Curtis. "Report: Black People Are Still Killed by Police at a Higher Rate Than Other Groups." *NBC News*, March 3, 2022. https://www .nbcnews.com/news/nbcblk/report-black-people-are-still-killed-police-higher-rate-groups-rcna17169 [https://perma.cc/2CA4-JG29].

Burke, Kenneth. *The Philosophy of Literary Form: Studies in Symbolic Action*. Baton Rouge: Louisiana State University Press, 1941.

Cinelli, Matteo, Gianmarco De Francisci Morales, Alessandro Galeazzi, and Michele Starnini. "The Echo Chamber Effect on Social Media." *Proceedings of the National Academy of Sciences* 118, no. 9 (2021): e2023301118. https://doi.org/10.1073/pnas.2023301118.

Delker, Brianna C., Rowan Salton, Kate C. McLean, and Moin Syed. "Who Has to Tell Their Trauma Story and How Hard Will It Be? Influence of Cultural Stigma and Narrative Redemption on the Storying of Sexual Violence." *PLoS One* 15, no. 6 (2020): e0234201. https://doi.org/10.1371/journal.pone.0234201.

Desai, Rajvi. "Stop Looking for the Perfect #MeToo Victim." *The Swaddle*, November 28, 2019. https://theswaddle.com/stop-looking-for-the-perfect-metoo-victim/ [https://perma.cc/WBH5-LA3A].

Dobbs v. Jackson Women's Health Organization, 142 S. Ct. 2228 (2022).

Foster-Frau, Silvia, Arelis R. Hernandez, Scott Clement, and Emily Guskin. "Poll: Black Americans Fear More Racist Attacks after Buffalo Shooting." *Washington Post*, May 21, 2022. https://www.washingtonpost.com/nation/2022/05/21/post-poll-black-americans/ [https://perma.cc/VP3U-U6AM].

Geer, John, and Mary Catherine Sullivan. "How Politically Divided Is the U.S.? It's Complicated but Quantifiable." *Washington Post*, June 7, 2022. https://www.washingtonpost.com/politics/2022/06/07/public-opinion-polarization-partisan-republicans-democrats [https://perma .cc/665G-WDU4].

Greenberg, Will. "'You Say the Wrong Thing Then Suddenly You are a Racist': Voices on MTV's 'White People.'" *Washington Post*, July 9, 2015. https://www.washingtonpost.com/news/morning-mix/wp /2015/07/09/you-say-the-wrong-thing-then-suddenly-you-are-a -racist-voices-on-mtvs-white-people/ [https://perma.cc/2K64-MHHQ].

Heritage Foundation. "Heritage Explains: BLM Is in Trouble, but Still Making Our Lives Worse." February 13, 2022. https://www.heritage .org/progressivism/heritage-explains/blm-trouble-still-making-our -lives-worse [https://perma.cc/724C-WMAU].

Hill, Latoya, and Samantha Artiga. "COVID-19 Cases and Deaths by Race/ Ethnicity: Current Data and Changes Over Time." Kaiser Family Foundation, August 22, 2022. https://www.kff.org/coronavirus -covid-19/issue-brief/covid-19-cases-and-deaths-by-race-ethnicity -current-data-and-changes-over-time/ [https://perma.cc/R7FR-G45F].

"How Do We Overcome Our Fear of Talking about Racism?" Vice President Finance and Operations Portfolio, University of British Columbia, March 15, 2021. https://vpfo.ubc.ca/2021/03/how-do-we -overcome-our-fear-of-talking-about-racism/ [https://perma.cc /PLT3-Q3XX].

Horowitz, Juliana Menasce, Kiley Hurst, and Dana Braga. *Support for the Black Lives Matter Movement Has Dropped Considerably from Its Peak in 2020*. Pew Research Center, June 14, 2023. https://www. pewresearch.org/social-trends/2023/06/14/support-for-the-black-lives -matter-movement-has-dropped-considerably-from-its-peak-in-2020 [https://perma.cc/R4EG-TZVM]

Hurst, Kiley. "U.S. Teens Are More Likely Than Adults to Support the Black Lives Matter Movement." Pew Research Center, June 15, 2022. https://www.pewresearch.org/fact-tank/2022/06/15/u-s-teens-are -more-likely-than-adults-to-support-the-black-lives-matter -movement/ [https://perma.cc/QX84-FRC8].

Inniss, Lolita Buckner. "Toward a Sui Generis View of Black Rights in Canada? Overcoming the Difference-Denial Model of Countering Anti-Black Racism." *Berkeley Journal of African-American Law and Policy* 9, no. 1 (2007): 32–73.

Kelleher, Susan. "Telling a #MeToo Story Can Help Survivors' Health." *Seattle Times*, March 23, 2018. https://www.seattletimes.com/seattle- news/telling-the-metoo-story-can-lighten-a-victims-burden/ [https:// perma.cc/DZG3-L9MD].

LaMotte, Sandee. "For Some, #MeToo Sexual Assault Stories Trigger Trauma Not Empowerment." *CNN*, October 19, 2017. https://www.cnn .com/2017/10/19/health/me-too-sexual-assault-stories-trigger-trauma /index.html [https://perma.cc/WST3-9PYR].

Lazarus, Simon. "How to Rein In Partisan Supreme Court Justices." Brookings Institute, March 23, 2022. https://www.brookings.edu /articles/how-to-rein-in-partisan-supreme-court-justices/ [https:// perma.cc/DX6N-XA4Z].

Morrison, Melanie S. "Becoming Trustworthy White Allies." Yale Divinity School. *Reflections*, Spring 2013. https://reflections.yale.edu/article

/future-race/becoming-trustworthy-white-allies [https://perma.cc
/JL2Y-QEDL].

Nguyen, Tina. "'Conservative Women Don't Feel Victimized': How the
Kavanaugh Nomination Underscored the Right's Complex Inability to
Cope with the #MeToo Reckoning." *Vanity Fair*, October 10, 2018.
https://www.vanityfair.com/news/2018/10/kavanaugh-nomination
-conservative-women-metoo-reckoning [https://perma.cc
/8DFQ-QJZF].

Petrusich, Amanda. "One Year of #MeToo: A Younger Generation's
Remedy for Rage." *New Yorker*, October 10, 2018. https://www
.newyorker.com/culture/culture-desk/one-year-of-metoo-a-younger
-generations-remedy-for-rage [https://perma.cc/7KFL-TW32].

Safronova, Valeriya. "Catherine Deneuve and Others Denounce the
#MeToo Movement." *New York Times*, January 9, 2018. https://www
.nytimes.com/2018/01/09/movies/catherine-deneuve-and-others
-denounce-the-metoo-movement.html [https://perma.cc
/5K2T-KBYM].

Sievert, Joel, and Seth C. McKee. "Nationalization in US Senate and
Gubernatorial Elections." *American Politics Research* 47, no. 5 (2019):
1055–80.

Silva, Christianna. "Black Activist Burnout: 'You Can't Do This Work If
You're Running On Empty.'" *NPR*, August 10, 2020. https://www.npr
.org/2020/08/10/896695759/black-activist-burnout-you-can-t-do-this
-work-if-you-re-running-on-empty [https://perma.cc/SWN7-LAW8].

Takagi, Dana Y. *The Retreat from Race: Asian-American Admissions and
Racial Politics.* New Brunswick, NJ: Rutgers University Press, 1992.

Vanderbilt Project on Unity and American Democracy. *Vanderbilt Unity
Index White Paper.* Nashville, TN: Vanderbilt University, 2022. https://
www.vanderbilt.edu/unity/wp-content/uploads/sites/380/2022/06
/Vanderbilt-Unity-Index-White-Paper.pdf [https://perma.cc
/6J5J-3NH2o].

Selected Key Readings

For a reader who seeks general sources and materials that might inform their reading of this book, we have compiled this list of selected key readings. Far from a comprehensive bibliography of all that has been written about the two movements, this (admittedly) idiosyncratic and subjective list comprises sources that can provide the reader with basic information, provoke deeper thinking, or both.

Akbar, Amna A. "Toward a Radical Imagination of Law." *New York University Law Review* 93, no. 3 (2018): 405–79.

Black Lives Matter (website). https://blacklivesmatter.com.

Burke, Tarana. *TaranaBurke.com* (archived website). [https://perma.cc /E53U-HLAZ].

"Civil Rights Movement." *History.com*. Updated January 24, 2024. https://www.history.com/topics/black-history/civil-rights-movement [https://perma.cc/TS2E-8PMH].

Crawford, Bridget J. "Toward a Third-Wave Feminist Legal Theory: Young Women, Pornography and the Praxis of Pleasure." *Michigan Journal of Gender and Law* 14, no. 1 (2007): 99–168.

Crenshaw, Kimberlé. "Demarginalizing the Intersection of Race and Sex: A Black Feminist Critique of Antidiscrimination Doctrine, Feminist Theory and Antiracist Politics." *University of Chicago Legal Forum* (1989): 139–67.

———. "Mapping the Margins: Intersectionality, Identity Politics, and Violence against Women of Color." *Stanford Law Review* 43 (1991): 1241–99.

Fielborn, Biana, and Rachel Loney-Howes. *#MeToo and the Politics of Social Change.* New York: Palgrave Macmillan, 2019.

Forin, Jacey. "Critical Race Theory: A Brief History." *New York Times,* November 8, 2021. https://www.nytimes.com/article/what-is-critical-race-theory.

Francis, Megan Ming. "The Price of Civil Rights: Black Lives, White Funding, and Movement Capture." *Law and Society Review* 53, no. 1 (2019): 275–309.

Henderson, Taja-Nia Y., and Jamila Jefferson Jones. "#LivingWhileBlack: Blackness as Nuisance." *American University Law Review* 69, no. 3 (2020): 863–914.

Hill, Anita. *Speaking Truth to Power.* New York: Anchor Books, 1998.

Hillstrom, Laurie Collier. *Black Lives Matter: From a Moment to a Movement.* Santa Barbara, CA: ABC-CLIO, 2019.

———. *The #MeToo Movement.* Santa Barbara, CA: ABC-CLIO, 2018.

Hobson, Janell, ed. *Are All the Women Still White? Rethinking Race, Expanding Feminisms.* Albany: State University of New York Press, 2016.

hooks, bell. *Feminist Theory: From Margin to Center.* 2nd ed. Boston, MA: South End Press, 2000.

Inniss, Lolita Buckner. "Race, Space, and Surveillance: A Response to *#LivingWhileBlack: Blackness as Nuisance.*" *American University Law Review Forum* 69 (2020): 213–32.

Kurtzleben, Danielle. "The Trailblazers and Turning Points on the Road to #MeToo." *Washington Post,* July 5, 2019. https://www.washingtonpost.com/outlook/the-trailblazers-and-turning-points-along-the-road-to-metoo/2019/07/05/5a027b42–9457–11e9-b570-6416efdc0803_story.html.

Lebron, Christopher J. *The Making of Black Lives Matter.* Oxford: Oxford University Press, 2017.

Levit, Nancy, and Robert R. M. Verchick. *Feminist Legal Theory: A Primer.* 2nd ed. New York: New York University Press, 2015.

MacKinnon, Catharine A. *Feminism Unmodified: Discourses on Life and Law*. Cambridge, MA: Harvard University Press, 1988.

McGinley, Ann C., and Frank Rudy Cooper, eds. *Masculinities and the Law: A Multidimensional Approach*. New York: New York University Press, 2012.

National Women's Law Center. "Legal Help for Discrimination and Harassment." Accessed April 24, 2024. https://nwlc.org/times-up-legal -defense-fund/legal-help-for-sex-discrimination-and-harassment/ [https://perma.cc/UHW3-SD3W].

New York Historical Society. "Women and the American Story." Accessed April 24, 2024. https://wams.nyhistory.org/?_ga = 2.264457359.180142984 .1646929695-1492925239.1646405585 [https://perma.cc/JZ6W-Y73X].

Project Implicit. Accessed February 27, 2023. https://www.projectimplicit .net/ [https://perma.cc/FBC7-EYXK].

Ransby, Barbara. *Making All Black Lives Matter*. Berkeley: University of California Press, 2018.

Scales, Ann. *Legal Feminism: Activism, Lawyering, and Legal Theory*. New York: New York University Press, 2006.

Serwer, Adam. "The Coronavirus Was an Emergency until Trump Found Out Who Was Dying." *The Atlantic*, May 8, 2020. https://www .theatlantic.com/ideas/archive/2020/05/americas-racial-contract -showing/611389 [https://perma.cc/G4TA-TZYY].

Sullivan, Patricia. *Lift Every Voice: The NAACP and the Making of the Civil Rights Movement*. New York: New Press, 2009.

Taylor, Keeanga-Yamahtta. "Did Last Summer's Black Lives Matter Protests Change Anything?" *New Yorker*, August 6, 2021. https://www .newyorker.com/news/our-columnists/did-last-summers-protests -change-anything [https://perma.cc/ZMM8-DFDH].

———. *From #BlackLives Matter to Black Liberation*. Chicago: Haymarket Books, 2016.

TMI Project. "Black Stories Matter." Accessed March 8, 2024. https://www .tmiproject.org/blackstoriesmatter [https://perma.cc/58F6-XWY2].

Traister, Rebecca, "The Toll of Me Too: Assessing the Costs for Those Who Came Forward." *The Cut*, September 30, 2019. https://www .thecut.com/2019/09/the-toll-of-me-too.html [https://perma.cc /5C2A-78BS].

Watters, Jessica. "Pink Hats and Black Fists: The Role of Women in the Black Lives Matter Movement." *William and Mary Journal of Women and the Law* 24, no. 1 (2017/2018): 199–207.

Wexler, Lesley. "#MeToo and Law Talk." *University of Chicago Legal Forum* (2019): 343–69.

Wilkins, Denise J., Andrew G. Livington, and Mark Levine. "Whose Tweets? The Rhetorical Functions of Social Media Use in Developing the Black Lives Matter Movement." *British Journal of Social Psychology* 58, no. 6 (2019): 786–805.

"Women's Suffrage." *History.com.* https://www.history.com/topics /womens-history/the-fight-for-womens-suffrage [https://perma.cc /W7G2-CM2X].

Figure Credits

Figure 1, p. 54   Jamelle Bouie, "Memorial to Michael Brown." https://commons.wikimedia.org/wiki/File:Memorial_to_Michael_Brown.jpg. Creative Commons Attribution 2.0 Generic.

Figure 2, p. 56   S. Pakhrin, "Women's March—Washington, DC, 2017." https://commons.wikimedia.org/wiki/File:Women%27s_March_-_Washington_DC_2017_(32203905350).jpg. Creative Commons Attribution 2.0.

Figure 3, p. 75   Johnny Silvercloud, "Black Lives Matter protesters in Washington, DC." https://commons.wikimedia.org/wiki/File:Black_Lives_Matter_(31136492043).jpg. Creative Commons Attribution Share-Alike 2.0.

Figure 4, p. 79   Michael R. Jenkins, "Anita Hill testifying in front of the Senate Judiciary Committee during Clarence Thomas's Supreme Court confirmation hearing." Library of Congress Prints and Photographs Division, Washington, DC. https://www.loc.gov/item/2019646369.

Figure 5, p. 81   Screenshot from "RWU Presidents Distinguished Lecture Series Tarana Burke." RWUEDU, https://youtu.be/sWszy

Index